FAME &
FOLLY

FAME &
FOLLY

Essays by

CYNTHIA OZICK

ALFRED A. KNOPF
New York 1996

Copyright © 1996 by Cynthia Ozick
All rights reserved under International and Pan-American
Copyright Conventions. Published in the United States
by Alfred A. Knopf, Inc., New York, and simultaneously
in Canada by Random House of Canada Limited, Toronto.
Distributed by Random House, Inc., New York.

Most of the essays in this collection were originally
published in *American Poetry Review, Antaeus, Commentary, The New
Criterion, The New Republic, The New York Times Book Review, The
New Yorker, Partisan Review,* and *The Washington Post Book Review.*

"Alfred Chester's Wig," "Rushdie in the Louvre," and "The Break"
were chosen for *Best American Essays 1993, 1994,* and *1995.*

"Annals of the Temple" is a chapter from the forthcoming
A Century of Arts and Letters, a history of the American Academy of Arts
and Letters to be published by Columbia University Press.

Owing to limitations of space, all permissions to reprint previously
published material can be found on pages 288–9.

Library of Congress Cataloging-in-Publication Data
Ozick, Cynthia.
Fame & folly : essays / by Cynthia Ozick. — 1st ed.
p.   cm.
ISBN 0-679-44690-7
1. American literature—History and criticism.   2. English
literature—History and criticism.   I. Title.
PS121.096   1996
810.9—dc20   95-44429   CIP

Manufactured in the United States of America
First Edition

For Rachel (again),
for Alex,
and for Samuel Joseph

Contents

Foreword

The impartial Law enrolled a name
For my especial use:
My rights in it would rest the same
Whether I puffed it into fame
Or sank it in abuse.

—Robert Graves, *"My Name and I"*

"NO PREFACES," someone admonished me long ago, and he may have been right, though I'm not exactly sure how or why. Is it because of what the lawyers say: *res ipsa loquitur*—whatever the thing is, let it speak for itself? Or because prefaces and introductions can be mistaken for a summary of a book's contents, or, worse yet, for a writer's credo—either one of which is guaranteed to irritate, the capsule for being superfluous, the credo for being grandiose?

So that is why this collection of mostly literary pieces comes without an introduction (which is usually one more essay pretending not to be) and without a preface (pretty much the same thing as an introduction). I hope "Foreword" will suggest something a lot more modest—at any rate, nothing so tyrannical as a Procrustean bed, to which a volume's wandering touchstones must be made to conform. (That notorious Greek bed, by the way, turns up in Jewish legend, too: it's precisely the kind of hospitality the burghers of Sodom are said to have offered their guests, and is probably the *real* meaning of sodomy.)

The point, then, of these words positioned before all the other words herein (and written afterward, it goes without saying) is only to muse a little on the title of this book. And I trust the point won't be *too* pointed, and will allow some leeway for a drizzle of uncertainty; it may be that Robert Graves, in the epigraph above, has done all the musing necessary on the subject of fame and folly. "My name will take less thought for me," he concludes in a later stanza, "In worlds of men I cannot see, / Than ever I for him." The assumption is the persistence of the poet's fame—that it will be known to posterity—whether or not it is connected with (damaged by) folly. Graves may have been too sanguine about the fate of his repute; for some (though not for me), especially for those who are a generation or two distant, he has already passed into that immense and glorious company of the Ephemeral. No noteworthy wickedness attaches to him; unlike some other poets even more illustrious, and more durable, Graves never labored toward sinking his name in abuse.

The list of famous literary figures in our famously rotten century who have been associated with one sort of folly or another is long enough without him. And yet certain of their names outlive, and outshine, their folly. Ezra Pound was incontrovertibly insane, but the form his madness chose (he might have gone harmlessly chasing butterflies, or posed as a Chinese sage) is a lasting stain on civilization. Posterity—that means us—appears to overlook the stain. Heidegger as philosopher outlives and outshines Heidegger as dedicated Nazi. T. S. Eliot (who takes my concentrated gaze in these pages) is less remembered for bigotry and an attraction to fascism than for his position as modernist poet-prophet. And not all of this amnesia—very little, in fact—is owed to what we may be tempted to call whitewash. Isaac Babel, murdered by the iron-hearted utopian regime he had himself subscribed to, began by carrying the whitewash in his own pail. More recently, a prominent writer of the former German Democratic Republic, celebrated by the West as a "dissident," did, after all, know what she was doing when she informed for the secret police.

There is the folly from within and the folly from without. The difference is sometimes hard to see. Even the clarity of Salman Rushdie's condition—a terrorist threat by external forces whose aims are plainly and fanatically extra-literary—is blurred by his earlier record of silence concerning any Middle Eastern terror that claimed to be "anti-imperialist." But such ironies are not to be relished by anyone; chiefly, I forbid them to myself. That stone-throwers may themselves occasionally vacation in glass houses is disappointing but unsurprising. Mark Twain, scourge of human folly, excoriator of bigots and their canards, himself committed an essay (I discuss it here) that reproduces some malicious old canards. It hurts, but never mind: he remains the radiant Mark Twain—a bit blemished. And Rushdie, heroic and combative in his denunciation of terror, has left all blemish behind.

Locally, there has for some time been an effort to sideline writers—including a Nobel luminary—who are known for a (largely private) resistance to whatever segment of the political spectrum currently prevails among dominant intellectuals. (And some intellectuals *are* more equal than others, as any writers' powwow-for-a-cause will demonstrate.) A literary periodical, for instance, will choose to ignore a writer's work, no matter how distinguished, even when the work itself has no political coloration. An audience at a literary conference, expressing its ideological solidarity, will lustily hiss and boo; or else, more subtly, it is the moderator who will suppress any disagreement. All this would seem to conform to the American principle of the (rough) play of ideas, and violates nothing; but the result is a certain "atmosphere." The consecration of a particular political impulse or pattern, unkindly and uniformly imposed, can engender its own fame-derived folly, though of a minor sort: the snubs of the sanctified.

Internal folly—of the kind that involves itself with fame—is stronger and stranger than *fatwa* or heritable malice or the lighting of what Saul Bellow calls "the ideological fuse." Think of Henry James's nervous breakdown (to use our own lingo for it) in the face of a raucous humiliation he had never before experienced: the exalted man of letters, the very Master, getting hooted off a stage. Indignity was a wound too horrible to bear—and why was that, given James's self-recognition and the clear interior resplendence of his powers? This amazing Jamesian plot (recounted in this volume) is mainly hidden in a corner of biography, a secret folly scarcely able to breathe its little fog on the great bright mirror, and armor, of James's renown.

Trollope's folly, the story goes, lay in his confessing in his *Autobiography* that he wrote for productivity, like a businessman, with his timepiece on his table. Though Trollope belongs with the permanent enchanting few (he educates domestically in the manner of Jane Austen, and in a worldly sense in the manner of Balzac), he has been a diminished figure ever since—except in the unbiased regions of literary truth. But didn't he bring it on himself, according to the legend at least, through needless arithmetical public bragging, so many words per hour?

By contrast, and to arrive at the proportionally lesser: my friend Chester's folly, all of his own making, succeeded in submerging altogether the upward flight of his reputation; it's likely you wouldn't have suspected his existence if not for my own mournful memoir (it looms ahead), and the mournful memoirs of a handful of others. But who, and what, *isn't* transitory, fleeting, perishable?

—An explosion. Ah, I hear you! "Don't," you're exploding, "*please* don't start on all that, the decay of civilizations, the vanishing of empires, where now are the scribes of Sumer and the snows of yesteryear—all that stuff. Besides," you're saying, "God knows fame isn't by any measure a literary subject, so why does it matter? Listen," you're saying, "it's folly that's *really* interesting. Forget the fame part. Concentrate on the folly."

I've done that, I think. With an exception here and there: a bit of homage when needed.

September 1995

FAME &
FOLLY

T. S. ELIOT
AT 101

"The Man Who
Suffers and the Mind
Which Creates"

Thomas Stearns Eliot, poet and preëminent modernist, was born one hundred and one years ago.* His centennial in 1988 was suitably marked by commemorative reporting, literary celebrations in New York and London, and the publication of a couple of lavishly reviewed volumes: a new biography and a collection of the poet's youthful letters. Probably not much more could have been done to distinguish the occasion; still, there was something subdued and bloodless, even superannuated, about these memorial stirrings. They had the quality of a slightly tedious reunion of aging alumni, mostly spiritless by now, spurred to animation by old exultation recollected in tranquility. The only really fresh excitement took place in London, where representatives of the usually docile community of British Jews, including at least one prominent publisher, condemned Eliot for antisemitism and protested the public fuss. Elsewhere, the moment passed modestly, hardly noticed at all by the bookish young—who, whether

*This essay was written in 1989.

absorbed by recondite theorizing in the academy, or scampering after newfangled writing careers, have long had their wagons hitched to other stars.

In the early Seventies it was still possible to uncover, here and there, a tenacious English department offering a vestigial graduate seminar given over to the study of Eliot. But by the close of the Eighties, only "The Love Song of J. Alfred Prufrock" appears to have survived the indifference of the schools—two or three pages in the anthologies, a fleeting assignment for high school seniors and college freshmen. "Prufrock," and "Prufrock" alone, is what the latest generations know—barely know: not "The Hollow Men," not "La Figlia che Piange," not "Ash-Wednesday," not even *The Waste Land*. Never *Four Quartets*. And the mammoth prophetic presence of T. S. Eliot himself—that immortal sovereign rock—the latest generations do not know at all.

To anyone who was an undergraduate in the Forties and Fifties (and possibly even into the first years of the Sixties), all that is inconceivable—as if a part of the horizon had crumbled away. When, four decades ago, in a literary period that resembled eternity, T. S. Eliot won the Nobel Prize for literature, he seemed pure zenith, a colossus, nothing less than a permanent luminary fixed in the firmament like the sun and the moon—or like the New Criticism itself, the vanished movement Eliot once magisterially dominated. It was a time that, for the literary young, mixed authority with innovation: authority *was* innovation, an idea that reads now, in the wake of the anti-establishment Sixties, like the simplest contradiction. But modernism then was an absolute ruler—it had no effective intellectual competition and had routed all its predecessors; and it was modernism that famously carried the "new."

The new—as embodied in Eliot—was difficult, preoccupied by parody and pastiche, exactingly allusive and complex, saturated in manifold ironies and inflections, composed of "layers," and pointedly inaccessible to anybody expecting run-of-the-mill coherence. The doors to Eliot's poetry were not easily opened. His lines and themes were not readily understood. But the young who flung themselves through those portals were lured by unfamiliar enchantments and bound by pleasurable ribbons of ennui. "April is the cruel-lest month," Eliot's voice, with its sepulchral cadences, came spiralling out of 78 r.p.m. phonographs, "breeding / Lilacs out of the dead land, mixing / Memory and desire . . ." That toney British accent—flat, precise, steady, unemotive, surprisingly high-pitched, bleakly passive—coiled through awed English departments and worshipful dormitories, rooms where the walls had pin-up Picassos, and Pound and Eliot and *Ulysses* and Proust shouldered one another higgledy-piggledy in the rapt late-adolescent breast. The voice was, like the poet himself, nearly sacerdotal, impersonal, winding and winding across the country's campuses like a spool of blank robotic woe. "Shantih shantih shantih," "not with a bang but a whimper," "an old man in a dry month," "I shall wear the bottoms of my trousers rolled"—these were the devout chants of the literarily passionate in the Forties and Fifties, who in their own first verses piously copied Eliot's tone: its restraint, gravity, mystery; its invasive remoteness and immobilized disjointed despair.

There was rapture in that despair. Wordsworth's nostalgic cry over the start of the French Revolution—"Bliss was it in that dawn to be alive, / But to be young was very heaven!"—belongs no doubt to every new generation; youth's heaven lies in its quitting, or sometimes spiting, the past, with or without a historical crisis. And though Eliot's impress—the bliss he evoked—had little to do with political rupture, it was revolutionary enough in its own way. The young who gave homage to Eliot were engaged in a self-contradictory double maneuver: they were willingly authoritarian even as they jubilantly rebelled. On the one hand, taking on the puzzlements of modernism, they were out to tear down the Wordsworthian tradition itself, and on the other they were ready to fall on their knees to a god. A god, moreover, who despised free-thinking, democracy, and secularism: the very conditions of anti-authoritarianism.

How T. S. Eliot became that god—or, to put it less extravagantly, how he became a commanding literary figure who had no successful rivals and whose formulations were in fact revered—is almost as mysterious a proposition as how, in the flash of half a lifetime, an immutable majesty was dismantled, an immutable glory dissipated. It is almost impossible nowadays to imagine such authority accruing to a poet. No writer today—Nobel winner or no—holds it or can hold it. The four* most recent American Nobel laureates in literature—Czeslaw Milosz, Saul Bellow, Isaac Bashevis Singer, and Joseph Brodsky (three of whom, though citizens of long standing, do not write primarily in English)—are much honored, but they are not looked to for manifestos or pronouncements, and their comments are not studied as if by a haruspex. They are as far from being cultural dictators as they are from filling football stadiums.

Eliot *did* once fill a football stadium. On April 30, 1956, fourteen thousand people came to hear him lecture on "The Frontiers of Criticism" at the University of Minnesota, in Minneapolis. By then he was solidly confirmed as "the Pope of Russell Square," as his London admirer Mary Trevelyan began to call him in 1949. It was a far-reaching papacy, effective even among students in the American Midwest; but if the young flocked to genuflect before the papal throne, it was not they who had enthroned Eliot, nor their teachers. In the Age of Criticism (as the donnish "little" magazines of the time dubbed the Forties and Fifties), Eliot was ceded power, and accorded veneration, by critics who were themselves minor luminaries. "He has a very penetrating influence, perhaps not unlike an east wind," wrote William Empson, one of whose titles, *Seven Types of Ambiguity*, became an academic catchphrase alongside Eliot's famous "objective correlative." R. P. Blackmur said of "Prufrock" that its "obscurity is like that of the womb"; Eliot's critical essays, he claimed, bear a "vital relation" to Aristotle's *Poetics*. Hugh Kenner's comparison is with still another monument: "Eliot's work, as he once noted of Shakespeare, is in important respects one continuous poem," and for Kenner the shape of Eliot's own monument turns out to be "the Arch which stands when the last marcher has left, and endures when the last centurion or sergeant-major is dust." F. R. Leavis, declaring Eliot "among the

*There is, of course, now a fifth: Toni Morrison.

greatest poets of the English language," remarked that "to have
gone seriously into the poetry is to have had a quickening insight
into the nature of thought and language." And in Eliot's hands,
F. O. Matthiessen explained, the use of the symbol can "create
the illusion that it is giving expression to the very mystery of life."

These evocations of wind, womb, thought and language, the
dust of the ages, the very mystery of life, not to mention the
ghosts of Aristotle and Shakespeare: not since Dr. Johnson has a
man of letters writing in English been received with so much adulation, or seemed so formidable—almost a marvel of nature
itself—within his own society.

Nevertheless there was an occasional dissenter. As early as
1929, Edmund Wilson was complaining that he couldn't stomach
Eliot's celebrated conversion to "classicism, royalism, and Anglo-
Catholicism." While granting that Eliot's essays "will be read by
everybody interested in literature," that Eliot "has now become
the most important literary critic in the English-speaking world,"
and finally that "one can find no figure of comparable authority,"
it was exactly the force of this influence that made Wilson "fear
that we must give up hope." For Wilson, the argument of Eliot's
followers "that, because our society at the present time is badly off
without religion, we should make an heroic effort to swallow medieval theology, seems . . . utterly futile as well as fundamentally
dishonest." Twenty-five years later, when the American intellectual center had completed its shift from freelance literary work
like Wilson's—and Eliot's—to the near-uniformity of university
English departments, almost no one in those departments would
dare to think such unfastidious thoughts about Eliot out loud. A
glaze of orthodoxy (not too different from the preoccupation with
deconstructive theory currently orthodox in English departments)
settled over academe. Given the normal eagerness of succeeding
literary generations to examine new sets of entrails, it was inevitable that so unbroken a dedication would in time falter and decline.
But until that happened, decades on, Eliot studies were an unop-
posable ocean; an unstoppable torrent; a lava of libraries.

It may be embarrassing for us now to look back at that nearly
universal obeisance to an autocratic, inhibited, depressed, rather

narrow-minded and considerably bigoted fake Englishman—
especially if we are old enough (as I surely am) to have been part
of the wave of adoration. In his person, if not in his poetry, Eliot
was, after all, false coinage. Born in St. Louis, he became indistinguishable (though not to shrewd native English eyes), in his dress,
his manners, his loyalties, from a proper British Tory. Scion of un-
doctrinaire rationalist New England Unitarianism (his grandfather
had moved from Boston to Missouri to found Washington University), he was possessed by guilty notions of sinfulness and martyr-
dom and by the monkish disciplines of asceticism, which he
pursued in the unlikely embrace of the established English church.
No doubt Eliot's extreme self-alterations should not be dismissed
as ordinary humbug, particularly not on the religious side; there
is a difference between impersonation and conversion. Still, self-
alteration so unalloyed suggests a hatred of the original design.
And certainly Eliot condemned the optimism of democratic
American meliorism; certainly he despised Unitarianism, centered
less on personal salvation than on the social good; certainly he had
contempt for Jews as marginal if not inimical to his notions of
Christian community. But most of all, he came to loathe himself,
a hollow man in a twilight kingdom.

In my undergraduate years, between seventeen and twenty-
one, and long after as well, I had no inkling of any of this. The
overt flaws—the handful of insults in the poetry—I swallowed
down without protest. No one I knew protested—at any rate, no
professor ever did. If Eliot included lines like "The rats are underneath the piles. / The jew [sic] is underneath the lot," if he had his
Bleistein, "Chicago Semite Viennese," stare "from the protozoic
slime" while elsewhere "The jew squats on the windowsill, the
owner" and "Rachel *née* Rabinovitch / Tears at the grapes with
murderous paws"—well, that, sadly, was the way of the world and
to be expected, even in the most resplendent poet of the age. The
sting of those phrases—the shock that sickened—passed, and the
reader's heart pressed on to be stirred by other lines. What was
Eliot to me? He was not the crack about "Money in furs," or
"Spawned in some estaminet in Antwerp." No, Eliot was "The
Lady is withdrawn / In a white gown, to contemplation, in a

white gown" and "Then spoke the thunder/ DA / *Datta*: what have we given?" and "Afternoon grey and smoky, evening yellow and rose"; he was incantation, mournfulness, elegance; he was liquescence, he was staccato, he was quickstep and oar, the hushed moan and the sudden clap. He was lyric shudder and roseburst. He was, in brief, poetry incarnate; and poetry was what one lived for.

And he was something else beside. He was, to say it quickly, absolute art: high art, when art was at its most serious and elitist. The knowledge of that particular splendor—priestly, sacral, a golden cape for the initiate—has by now ebbed out of the world, and many do not regret it. Literary high art turned its back on egalitarianism and prized what is nowadays scorned as "the canon": that body of anciently esteemed texts, most of them difficult and aristocratic in origin, which has been designated Western culture. Modernism—and Eliot—teased the canon, bruised it, and even sought to astonish it by mocking and fragmenting it, and also by introducing Eastern infusions, such as Eliot's phrases from the Upanishads in *The Waste Land* and Pound's Chinese imitations. But all these shatterings, dislocations, and idiosyncratic juxtapositions of the old literary legacies were never intended to abolish the honor in which they were held, and only confirmed their centrality. Undoing the canon is the work of a later time—of our own, in fact, when universal assent to a central cultural standard is almost everywhere decried. For the moderns, and for Eliot especially, the denial of permanently agreed-on masterworks—what Matthew Arnold, in a currency now obsolete beyond imagining, called "touchstones"—would have been unthinkable. What one learned from Eliot, whose poetry skittered toward disintegration, was the power of consolidation: the understanding that literature could genuinely *reign*.

One learned also that a poem could actually be penetrated to its marrow—which was not quite the same as comprehending its meaning. In shunting aside or giving up certain goals of ordinary reading, the New Criticism installed Eliot as both teacher and subject. For instance, following Eliot, the New Criticism would not allow a poem to be read in the light of either biography or psychology. The poem was to be regarded as a thing-in-itself; nothing environmental or causal, including its own maker, was permitted to illuminate or explain it. In that sense it was as impersonal as a jar or any other shapely artifact that must be judged purely by its externals. This objective approach to a poem, deriving from Eliot's celebrated "objective correlative" formulation, did not dismiss emotion; rather, it kept it at a distance, and precluded any speculation about the poet's own life, or any other likely influence on the poem. "The progress of an artist is a continual self-sacrifice, a continual extinction of personality," Eliot wrote in his landmark essay, "Tradition and the Individual Talent." "Emotion . . . has its life in the poem and not in the history of the poet." And, most memorably: "The more perfect the artist, the more completely separate in him will be the man who suffers and the mind which creates." This was a theory designed to prevent old-fashioned attempts to read private events into the lines on the page. Artistic inevitability, Eliot instructed, "lies in this complete adequacy of the external to the emotion" and suggested a series of externals that might supply the "exact equivalence" of any particular emotion: "a set of objects, a situation, a chain of events." Such correlatives—or "objective equivalences"—provided, he insisted, the "only way of expressing emotion in the form of art." The New Criticism took him at his word, and declined to admit any other way. Not that the aesthetic scheme behind Eliot's formulation was altogether new. Henry James, too, had demanded—"Dramatize, dramatize!"—that the work of art resist construing itself in public. When Eliot, in offering his objective correlative, stopped to speak of the *"données* of the problem"—*donnée* was one of James's pet Gallicisms—he was tipping off his source. No literary figure among James's contemporaries had paid any attention to this modernist dictum, often not even James himself. Emerging in far more abstruse language from Eliot, it became a papal bull. He was thirty-five at the time.

The method used in digging out the objective correlative had a Gallic name of its own: *explication de texte.* The sloughing off of what the New Criticism considered to be extraneous had the effect of freeing the poem utterly—freeing it for the otherwise undistracted mind of the reader, who was released from "psychology" and similar blind alleys in order to master the poem's components. The New Criticism held the view that a poem could indeed be mastered: this was an act of trust, as it were, between poem and reader. The poem could be relied on to yield itself up to the reader—if the reader, on the other side of the bargain, would agree to a minutely close *"explication,"* phrase by phrase: a process far more meticulous than "interpretation" or the search for any identifiable meaning or definitive commentary. The search was rather for architecture and texture—or call it resonance and intricacy, the responsive web-work between the words. *Explication de texte*, as practiced by the New Critics and their graduate-student disciples, was something like watching an ant maneuver a bit of leaf. One notes first the fine veins in the leaf, then the light speckled along the veins, then the tiny glimmers charging off the ant's various surfaces, the movements of the ant's legs and other body parts, the lifting and balancing of the leaf, all the while scrupulously aware that ant and leaf, though separate structures, become—when linked in this way—a freshly imagined structure.

A generation or more was initiated into this concentrated scrutiny of a poem's structure and movement. High art in literature—which had earlier been approached through the impressionistic "appreciations" that commonly passed for critical reading before the New Criticism took hold—was seen to be indivisible from *explication de texte*. And though the reverence for high art that characterized the Eliot era is now antiquated—or dead—the close reading that was the hallmark of the New Critics has survived, and remains the sine qua non of all schools of literary theory. Currently it is even being applied to popular culture; hamburger advertisements and television sitcoms can be serious objects of up-to-date critical examination. Eliot was hugely attracted to popular culture as an innovative ingredient of pastiche—"Sweeney Agonistes," an unfinished verse drama, is saturated in it. But for Eliot and the New Critics, popular culture or "low taste" contributed to a literary technique; it would scarcely have served as a literary subject, or "text," in its own right. Elitism ruled. Art was expected to be strenuous, hard-earned, knotty. Eliot explicitly said so, and the New Critics faithfully concurred. "It is not a permanent necessity that poets should be interested in philosophy," Eliot wrote (though he himself had been a graduate student in philosophy at Harvard and Oxford, and had completed a thesis on F. H. Bradley, the British idealist). "We can only say that it appears likely that poets in our civilization, as it exists at present, must be *difficult*. Our civilization comprehends great variety and complexity, and this variety and complexity, playing upon a refined sensibility, must produce various and complex results. The poet must become more and more comprehensive, more allusive, more indirect, in order to force, to dislocate if necessary, language into his meaning."

He had another requirement as well, and that was a receptiveness to history. Complexity could be present only when historical consciousness prevailed. He favored history over novelty, and tradition over invention. While praising William Blake for "a remarkable and original sense of language and the music of language, and a gift of hallucinated vision," Eliot faulted him for his departures from the historical mainstream. "What his genius required, and what it sadly lacked, was framework of accepted and traditional ideas which would have prevented him from indulging in a philosophy of his own." And he concluded, "The concentration resulting from a framework of mythology and theology and philosophy is one of the reasons why Dante is a classic, and Blake only a poet of genius." Genius was not enough for Eliot. A poet, he said in "Tradition and the Individual Talent," needs to be "directed by the past." The historical sense "compels a man to write not merely with his own generation in his bones, but with the feeling that the whole of the literature of Europe from Homer and within it the whole of the literature of his own country has a simultaneous existence and composes a simultaneous order."

A grand view; a view of grandeur; high art defined: so high that even the sublime Blake fails to meet its measure. It is all immensely elevated and noble—and, given the way many literary academics and critics think now, rare and alien. Aristocratic ideas of this kind, which some might call Eurocentric and obscurantist, no longer engage most literary intellectuals; nor did they, sixty years ago, engage Edmund Wilson. But they were dominant for decades, and in the reign of Eliot they were law. Like other postulates, they brought good news and bad news; and we know that my good news may well be your bad news. Probably the only legacy of the Eliot era that everyone can affirm as enduringly valuable is the passionate, yet also disinterested, dissection of the text, a nuanced skill that no critical reader, taking whatever ideological stand, can do without. This exception aside, the rest is all disagreement. As I see it, what appeared important to me at twenty-one is still important; in some respects I admit to being arrested in the Age of Eliot, a permanent member of it, unregenerate. The etiolation of high art seems to me to be a major loss. I continue to suppose that some texts are worthier than other texts. The same with the diminishment of history and tradition: not to incorporate into an educable mind the origins and unifying principles of one's own civilization strikes me as a kind of cultural autolobotomy. Nor am I ready to relinquish Eliot's stunning declaration that the reason we know so much more than the dead writers knew is that "they are that which we know." As for that powerful central body of touchstone works, the discredited "canon," and Eliot's strong role in shaping it for his own and the following generation, it remains clear to me—as Susan Sontag remarked at the 1986 International PEN Convention—that literary genius is not an equal opportunity employer; I would not wish to drop Homer or Jane Austen or Kafka to make room for an Aleutian Islander of lesser gifts, however unrepresented her group may be on the college reading list.

In today's lexicon these are no doubt "conservative" notions, for which Eliot's influence can be at least partly blamed or—depending on your viewpoint—credited. In Eliot himself they have a darker side—the bad news. And the bad news is very bad. The gravity of high art led Eliot to envision a controlling and exclusionary society that could, presumably, supply the conditions to produce that art. These doctrinal tendencies, expressed in 1939 in a little book called *The Idea of a Christian Society*, took Eliot—on the eve of Nazi Germany's ascendancy over Europe—to the very lip of shutting out, through "radical changes," anyone he might consider ineligible for his "Community of Christians." Lamenting "the intolerable position of those who try to lead a Christian life in a non-Christian world," he was indifferent to the position of those who would try to thrive as a cultural minority within his contemplated Utopia. (This denigration of tolerance was hardly fresh. He had argued in a lecture six years before that he "had no objection to being called a bigot.") In the same volume, replying to a certain Miss Bower, who had frowned on "one of the main tenets of the Nazi creed—the relegation of women to the sphere of the kitchen, the children, and the church," Eliot protested "the implication that what is Nazi is wrong, and need not be discussed on its own merits." Nine years afterward, when the fight against Germany was won, he published *Notes Toward the Definition of Culture*, again proposing the hegemony of a common religious culture. Here he wrote—at a time when Hitler's ovens were just cooled and the shock of the Final Solution just dawning—that "the scattering of Jews amongst peoples holding the Christian faith may have been unfortunate both for these peoples and for the Jews themselves," because "the effect may have been to strengthen the illusion that there can be culture without religion." An extraordinary postwar comment. And in an Appendix, "The Unity of European Culture," a radio lecture broadcast to Germany in 1946, one year after the Reich was dismantled, with Europe in upheaval, the death camps exposed, and displaced persons everywhere, he made no mention at all of the German atrocities. The only reference to "barbarism" was hypothetical, a worried projection into a potentially barren future: "If Christianity goes, the whole of our culture goes," as if the best of European civilization (including the merciful tenets of Christianity) had not already been pulverized to ash throughout the previous decade. So much for where high art and traditional culture landed Eliot.

There is bad news, as it happens, even in the objective correlative. What was once accepted as an austere principle of poetics is suddenly decipherable as no more than a device to shield the poet from the raw shame of confession. Eliot is now unveiled as a confessional poet above all—one who was driven to confess, who *did* confess, whose subject was sin and guilt (his own), but who had no heart for the act of disclosure. That severe law of the impersonality of the poem—the masking technique purported to displace emotion from its crude source in the poet's real-life experience to its heightened incarnation in "a set of objects, a situation, a chain of events"—turns out to be motivated by something less august and more timorous than pure literary theory or a devotion to symbol. In the name of the objective correlative, Eliot had found a way to describe the wound without the embarrassment of divulging who held the knife. This was a conception far less immaculate than the practitioners of the New Criticism ever supposed; for thirty years or more Eliot's close readers remained innocent of—or discreet about—Eliot's private life. Perhaps some of them imagined that, like the other pope, he had none.

The assault on the masking power of the objective correlative—the breach in Eliot's protective wall—came about in the ordinary way: the biographies began. They began because time, which dissolves everything, at last dissolved awe. Although the number of critical examinations of Eliot, both book-length and in periodicals, is beyond counting, and although there are a handful of memoirs by people who were acquainted with him, the first true biography did not appear until a dozen years after his death. In 1977 Lyndall Gordon published *Eliot's Early Years*, an accomplished and informative study taking Eliot past his failed first marriage and through the composition of *The Waste Land*. Infiltrated by the familiar worshipfulness, the book is a tentative hybrid, part dense critical scrutiny and part cautious narrative—self-conscious about the latter, as if permission has not quite been granted by the author to herself. The constraints of awe are still there. Nevertheless the poetry is advanced in the light of Eliot's personal religious development, and these first illuminations are potent. In 1984 a second biography arrived, covering the life entire; by now awe has been fully dispatched. Peter Ackroyd's *T. S. Eliot: A Life* is thorough, bold, and relaxed about its boldness—even now and then a little acid. Not a debunking job by any means, but admirably straightforward. The effect is to bring Eliot down to recognizably human scale—disorienting to a reader trained to Eliot-adulation and ignorant until now of the nightmare of Eliot's youthful marriage and its devastating evolution. Four years on, Eliot's centenary saw the publication of *Eliot's New Life*, Lyndall Gordon's concluding volume, containing augmented portraits—in the nature of discoveries—of two women Ackroyd had touched on much less intensively; each had expected Eliot to marry her after the death of his wife in a mental institution. Eliot was callous to both. Eleven years following her first study, Gordon's manner continues respectful and her matter comprehensive, but the diffidence of the narrative chapters is gone. Eliot has acquired fallibility, and Gordon is not afraid to startle herself, or the long, encrusted history of deferential Eliot scholarship. Volume Two is daring, strong, and psychologically brilliant. Finally, 1988 also marked the issuance of a fat book of letters, *The Letters of T. S. Eliot, Vol. I: 1898–1922*, from childhood to age thirty-five (with more to come), edited by Eliot's widow, Valerie Eliot, whom he married when she was thirty and he sixty-eight.

"The man who suffers and the mind which creates"—these inseparables, sundered long ago by Eliot himself, can now be surgically united.

IF ELIOT HID his private terrors behind the hedge of his poetry, the course of literary history took no notice of it. Adoration, fame, and the Nobel Prize came to him neither in spite of nor because of what he left out; his craft was in the way he left it out. And he had always been reticent; he had always hidden himself. It can even be argued that he went to live in England in order to hide from his mother and father.

His mother, Charlotte Stearns Eliot, was a frustrated poet who wrote religious verse and worked for the civic good. His father, Henry Ware Eliot, was an affluent businessman who ran a St. Louis brick-manufacturing company. Like any entrepreneur, he liked to see results. His father's father, an intellectual admired by Dickens, was good at results—though not the conventional kind. He had left the family seat in blueblood Boston to take the enlightenment of Unitarianism to the American West; while he was at it he established a university. Both of Eliot's parents were strong-willed. Both expected him to make a success of himself. Both tended to diminish his independence. Not that they wanted his success on any terms but his own—it was early understood that this youngest of six siblings (four sisters, one of whom was nineteen years older, and a brother almost a decade his senior) was unusually gifted. He was the sort of introspective child who is photographed playing the piano or reading a book or watching his girl cousins at croquet (while himself wearing a broad-brimmed straw hat and a frilly dress, unremarkable garb for upper-class nineteenth-century male tots). His mother wrote to the headmaster of his prep school to ensure that he would not be allowed to participate in sports. She wrote again to warn against the dangers of swimming in quarry ponds. She praised Eliot's schoolboy verse as better than her own, and guaranteed his unease. "I knew what her verses meant to her. We did not discuss the matter further," he admitted long afterward. At his Harvard commencement in 1910, the same year as the composition of "Portrait of a Lady" and a year before "Prufrock," he delivered the farewell ode in a style that may have been a secret parody of his mother's: "For the hour that is left us Fair Harvard, with thee, / Ere we face the importunate years . . ." His mother was sympathetic to his ambitions as a poet—too sympathetic: it was almost as if his ambitions were hers, or vice versa. His father took a brisk view of Eliot's graduate studies in philosophy: they were the ticket to a Harvard professorship, a recognizably respectable career.

But Eliot would not stay put. To the bewilderment of his parents—the thought of it gave his mother a "chill"—he ran off to Paris, partly to catch the atmosphere of Jules Laforgue, a French poet who had begun to influence him, and partly to sink into Europe. In Paris he was briefly attracted to Henri Bergson, whose lectures on philosophy he attended at the Collège de France, but then he came upon Charles Maurras; Maurras's ideas—*"classique, catholique, monarchique"*—stuck to him for life, and were transmuted in 1928 into his own "classicist, royalist, Anglo-Catholic." In 1910 the word "fascist" was not yet in fashion, but that is exactly what Maurras was: later on he joined the pro-Nazi Vichy regime, and went to jail for it after World War II. None of this dented Eliot's enduring admiration; *Hommage à Charles Maurras* was written as late as 1948. When Eliot first encountered him, Maurras was the founder of an anti-democratic organization called Action Française, which specialized in student riots and open assaults on free-thinkers and Jews. Eliot, an onlooker on one of these occasions, did not shrink from the violence. (Ackroyd notes that he "liked boxing matches also.")

After Paris he obediently returned to Harvard for three diligent years, doing some undergraduate teaching and working on his doctoral degree. One of his courses was with Bertrand Russell, visiting from England. Russell saw Eliot at twenty-five as a silent young dandy, impeccably turned out, but a stick without "vigour or life—or enthusiasm." (Only a year later, in England, the diffident dandy—by then a new husband—would move with his bride right into Russell's tiny flat.) During the remainder of the Harvard period, Eliot embarked on Sanskrit, read Hindu and Buddhist sacred texts, and tunneled into the investigations that would culminate in his dissertation, *Experience and the Objects of Knowledge in the Philosophy of F. H. Bradley.* Screened by this busy academic program, he was also writing poetry. When Harvard offered him a traveling scholarship, he set off for Europe, and never again came back to live in the country of his birth. It was the beginning of the impersonations that were to become transformations.

He had intended an extensive tour of the Continent, but, in August of 1914, when war broke out, he retreated to England and enrolled at Oxford, ostensibly to continue his studies in philosophy. Oxford seemed an obvious way station for a young man headed for a professorial career, and his parents, shuttling between St. Louis and their comfortable New England summer house, ineradicably American in their habits and point of view, could not have judged otherwise, or suspected a permanent transatlantic removal. But what Eliot was really after was London: the literary life of London, in the manner of Henry James's illustrious conquest of it three decades before. He was quiet, deceptively passive, always reserved, on the watch for opportunity. He met Ezra Pound almost immediately. Pound, a fellow expatriate, was three years older and had come to London five years earlier. He had already published five volumes of poetry. He was idiosyncratic, noisy, cranky, aggressive, repetitively and tediously humorous as well as perilously unpredictable, and he kept an eye out for ways to position himself at the center of whatever maelstrom was current or could be readily invented. By the time he and Eliot discovered each other, Pound had been through Imagism and was boosting Vorticism; he wanted to shepherd movements, organize souls, administer lives. He read a handful of Eliot's Harvard poems, including "Portrait of a Lady" and "Prufrock," and instantly anointed him as the real thing. To Harriet Monroe in Chicago, the editor of *Poetry*, then the most distinguished—and coveted—American journal of its kind, he trumpeted Eliot as the author of "the best poem I have yet had or seen from an American," and insisted that she publish "Prufrock." He swept around London introducing his new protégé and finding outlets for his poems in periodicals with names like *Others* and *BLAST* (a Vorticist effort printed on flamingo-pink paper and featuring eccentric typography).

Eliot felt encouraged enough by these successes to abandon both Oxford and Harvard, and took a job teaching in a boy's secondary school to support the poet he was now heartened to become. His mother, appalled by such recklessness, directed her shock not at Eliot but at his former teacher, Bertrand Russell (much as she had gone to the headmaster behind the teen-age Eliot's back to protest the risks of the quarry pond): "I hope Tom will be able to carry out his purpose of coming on in May to take his degree. The Ph.D. is becoming in America . . . almost an essential condition for an Academic position and promotion therein. The male teachers in our secondary schools are as a rule inferior to the women teachers, and they have little social position or distinction. I hope Tom will not undertake such work another year—it is like putting Pegasus in harness." Eliot's father, storming behind the scenes, was less impressed by Pegasus. The appeal to Russell concluded, "As for 'The *BLAST*,' Mr. Eliot remarked when he saw a copy he did not know there were enough lunatics in the world to support such a magazine."

Home, in short, was seething. Within an inch of his degree, the compliant son was suddenly growing prodigal. A bombardment of cables and letters followed. Even the war conspired against the prodigal's return; though Pound was already preparing to fill

Eliot's luggage with masses of Vorticist material for a projected show in New York, the danger of German U-boats made a journey by sea unsafe. Russell cabled Eliot's father not to urge him to sit for his exams "UNLESS IMMEDIATE DEGREE IS WORTH RISKING LIFE." "I was not greatly pleased with the language of Prof. Russell's telegram," Eliot's father complained in a letter to Harvard. "Mrs. Eliot and I will use every effort to induce my son to take his examinations later. Doubtless his decision was much influenced by Prof. Russell." Clearly the maternal plea to Russell had backfired. Meanwhile Harvard itself, in the person of James H. Woods, Eliot's mentor in the philosophy department, was importuning him; Woods was tireless in offering an appointment. Eliot turned him down. Three years on, the family campaign to lure him home was unabated: the biggest gun of all was brought out—Charles W. Eliot, eminent educational reformer, recently President of Harvard, architect of the "five-foot shelf" of indispensable classics, and Eliot's grandfather's third cousin once removed. "I conceive that you have a real claim on my attention and interest," he assured his wayward young relative.

> It is, nevertheless, quite unintelligible to me how you or any other young American scholar can forego the privilege of living in the genuine American atmosphere—a bright atmosphere of freedom and hope. I have never lived long in England—about six months in all—but I have never got used to the manners and customs of any class in English society, high, middle, or low. After a stay of two weeks or two months in England it has been delightful for me to escape . . .
>
> Then, too, I have never been able to understand how any American man of letters can forego the privilege of being of use primarily to Americans of the present and future generations, as Emerson, Bryant, Lowell, and Whittier were. Literature seems to me highly climatic and national . . . You mention in your letter the name of Henry James. I knew his father well, and his brother William very well; and I had some conversation with Henry at different times during his life. I have a vivid remembrance of a talk with him during his last visit to America. It seemed to me all along that his English residence for so many

years contributed neither to the happy development of his art nor to his personal happiness.

. . . My last word is that if you wish to speak through your work to people of the "finest New England spirit" you had better not live much longer in the English atmosphere. The New England spirit has been nurtured in the American atmosphere.

What Eliot thought—three years before the publication of *The Waste Land*—of this tribal lecture, and particularly of its recommendation that he aspire to the mantle of the author of "Thanatopsis," one may cheerfully imagine. In any case it was too late, and had long been too late. The campaign was lost before the first parental shot. Eliot's tie to England was past revocation. While still at Oxford he was introduced to Vivien Haigh-Wood, a high-spirited, high-strung, artistic young woman, the daughter of a cultivated upper-class family; her father painted landscapes and portraits. Eliot, shy and apparently not yet relieved of his virginity, was attracted to her rather theatrical personality. Bertrand Russell sensed in her something brasher, perhaps rasher, than mere vivaciousness—he judged her light, vulgar, and adventurous. Eliot married her only weeks after they met. The marriage, he knew, was the seal on his determination to stay in England, the seal his parents could not break and against which they would be helpless. After the honeymoon, Russell (through pure chance Eliot had bumped into him on a London street) took the new couple in for six months, from July to Christmas—he had a closet-size spare room—and helped them out financially in other ways. He also launched Eliot as a reviewer by putting him in touch with the literary editor of the *New Statesman*, for whom Eliot now began to write intensively. Probably Russell's most useful service was his arranging for Eliot to be welcomed into the intellectual and literary circle around Lady Ottoline Morrell at Garsington, her country estate. Though invitations went to leading artists and writers, Garsington was not simply a salon: the Morrells were principled pacifists who provided farm work during the war for conscientious objectors. Here Eliot found Aldous Huxley, D. H. Lawrence, Lytton Strachey, Katherine Mansfield, the painter Mark Gertler,

Clive Bell, and, eventually, Leonard and Virginia Woolf. Lady Ottoline complained at first that Eliot had no spontaneity, that he barely moved his lips when he spoke, and that his voice was "mandarin." But Russell had carried him—in his arms, as it were—into the inmost eye of the most sophisticated whorl of contemporary English letters. The American newcomer who had left Harvard on a student fellowship in 1914 was already, by the middle of 1915, at the core of the London literary milieu he had dreamed of. And with so many models around him, he was working on disposing of whatever remnants of St. Louis remained lodged in his mouth, and perfecting the manner and accent of a high-born Englishman. (If he was grateful to Russell for this happy early initiation into precisely the society he coveted, by 1931—in "Thoughts After Lambeth," an essay on the idea of a national English church—he was sneering, in italics, at Russell's *gospel of happiness*.")

Meanwhile his parents required placating. A bright young man in his twenties had gone abroad to augment his studies; it was natural for him to come home within a reasonable time to get started on real life and his profession. Instead, he had made a precipitate marriage, intended to spend the rest of his days in a foreign country, and was teaching French and arithmetic in the equivalent of an American junior high school. Not surprisingly, the brick manufacturer and his piously versifying wife could not infer the sublime vocation of a poet from these evidences. Eliot hoped to persuade them. The marriage to Vivien took place on June 26, 1915; on June 28 Ezra Pound wrote a very long letter to Eliot's father. It was one of Eliot's mother's own devices—that of the surrogate pleader. As his mother had asked Russell to intervene with Eliot to return him to Harvard, so now Eliot was enlisting Pound to argue for London. The letter included much information about Pound's own situation, which could not have been reassuring, since—as Pound himself remarked—it was unlikely that the elder Eliot had ever heard of him. But he sweetened the case with respectable references to Edgar Lee Masters and Robert Browning, and was careful to add that Robert Frost, another American in London, had "done a book of New England eclogues." To the heartbroken father who had looked forward to a distinguished university career for his son, Pound said, "I am now much better off than if I had kept my professorship in Indiana"—empty comfort, considering it was Fair Harvard that was being mourned; what Pound had relinquished was Wabash College in a place called Crawfordsville. What could it have meant to Eliot's father that this twenty-nine-year-old contributor to the lunatic *BLAST* boasted of having "engineered a new school of verse now known in England, France and America," and insisted that "when I make a criticism of your son's work it is not an amateur criticism"? "As to his coming to London," Pound contended,

> anything else is a waste of time and energy. No one in London cares a hang what is written in America. After getting an American audience a man has to begin all over again here if he plans for an international hearing . . . The situation has been very well summed up in the sentence: "Henry James stayed in Paris and read Turgenev and Flaubert, Mr. Howells returned to America and read Henry James." . . . At any rate if T.S.E. is set on a literary career, this is the place to begin it and any other start would be very bad economy.

"I might add," he concluded, "that a literary man's income depends very much on how rigidly he insists on doing exactly what he himself wants to do. It depends on his connection, which he makes himself. It depends on the number of feuds that he takes on for the sake of his aesthetic beliefs. T.S.E. does not seem to be so pugnacious as I am and his course should be smoother and swifter."

The prediction held. The two-year eruption that was Vorticism waned, and so did Pound's local star; he moved on to Paris—leaving London, as it would turn out, in Eliot's possession. Pound's letter to the elder Eliot was not all bluster: he may have been a deft self-promoter, but he was also a promoter of literary ideas, and in Eliot's work he saw those ideas made flesh. The exuberance that sent Pound bustling through London to place Eliot here and there was the enthusiasm of an inventor whose thingamajig is just beginning to work in the world at large, in the breakthrough spirit of Alexander Graham Bell's "Mr. Watson, come here." In Pound's mind Eliot was Pound's invention. Certainly the excisions he demanded in *The Waste Land* radically "modernized" it in the direction of the objective correlative by keeping in the symbols and chopping out context and narrative, maneuvering the poem toward greater obliqueness and opacity. He also maneuvered Eliot. A determined literary man must go after his own "connection," he had advised Eliot's father, but the boisterous Pound served the reticent Eliot in a network of useful connections that Eliot would not have been likely to make on his own—including John Quinn, a New York literary philanthropist who became his (unpaid) agent in America and shored him up from time to time with generous money contributions.

Eliot was dependent on Pound's approval, or for a long while behaved as if he was. It was Pound who dominated the friendship, periodically shooting out instructions, information, scalawag counsel and pontification. "I value his verse far higher than that of any other living poet," Eliot told John Quinn in 1918. Gradually, over a span of years, there was a reversal of authority and power. Eliot rose and Pound sank. Under the pressure of his marriage (Vivien never held a job of any kind, nor could she have, even if it had been expected of her), Eliot ascended in the pragmatic world as well. He gave up teaching secondary school—it required him to supervise sports—and tried evening adult extension-course lecturing. The preparation was all-consuming and the remuneration paltry. Finally he recognized—he was, after all, his father's son—that this was no way to earn a living. A friend of Vivien's family recommended him to Lloyds Bank, where he turned out to be very good at the work—he had a position in the foreign department—and was regularly praised and advanced. Eventually he joined Faber & Gwyer, the London publishing house (later Faber & Faber), and remained associated with it until the end of his life. And then it was Pound who came to Eliot with his manuscripts. Eliot published them, but his responses, which had once treated Pound's antics with answering foolery, became heavily businesslike and impatient. As founder and editor of a literary journal Vivien had named *The Criterion*, Eliot went on commissioning

pieces from Pound, though he frequently attempted to impose coherence and discipline; occasionally he would reject something
outright. In 1922 Pound had asserted that "Eliot's *Waste Land* is I
think the justification of the 'movement,' of our modern experiment, since 1900," but by 1930 he was taunting Eliot for having "arrived at the supreme Eminence among English critics largely
through disguising himself as a corpse." Admiration had cooled
on both sides. Still, Eliot's loyalty remained fundamentally steadfast, even when he understood that Pound may have been approaching lunacy. After the Second World War, when Pound was
a patient in St. Elizabeth's Federal Hospital for the Insane in Washington, D.C.—the United States government's alternative to jail-
ing him for treason—Eliot signed petitions for his release and
made sure to see him on visits to America. Eliot never publicly
commented on the reason for Pound's incarceration: Pound had
supported the Axis and had actively aided the enemy. On Italian
radio, in Mussolini's employ, he had broadcast twice-weekly at-
tacks on Roosevelt, Churchill, and the Jews (whom he vilified in
the style of Goebbels).

Though in the long run the friendship altered and attenuated—
especially as Eliot grew more implicated in his Christian commitment and Pound in his self-proclaimed paganism—Eliot learned
much from Pound. He had already learned from Laforgue the
technique of the ironically illuminated persona. The tone of
youthful ennui, and the ageless though precocious recoil from the
world of phenomena, were Eliot's own. To these qualities of negation Pound added others: indirection, fragmentation, suggestibil-
ity, the force of piebald and zigzag juxtaposition—what we have
long recognized as the signs of modernism, that famous alchemy
of less becoming more. But even as he was tearing down the conventional frame of art, Pound was instructing Eliot in how to
frame a career: not that Eliot really needed Pound in either
sphere. Poets and critics may fabricate "movements," but no one
can invent the Zeitgeist, and it was the Zeitgeist that was promul-
gating modernism. Eliot may well have been headed there with or
without Pound at the helm. That Pound considered Eliot a creature of his own manufacture—that he did in fact tinker with the

design—hardly signifies, given that Eliot's art was anyhow likely to fall into the rumbling imperatives of its own time. As for Eliot's advancement into greater and greater reputation, even pushy Pound could not push a miracle into being. Still, it was evident early on that Pound's dictates were in full operation. "Now I am going to ask you to do something for me," Eliot informs his brother Henry in 1915,

> in case you are in Boston or New York this summer. These are suggestions of Ezra Pound's, who has a very shrewd head, and has taken a very great interest in my prospects. There will be people to be seen in Boston and New York, editors with whom I might have some chance . . . As you are likeliest to be in Boston, the first thing is the *Atlantic Monthly*. Now Pound considers it important, whenever possible, to secure introductions to editors from people of better social position than themselves,

and he goes on to propose that Isabella Stewart Gardner, an influential blueblood connection of his, be dragooned into sending a note to the editor of the *Atlantic* on Eliot's behalf. A few days later he is writing to Mrs. Gardner herself, announcing the imminent arrival of his brother, "in order that he may get your advice." To Henry he admits he has only a handful of poems to show, including "some rather second rate things," but anyhow he asks him to try for an opening at *Harper's, Century, Bookman*, and the *New Republic*. "Nothing needs to be done in Chicago, I believe."

Thus, Pound's training in chutzpah. Yet much of it was native to Eliot, picked up at the parental knee. Not for nothing was he the offspring of a mother who was a model of the epistolary maneuver, or of a father who demanded instant success. He had been reared, in any event, as one of the lords of creation in a conscious American aristocracy that believed in its superior birthright—a Midwestern enclave of what Cousin Charles Eliot had called "the finest New England spirit." In the alien precincts of London, where his credentials were unknown or immaterial, the top could not be so easily guaranteed; it would have to be cajoled, manipulated, seduced, dared, commanded, now and then dodged; it would have to be pressed hard, and cunningly. All this Eliot saw for himself, and rapidly. Reserve shored up cunning. It scarcely required Pound to teach him how to calculate the main chance, or how to scheme to impose his importance. He was actually better at it than Pound, because infinitely silkier. Whereas Pound had one voice to assault the barricades with—a cantankerous blast in nutty frontiersman spelling ("You jess set and hev a quiet draw at youh cawn-kob") that was likely to annoy, and was intended to shake you up—Eliot had dozens of voices. His early letters— where he is sedulously on the make—are a ventriloquist's handbook. To Mrs. Gardner he purrs as one should to a prominent patroness of the arts, with friendly dignity, in a courteously appreciative tone, avoiding the appearance of pursuit. Addressing the irascibly playful Pound, he is irascibly playful, and falls into identical orthographical jokiness. To his benefactor John Quinn he is punctiliously—though never humbly—grateful, recording the state of his literary barometer with a precision owed to the chairman of the board; nor does he ever fail to ask after Quinn's health. To his father he writes about money, to his mother about underwear and overcoats. Before both of them, anxiety and dutifulness prevail; he is eager to justify himself and to tot up his triumphs. He means to show them how right he was in choosing a London life; he is not a disappointment after all. "I am staying in the bank," he reports (he had been offered an editorship on a literary journal)— this alone will please his father, but there is much more:

> As it is, I occupy rather a privileged position. I am out of the intrigues and personal hatreds of journalism, and everyone respects me for working in a bank. My social position is quite as good as it would be as editor of a paper. I only write what I want to—now—and everyone knows that anything I do write is good. I can influence London opinion and English literature in a better way. I am known to be disinterested. Even through the *Egoist* I am getting to be looked up to by people who are far better known to the general public than I. There is a small and select public which regards me as the best living critic, as well as the best living poet, in England. I shall of course write for the *Ath.* [*The Athenaeum*] and keep my finger in it. I am much in sympathy with the editor, who is one of my most cordial admirers. With that and the *Egoist* and a young quarterly review which I am interested in, and which is glad to take anything I

will give, I can have more than enough power to satisfy me. I really think that I have far more *influence* on English letters than any other American has ever had, unless it be Henry James. I know a great many people, but there are many more who would like to know me, and I can remain isolated and detached.

All this sounds very conceited, but I am sure it is true, and as there is no outsider from whom you would hear it, and America really knows very little of what goes on in London, I must say it myself. Because it will give you pleasure if you believe it, and it will help to explain my point of view.

This was surely the voice of a small boy making his case to his skeptical parents: *it will give you pleasure if you believe it.* He was thirty years old. The self-assurance—or call it, as others did, the arrogance—was genuine, and before his father and mother he was unashamed of speaking of the necessity of power. Such an aspiration was axiomatic among Eliots. What he had set himself to attain was the absolute pinnacle—a place inhabited by no one else, where he could "remain isolated and detached." Fate would give him his wish exactly and with a vengeance, though not quite yet. If he was puffing London to St. Louis, and representing himself there as "the best living critic, as well as the best living poet, in England," two months later he was telling Lytton Strachey that he regarded "London with disdain," and divided "mankind into supermen, termites, and wireworms. I am sojourning among the termites."

In all this there is a wonder and an enigma: the prodigy of Eliot's rocketlike climb from termite to superman. London (and New York and Boston) was swarming with young men on a course no different from Eliot's. He was not the only one with a hotly ambitious pen and an appetite for cultivating highly-placed people who might be useful to him. John Middleton Murry and Wyndham Lewis, for example, both of whom were in Eliot's immediate circle, were equally striving and polished, and though we still know their names, we know them more in the nature of footnotes than as the main text. All three were engaged in the same sort of essayistic empire-building in the little magazines, and at the same time. Lewis published Eliot in *BLAST*, Murry published him in the *Athenaeum*, and later Eliot, when he was editing the *Criterion*, published Lewis. Yet Eliot very quickly overshadowed the others. The disparity, it can be argued, was that Eliot was primarily a poet; or that Eliot's talent was more robust. But even if we believe, as most of us do, that genius of its own force will sooner or later leap commandingly out (Melville's and Dickinson's redemption from obscurity being our sacred paradigms), the riddle stands: why, for Eliot, so soon? His termite days were a brevity, a breath; he was superman in an instant. What was it that singled Eliot out to put him in the lead so astoundingly early? That he ferociously *willed* it means nothing. Nearly all beginning writers have a will for extreme fame; will, no matter how resilient, is usually no more efficacious in the marketplace than daydream.

If there is any answer to such questions—and there may not be—it may lie hidden in one of Eliot's most well-appointed impersonations: the voice he employed as essayist. That charm of intimacy and the easy giving of secrets that we like to associate with essayists—Montaigne, Lamb, Hazlitt, George Orwell, Virginia Woolf when the mood struck her—was not Eliot's. As in what is called the "familiar" essay, Eliot frequently said "I"—but it was an "I" set in ice cut from the celestial vault: uninsistent yet incontestable, serenely sovereign. It seemed to take its power from erudition, and in part it did; but really it took it from some proud inner figuration or incarnation—as if Literature itself had been summoned to speak in its own voice:

> I am not considering whether the language of Dante or Shakespeare is superior, for I cannot admit the question: I readily affirm that the differences are such as make Dante easier for a foreigner. Dante's advantages are not due to greater genius, but to the fact that he wrote when Europe was still more or less one. And even had Chaucer or Villon been exact contemporaries of Dante, they would still have been farther, linguistically as well as geographically, from the center of Europe than Dante.

Who could talk back to that? Such sentences appear to derive from a source of knowledge—a congeries of assumptions—indistinguishable from majesty. In short, Eliot would not *permit* himself to be ignored, because it was not "himself" he was representing, but the very flower of European civilization. And there may have been another element contributing to the ready acceptance of his authority: as a foreigner, he was drawn to synthesizing and summarizing in a way that insiders, who take their context for granted, never do. He saw principles where the natives saw only phenomena. Besides, he had a clear model for focused ascent: Henry James. Knowing what he meant to become, he was immune to distraction or wrong turnings. "It is the final perfection, the consummation of an American," Eliot (in one of his most autobiographical dicta) wrote of James, "to become, not an Englishman, but a European—something which no born European, no person of any European nationality, can become."

So much for the larger trajectory. He had mapped out an unimpeded ideal destination. In the lesser geography of private life, however, there was an unforeseen impediment. Henry James had never married; Eliot had married Vivien. In 1915 she was twenty-seven, slender, lively, very pretty, with a wave in her hair and a pleasant mouth and chin. By 1919, Virginia Woolf was describing her as "a washed out, elderly and worn looking little woman." She complained of illness from the very first, but otherwise there were few immediate hints of the devastation to come. She was absorbed in Eliot's career. He brought his newest work to her for criticism; she read proofs; she assisted in preparing the *Criterion*. She also did some writing of her own—short stories, and prose sketches that Eliot admired and published in the *Criterion*. She had energy enough at the start: there were excursions, dinners, visits to Garsington, dance halls, dance lessons, theater, opera; even a flirtation with Bertrand Russell that turned into a one-night stand. ("Hellish and loathsome," Russell called it.) A month after the wedding she told Russell that she had married Eliot because she thought she could "stimulate" him, but that it could not be done. She began to suffer from headaches, colitis, neuralgia, insomnia. "She is a person who lives on a knife edge," Russell said. Eliot himself often woke at night feeling sick. He was plagued by colds, flu, bronchial problems; he smoked too much and he consistently drank too much, though he held it well. Retreating from Vivien, he threw himself into the work at the bank and into developing his literary reputation. Vivien had nowhere to go but into resentment, ill-will, hysteria. In the mornings the bed linens were frequently bloody—she menstruated excessively, and became obsessed with washing the sheets. She washed them herself even when they stayed in hotels. Morphine was prescribed for her various symptoms; also bromides and ether (she swabbed her whole body with ether, so that she reeked of it), and mercilessly bizarre diets—a German doctor combined starvation with the injection of animal glands. She collapsed into one nervous illness after another. Eliot repeatedly sent her to the country to recuperate while he remained in town. When his mother, now an elderly widow, and one of his sisters came on a visit from America, Vivien was absent, and Eliot was obliged to manage the complications of hospitality on his own. Anxiety over Vivien crept into all his business and social correspondence: "my wife has been very ill"; "she is all right when she is lying down, but immediately she gets up is very faint"; "wretched today—another bad night"; "Have you ever been in such incessant and extreme pain that you felt your sanity going, and that you no longer knew reality from delusion? That's the way she is. The doctors have never seen so bad a case, and hold out no definite hope, and have so far done her no good. Meanwhile she is in screaming agony . . ."

She brought out in him all his responsibility, vigilance, conscientiousness, troubled concern; in brief, his virtue. Her condition bewildered him; nothing in his experience, and certainly nothing in his upbringing, had equipped him for it; her manifold sicknesses were unpredictable, and so was she. Her sanity was in fact going. Daily she made him consider and reconsider his conduct toward her, and her ironic, clever, assaultive, always embarrassing responses ran tumbling over his caution. He dreaded dinner parties in her company, and went alone or not at all. It became known that Eliot was ashamed of his wife. But he was also ashamed of his life. Little by little he attempted to live it without Vivien, or despite Vivien, or in the few loopholes left him by Vivien. She was in and out of sanitoria in England, France, and Switzerland; it was a relief to have her away. What had once been frightened solicitude was gradually transmuted into horror, and horror into self-preservation, and self-preservation into callousness, and callousness into a kind of moral brutality. She felt how, emotionally and spiritually, he was abandoning her to her ordeal. However imploringly she sought his attention, he was determined to shut her out; the more he shut her out, the more wildly, dramatically, and desperately she tried to recapture him. He was now a man hunted—and haunted—by a mad wife. He saw himself transmogrified into one of the hollow men of his own imagining, that scarecrow figure stuck together out of "rat's coat, crowskin, crossed staves":

> The eyes are not here
> There are no eyes here
> In this valley of dying stars
> In this hollow valley
> This broken jaw of our lost kingdoms

He carried this Golgothan self-portrait with him everywhere; his lost kingdoms were in the stony looks he gave to the world. Virginia Woolf was struck by "the grim marble face . . . mouth twisted and shut; not a single line free and easy; all caught, pressed, inhibited." "Humiliation is the worst thing in life," he told her. Vivien had humiliated him. Torment and victimization—she of him, and he of her—had degraded him. Bouts of drink depleted him. At times his behavior was as strange as hers: he took to wearing pale green face powder, as if impersonating the sickly cast of death. Virginia Woolf thought he painted his lips. In 1933, after eighteen years of accelerating domestic misery, he finally broke loose: he went to America for a series of angry lectures (published later as *After Strange Gods: A Primer of Modern Heresy*) in which he attacked Pound, D. H. Lawrence, liberalism, and "free-thinking Jews," complaining that the United States had been "invaded by foreign races" who had "adulterated" its population. In London, meanwhile, a remorseful Vivien was refurbishing the flat for his homecoming; she even offered to join him overseas. In the black mood of his lectures her letter shocked him into a quick cruel plan. Writing from America, he directed his London solicitors to prepare separation documents and to deliver them to Vivien in his absence. When he arrived back in England, the deed was done. Vivien in disbelief continued to wait for him in the reupholstered flat. He moved instead into the shabby guest rooms of the parish house of St. Stephen's, an Anglican congregation with a high-church bent. There, subdued and alone among celibate priests, he spent the next half-dozen years in penance, suffering the very isolation and detachment he had once prized as the influential poet's reward.

Yet Vivien was in pursuit. Though he kept his lodgings secret from her, with fearful single-mindedness she attempted to hunt him down, turning up wherever there might be a chance of confronting him, hoping to cajole or argue or threaten him into resuming with her. He contrived to escape her time after time. By now he had left the bank for Faber; she would burst into the editorial offices without warning, weeping and pleading to be allowed to talk to him. One of the staff would give some excuse and Eliot would find a way of sneaking out of the building without detection. She carried a knife in her purse—it was her customary flamboyance—to alarm him; but it was a theater knife, made of rubber. She sent Christmas cards in the name of "Mr. and Mrs. T. S. Eliot," as if they were still together, and she advertised in *The Times* for him to return. She called herself sometimes Tiresias, and sometimes Daisy Miller, after the doomed Jamesian heroine. In a caricature of what she imagined would please him, she joined the newly formed British Union of Fascists. One day she actually caught him; she went up to him after a lecture, handed him books to sign as if they were strangers, and begged him to go home with her. He hid his recoil behind a polite "How do you do?" When she got wind of a scheme to commit her to a mental hospital, she fled briefly to Paris. In 1938 she was permanently institutionalized, whether by her mother or her brother, or by Eliot himself, no one knows; but Eliot had to have been consulted, at the very least. When her brother visited her in 1946, a year before her death, he reported that she seemed as sane as he was. She had tried on one occasion to run away; she was captured and brought back. She died in the asylum a decade after her commitment. Eliot never once went to see her.

Out of this brutalizing history of grieving and loss, of misalliance, misfortune, frantic confusion, and recurrent panic, Eliot drew the formulation of his dream of horror—that waste land where

> . . . I Tiresias have foresuffered all
> . . . and walked among the lowest of the dead
> Here is no water but only rock . . .
> If there were only water amongst the rock
> Dead mountain mouth of carious teeth that cannot
>   spit
>
> . . . blood shaking my heart
> The awful daring of a moment's surrender
> Which an age of prudence can never retract
> By this, and this only, we have existed
> Which is not to be found in our obituaries
> Or in memories draped by the beneficent spider
> Or under seals broken by the lean solicitor
> In our empty rooms

He might have regarded his marriage and its trials as a regrettable accident of fallible youth—the awful daring of a moment's surrender—compounded by his initial sense of duty and loyalty. But he was shattered beyond such realism, and finally even beyond stoicism. He felt he had gazed too long on the Furies. The fiery brand he had plucked out of his private inferno seemed not to have been ignited in the ordinary world; it blackened him metaphysically, and had little to do with fractured expectations or the social difficulties of mental illness. What he knew himself to be was a sinner. The wretchedness he had endured was sin. Vivien had been abused—by doctors and their scattershot treatments, and by regimens Eliot could not have prevented. The truth was she had been drugged for years. And he had abused her himself, perhaps more horribly, by the withdrawal of simple human sympathy. It was she who had smothered his emotional faculties, but reciprocal humiliation had not earned reciprocal destinies. Vivien was confined. He was freed to increase his fame. Nevertheless—as if to compensate her—he lived like a man imprisoned; like a penitent; like a flagellant. He was consumed by ideas of sin and salvation, by self-loathing. The scourge that was Vivien had driven him to conversion: he entered Christianity seriously and desperately, like a soul literally in danger of damnation, or as though he believed he was already half-damned. The religiosity he undertook was a kind of brooding medieval monkishness: ascetic, turned altogether inward, to the sinful self. Its work was the work of personal redemption. In "Ash-Wednesday" he exposed the starting-point, the beginning of abnegation and confession:

> *Because these wings are no longer wings to fly*
> *But merely vans to beat the air*
> *The air which is now thoroughly small and dry*
> *Smaller and dryer than the will*
> *Teach us to care and not to care*
> *Teach us to sit still.*

And in a way he did learn to sit still. He was celibate. He was diligent and attentive in his office life while conducting an orderly if lonely domestic routine. He was at Mass every morning, and frequently went on retreat. During the night blitz of London in 1939, he served for a time as an air raid warden, often staying up till dawn. Then, to escape the exhausting bombings, like so many others he turned to commuting from the far suburbs, where he became the paying guest of a family of gentlewomen. In 1945, at the war's end, he made another unusual household arrangement, one that also had its spiritual side: he moved in with John Hayward, a gregarious wit and bookish extrovert whom disease had locked in a wheelchair. Eliot performed the necessary small personal tasks for his companion, wheeled him to the park on pleasant afternoons, and stood vigilantly behind his chair at the parties Hayward liked to preside over—Eliot reserved and silent under the burden of his secret wounds and his eminence, Hayward boisterous, funny, and monarchically at ease. In the evenings, behind the shut door of the darkest room at the back of the flat, Eliot recited the rosary, ate his supper from a tray, and limited himself to a single game of patience. This odd couple lived together for eleven years, until Eliot suddenly married his young secretary, Valerie Fletcher. She offered him the intelligent adoration of an infatuated reader who had been enchanted by his poetry and his fame since her teens; she had come to Faber & Faber with no other motive than to be near him. Vivien had died in 1947; the marriage to Valerie took place in 1957. After the long discipline of penance, he opened himself to capacious love for the first time. As he had known himself for a sinner, so now he knew himself for a happy man.

But the old reflex of recoil—and abandonment—appeared to have survived after all. From youth he had combined ingrained loyalty with the contrary habit of casting off the people who seemed likely to impede his freedom. He had fled over an ocean to separate himself from his demanding parents—though it was his lot ultimately to mimic them. He was absorbed by religion like his mother, and ended by writing, as she did, devotional poetry. Like his father, he was now a well-established businessman, indispensable to his firm and its most influential officer. (It developed that he copied his father even in trivia. The elder Eliot was given to playful doodlings of cats. The son—whose knack for cartooning exceeded the father's—wrote clever cat verses. These, in the form of the long-running Broadway musical, are nearly the whole sum of Eliot's current American renown: if today's undergraduates take spontaneous note of Eliot at all, it will be *Cats* on their tape cassettes, not *The Waste Land*.) Still, despite these evolving reversions, it was the lasting force of his repudiations that stung: his scorn for the family heritage of New England Unitarianism, his acquisition in 1927 of British citizenship. He had thrown off both the liberal faith of his fathers—he termed it a heresy—and their native pride of patriotism. He had shown early that he could sever what no longer suited. The selfless interval with John Hayward was cut off overnight: there is a story that Eliot called a taxi, told Hayward he was going off to be married, and walked out. After so prolonged a friendship—and a dependence—Hayward felt cruelly abandoned. He never recovered his spirit. Eliot was repeatedly capable of such calculated abruptness. His abandonment of Vivien—

the acknowledged sin of his soul, the flaming pit of his exile and suffering—was echoed in less theological tones in his careless dismissal of Emily Hale and Mary Trevelyan, the wounded women whose loving attachment he had welcomed for years. When Vivien died, each one—Emily Hale in America and Mary Trevelyan close at hand in London—believed that Eliot would now marry her.

Miss Hale—as she was to her students—was a connection of the New England cousins; Eliot had known her since her girlhood. Their correspondence, with its webwork of common associations and sensibilities, flourished decade after decade—she was a gifted teacher of drama at various women's colleges and private schools for girls, with a modest but vivid acting talent of her own. Eliot's trips to America always included long renewing visits with her, and she in turn traveled to England over a series of summer vacations to be with him. One of their excursions was to the lavish silent gardens of Burnt Norton, the unoccupied country mansion of an earl. (That single afternoon of sunlight and roses was transformed by "a grace of sense, a white light still and moving," into the transcendent incantations of "Burnt Norton," the first of the *Quartets.*) In America she waited, in tranquil patience and steady exultation, for the marriage that was never to come: generations of her students were informed of her friendship with the greatest of living poets. Eliot found in her, at a distance, unbodied love, half-elusive nostalgia, the fragility of an ideal. When she threatened, at Vivien's death, to become a real-life encumbrance, he diluted their intimacy; but when he married Valerie Fletcher he sloughed Emily off altogether—rapidly and brutally. Stunned and demoralized—they had been friends for fifty years—she gave up teaching and spiralled into a breakdown. She spent the rest of her life in the hope that her importance to Eliot would not go unrecognized. Her enormous collection of his letters (more than a thousand) she donated to Princeton University, and—Eliot-haunted and Eliot-haunting—she asked him to return hers. He did not reply; he had apparently destroyed them. The "man I loved," she wrote to Princeton, "I think, did not respond as he should have to my long trust, friendship and love." She stipulated that the

Princeton repository not be opened until 2019; she looked to her vindication then. Having been patient so long, she was willing to be patient even beyond the grave. Eliot may have bestowed his infirm old age on Miss Fletcher, but the future would see that he had loved Miss Hale in his prime.

As for Mary Trevelyan, she was a hearty pragmatist, a spunky activist, a bold managerial spirit. For nineteen years she was a prop against Eliot's depressions, a useful neighbor—she drove him all over in her car—and, to a degree, a confidante. From the beginning of Vivien's incarceration until his marriage to Valerie—i.e., from 1938 until 1957—Eliot and Mary were regularly together at plays, at parties, and, especially, at church. Their more private friendship centered on lunches and teas, domestic evenings cooking and listening to music in Mary's flat, her matter-of-fact solicitude through his illnesses and hypochondria. They made a point of mentioning each other in their separate devotions. Mary was at home in the pieties Eliot had taken on—she came of distinguished High Anglican stock, the elite of government, letters, and the cloth, with a strong commitment to public service. Her father was a clergyman who erected and administered churches; the historian G. M. Trevelyan was a cousin; her relatives permeated Oxford and Cambridge. (Humphrey Carpenter, author of a remarkably fine biography of Ezra Pound—fittingly published in Eliot's centenary year—represents the newest generation of this family.)

With Mary, Eliot could unbutton. He felt familiar enough to indulge in outbursts of rage or contemptuous sarcasm, and to display the most withering side of his character, lashing out at the people he despised. Through it all she remained candid, humorous, and tolerant, though puzzled by his unpredictable fits of withdrawal from her, sometimes for three months at a time. He drew lines of conduct she was never permitted to cross: for instance, only once did he agree to their vacationing together, and that was when he needed her—and the convenience of her driving—to help entertain his sister, visiting from America. Mary was accommodating but never submissive. During the war she organized a rest hostel in Brussels for soldiers on leave from the front; in 1944 she nursed hundreds of the wounded. After the war she traveled all over Asia for UNESCO, and founded an international house in London for foreign students. Plainly she had nothing in common with the wistful and forbearing Miss Hale of Abbot Academy for girls. But her expectations were the same. When Vivien died, Mary proposed marriage to Eliot—twice. When he refused her the first time, he said he was incapable of marrying anyone at all; she thought this meant his guilt over Vivien. The second time, he told her about his long attachment to Emily Hale, and how he was a failure at love; she thought this meant psychological exhaustion. And then he married Valerie. Only eight days before the wedding—held secretly in the early morning at a church Eliot did not normally attend—he and Mary lunched together for hours; he disclosed nothing. On the day of the wedding she had a letter from him commemorating their friendship and declaring his love for Valerie. Mary sent back two notes, the earlier one to congratulate him, the second an unrestrained account of her shock. Eliot responded bitterly, putting an end to two decades of companionship.

BUT ALL THIS—the years of self-denial in the parish house, the wartime domesticity among decorous suburban ladies, the neighborly fellowship with John Hayward and Mary Trevelyan, the break with Hayward, the break with Emily Hale, the break with Mary Trevelyan, the joyous denouement with Valerie Fletcher— all this, however consecrated to quietism, however turbulent, was aftermath and postlude. The seizure that animated the poetry had already happened—the seizure was Vivien. Through Vivien he had learned to recognize the reality of sin in all its influences and phases; she was the turning wind of his spiritual storm. Vivien herself understood this with the canniness of a seer: "As to Tom's *mind*," she once said, "I am his mind." The abyss of that mind, and its effect on Eliot as it disintegrated, led him first through a vortex of flight, and then to tormented contemplation, and finally to the religious calm of "Burnt Norton":

> Time present and time past
> Are both perhaps present in time future.
> And time future contained in time past.

Time past marked the psychological anarchy of his youthful work, that vacuous ignorance of sin that had produced "Prufrock," "Gerontion," "The Hollow Men," *The Waste Land*. Not to acknowledge the real presence of sin is to be helpless in one's degradation. Consequently Prufrock is a wraith "pinned and wriggling on the wall," uncertain how to "spit out all the butt-ends of my days and ways"; Gerontion is "a dry brain in a dry season"; the hollow men "filled with straw" cannot falter through to the end of a prayer—"For Thine is / Life is / For Thine is the"; the voice of *The Waste Land*—"burning burning burning burning"—is unable to imagine prayer. And the chastening "future contained in time past" is almost surely the inferno that was Vivien: what else could that earlier hollowness have arrived at if not a retributive burning? The waste land—a dry season of naked endurance without God— had earned him the ordeal with Vivien; but the ordeal with Vivien was to serve both time past and time future. Time past: he would escape from the formless wastes of past metaphysical drift only because Vivien had jolted him into a sense of sin. And time future: only because she had jolted him into a sense of sin would he uncover the means to future absolution—the genuine avowal of himself as sinner. To the inferno of Vivien he owed clarification of what had been. To the inferno of Vivien he owed clarification of what might yet be. If Vivien was Eliot's mind, she had lodged Medusa there, and Medusa became both raging muse and purifying savior. She was the motive for exorcism, confession, and penitence. She gave him "Ash-Wednesday," a poem of supplication. She gave him *Four Quartets*, a subdued lyric of near-forgiveness, with long passages of serenely prosaic lines (occasionally burned out into the monotone of philosophic fatigue), recording the threshold of the shriven soul:

> . . . *music heard so deeply*
> *That it is not heard at all, but you are the music*
> *While the music lasts. These are only hints and guesses,*
> *Hints followed by guesses; and the rest*
> *Is prayer, observance, discipline, thought and action.*
> *The hint half guessed, the gift half understood, is*
> *Incarnation.*

What makes such "reading backward" possible, of course, is the biographies. (I have relied on Peter Ackroyd and Lyndall Gordon for much of the narrative of Eliot's life.) Knowledge of the life interprets—decodes—the poems: exactly what Eliot's theory of the objective correlative was designed to prevent. Occasionally the illuminations cast by reading backward provoke the uneasy effect of looking through a forbidden keyhole with a flashlight:

> "My nerves are bad tonight. Yes, bad. Stay with
> me.
> "Speak to me. Why do you never speak? Speak.
> "What are you thinking of? What thinking? What?
> "I never know what you are thinking. Think."
>
> I think we are in rats' alley
> Where the dead men lost their bones.

That, wailing out of a jagged interval in *The Waste Land*, can only be Vivien's hysteria, and Eliot's recoil from it. But it hardly requires such explicitness (and there is little else that is so clearly explicit) to recognize that his biographers have broken the code of Eliot's reticence—that programmatic reticence embodied in his doctrine of impersonality. The objective correlative was intended to direct the reader to a symbolic stand-in for the poet's personal suffering—not Vivien but Tiresias. Secret becomes metaphor. Eliot's biographers begin with the metaphor and unveil the secret. When the personal is exposed, the objective correlative is annihilated.

And yet the objective correlative has won out, after all, in a larger way. If *The Waste Land* can no longer hide its sources in Eliot's private malaise, it has formidably sufficed as an "objective equivalence" for the public malaise of generations. Its evocations of ruin, loss, lamentation, its "empty cisterns and exhausted wells," are broken sketches of the discontents that remain when the traditional props of civilization have failed: for some (unquestionably for Eliot), a world without God; for others, a world without so much as an illusion of intelligibility or restraint. In 1867, contemplating the Victorian crisis of faith, Matthew Arnold saw "a darkling plain . . . where ignorant armies clash by night," but in

Eliot's echoing "arid plain" there is nothing so substantial as even a clash—only formlessness, "hooded hordes swarming," "falling towers"; hallucination succeeds hallucination, until all the crowns of civilization—"Jerusalem Athens Alexandria / Vienna London"—are understood to be "unreal."

In 1922 (a postwar time of mass unemployment, economic disintegration and political uncertainty), *The Waste Land* fell out upon its era as the shattered incarnation of dissolution, the very text and texture of modernism—modernism's consummate document and ode. In the almost seventy years since its first publication, it has taken on, as the great poems do (but not the very greatest), a bloom of triteness (as ripe truth can overmature into truism). It is no more "coherent" to its newest readers than it was to its astonished earliest readers, but it is much less difficult; tone and technique no longer startle. Post-Bomb, post-Holocaust, post-moonwalk, it may actually be too tame a poem to answer to the mindscape we now know more exhaustively than Eliot did. Professor Harry Levin, Harvard's eminent pioneer promulgator of Proust, Joyce, and Eliot, quipped a little while ago—not altogether playfully—that modernism "has become old-fashioned." *The Waste Land* is not yet an old-fashioned poem, and doubtless never will be. But it does not address with the same exigency the sons and daughters of those impassioned readers who ecstatically intoned it, three and four decades ago, in the belief that infiltration by those syllables was an aesthetic sacrament. Even for the aging generation of the formerly impassioned, something has gone out of the poem—not in *The Waste Land* proper, perhaps, but rather in that parallel work Eliot called "Notes on 'The Waste Land.' " This was the renowned mock-scholarly apparatus Eliot tacked on to the body of the poem, ostensibly to spell out its multiple allusions—a contrivance that once seemed very nearly a separate set of modernist stanzas: arbitrary, fragmented, dissonant, above all solemnly erudite. "The whole passage from Ovid," drones the sober professorial persona of the "Notes," "is of great anthropological interest." There follow nineteen lines of Latin verse. The procession of brilliantly variegated citations—Augustine, the Upanishads, Verlaine, Baudelaire, Hermann Hesse, Shakespeare,

Tarot cards, the Grail legend—suggests (according to Professor Levin) that context was to Eliot what conceit was to the meta-physical poets. A fresh reading of the "Notes" admits to something else—the thumbed nose, that vein in Eliot of the practical joker, released through Macavity the Mystery Cat and in masses of un-published bawdy verses (nowadays we might regard them as more racist than bawdy) starring "King Bolo's big black basssturd kween." In any case, whatever pose Eliot intended, no one can come to the "Notes" today with the old worshipful gravity. They seem drained of austerity—so emphatically serious that it is hard to take them seriously at all.

The same with the plays. With the exception of the first of the five, *Murder in the Cathedral*—a major devotional poem of orches-tral breadth—the plays are all collapsed into curios. From our per-spective, they are something worse than period pieces, since that is what they were—Edwardian drawing room dramas—when they were new. They hint at (or proclaim) a failure of Eliot's public ear. His aim was to write popular verse plays for the English stage—an aim worthy (though Eliot never had the hubris to say this) of Shakespeare. George Bernard Shaw had been content with prose—and the majestically cunning prose speeches in *Murder in the Cathedral* are reminiscent of nothing so much as Shaw's *Saint Joan*, including Shaw's preface to that play. The dialogue of en-jambment that is the style and method of *The Cocktail Party*, *The Confidential Clerk*, and *The Elder Statesman*, never attains the sound of verse, much less poetry. That was precisely Eliot's hope: he con-sidered *Murder in the Cathedral* too blatantly poetic, a "dead end." His goal was to bury the overt effects of poetry while drawing out of ordinary speech and almost ordinary situations a veil of transcendence—even, now and then, of mystical horror, as when (in *The Family Reunion*) the Furies suddenly appear, or when (in *The Cocktail Party*) a character we are meant to imagine as a saint and a martyr goes off to be a missionary among the "natives" and is eaten by ants. (Having first been crucified, it ought to be added. And though there are farcical moments throughout, the devour-ing anthill is not intended as one of them.) Nevertheless nothing transcendent manages to rise from any printed page of any of the last four plays—almost nothing suggestive of poetry, in fact, except an occasional "wisdom" patch in the semi-lyrical but largely prosy manner of the philosophical lines in *Four Quartets*. Possibly this is because the printed page is perforce bare of technical stagecraft, with its color and excitement. Yet—similarly unaccoutered—Shakespeare, Marlowe, and Shaw, in their greater and lesser written art, send out language with presence and power enough to equal absent actors, sets, lighting, costumes. Much of Eliot's dialogue, rather than achieving that simplicity of common speech he aspired to, plummets to the stilted, the pedestrian, the enervated:

> *Oh, Edward, when you were a little boy,*
> *I'm sure you were always getting yourself measured*
> *To prove how you had grown since the last holidays.*
> *You were always intensely concerned with yourself;*
> *And if other people grow, well, you want to grow too.*

Given only the text and nothing else, a reader of *The Cocktail Party*, say, will be perplexed by its extravagant performing history: in London and New York in the Fifties, it filled theaters and stunned audiences. Read now, these later plays are unmistakably dead, embalmed, dated beyond endurance—dated especially in the light of the vigorous Fifties, when the energetic spokesmen of the Angry Young Men were having their first dramatic hearing. As playwright, Eliot inexplicably eschewed or diluted or could not pull off his theory of demarcation between "the man who suffers and the mind which creates," so the plays are surprisingly confessional—the Furies harbor Vivien, a character is tormented by thinking he has killed his wife, Valerie turns up as a redemptive young woman piously named Monica, etc. Since Eliot's private life was not only closed but unguessed-at in those years, gossip could not have been the lure for theater-goers. The lure was, in part, skillful production: on the page, the Furies when they pop up seem as silly as the news of the hungry anthill, but their theatrical embodiment was electrifying. Fine performances and ingenious staging, though, were at bottom not what brought overflowing audiences to see Eliot's plays. They came because of the supremacy of Eliot's fame. They came because verse drama by T. S. Eliot was the most potent cultural vitamin of the age.

Inevitably we are returned to the issue (there is no escaping it at any point) of Eliot's renown. As a young man, he had hammered out the prestige of a critical reputation by means of essay after essay. By the time of the later plays he had become a world celebrity, an international feature story in newspapers and magazines. But neither the essays by themselves, nor (certainly) the plays—always excepting *Murder in the Cathedral*, which ought to count among the most lastingly resonant of the poems—could have won for Eliot his permanent place in English letters. The fame belongs to the poems. The rest, however much there might be of it, was spinoff. Yet the body of poems is amazingly small in the light of Eliot's towering repute. In 1958, for example, invited to Rome for an honorary degree, he was driven through streets mobbed with students roaring *"Viva* Eliot!" Mass adulation of this sort more often attaches to presidents and monarchs—or, nowadays, to rock stars. What did that roar rest on? Leaving aside the early Bolo ribaldry (which in any case never reached print), the fourteen cat verses, and the contents of a little posthumous collection called *Poems Written in Early Youth* (from ages sixteen to twenty-two), but not omitting two unfinished works—"Sweeney Agonistes" and "Coriolan"—Eliot's entire poetic oeuvre comes to no more than fifty-four poems. England, at least, is used to more abundant output from the poets it chooses to mark with the seal of permanence. My copy of Wordsworth's *Poetical Works* adds up to nine hundred and sixty-six pages of minuscule type, or approximately a thousand poems. The changes in the written culture between, say, the "Ode on Intimations of Immortality," published in 1807, and Eliot's *Waste Land*, published one hundred and fifteen years later, speak for themselves. Still, granting the impertinence of measuring by number, there remains something extraordinary—even uncanny—about the torrent of transoceanic adoration that, for Eliot, stemmed from fifty-four poems.

Eliot may have supposed himself a classicist, but really he is in the line of the Romantics: subjective, anguished, nostalgic, mystical, lyrical. The critic Harold Bloom's mild view is that he "does not derive from Dante and Donne, as he thought, but from Tennyson and Whitman"—a judgment that might have stung him. For Eliot to have believed himself an offspring of the cosmic Dante and the precision-worker Donne, and to end, if Professor Bloom is correct, as a descendant of the softer, lusher music of Tennyson, is no serious diminishment (Tennyson is permanent too)—though it *is* a diminishment. Lord Tennyson, the British Empire's laureate, may have seemed a weighty and universal voice to the Victorians. For us he is lighter and more parochial. It is in the nature of fame to undergo revision: Eliot appears now to be similarly receding into the parochial, even the sectarian (unlike the all-embracing Whitman, with whom he shares the gift of bel canto). His reach—once broad enough to incorporate the Upanishads—shrank to extend no farther than the neighborhood sacristy, and to a still smaller space: the closet of the self. His worship was local and exclusionary not simply in the limited sense that it expressed an astringent clerical bias, or that he observed the forms of a narrow segment of the Church of England—itself an island church, after all, though he did his best to link it with what he termed "the Universal Church of the World." What made Eliot's religiosity local and exclusive was that he confined it to his personal pain and bitterness: he allowed himself to become estranged from humanity. Feeling corrupt in himself, he saw corruption everywhere: "all times are corrupt," he wrote; and then again, "the whole of modern literature is corrupted by what I call Secularism." Demanding that faith—a particular credo—be recognized as the foundation of civilization, he went on to define civilization as extraneous to some of its highest Western manifestations—the principles of democracy, tolerance, and individualism. Despite his youthful study of Eastern religion and his poet's immersion in Hebrew scripture, he was finally unable to imagine that there might be rival structures of civilization not grounded in the doctrine of original sin, and yet intellectually and metaphysically exemplary. Even within the familial household of Christendom, he was quick to cry heretic. In any event, the style of his orthodoxy was, as Harry Levin put it, "a literary conception." As a would-be social theorist he had a backward longing for the medieval hegemony of cathedral spires—i.e., for a closed society. It was a ruefulness so poignant that it preoccupied much of the prose and seeped into the melancholy cadences of the poetry. As a modernist, Eliot was the last of the Romantics.

In the end he could not disengage the mind that created from the man who suffered; they were inseparable. But the mind and the man—the genius and the sufferer—had contributed, in influence and authority, more than any other mind and man (with the exception perhaps of Picasso) to the formation of the most significant aesthetic movement of the twentieth century. It was a movement so formidable that its putative successor cannot shake off its effects and is obliged to carry on its name; helplessly, we speak of the "postmodern." Whether postmodernism is genuinely a successor, or merely an updated variant of modernism itself, remains unresolved. Yet whichever it turns out to be, we do know for certain that we no longer live in the literary shadow of T. S. Eliot. "Mistah Kurtz—he dead"—the celebrated epigraph Eliot lifted from Conrad's *Heart of Darkness* and affixed to "The Hollow Men"—applies: the heart has gone out of what once ruled. High art is dead. The passion for inheritance is dead. Tradition is equated with obscurantism. The wall that divided serious high culture from the popular arts is breached; anything can count as "text." Knowledge—saturated in historical memory—is displaced by information, or memory without history: data. Allusiveness is crosscultural in an informational and contemporary way (from, say, beekeeping to film-making), not in the sense of connecting the present with the past. The relation of poets to history is that they can take it or leave it, and mostly they leave it, whether in prosody or in the idea of the venerable. If it is true that *The Waste Land* could not be written today because it is too tame for the savagery we have since accumulated, there is also a more compelling truth: because we seem content to live without contemplation of our formal beginnings, a poem like *The Waste Land,* mourning the loss of an integral tradition, is for us inconceivable. For the modernists, the center notoriously did not hold; for us (whatever *we* are), there is no recollection of a center, and nothing to miss, let alone mourn.

Was it the ever-increasing rush to what Eliot called "Secular-ism" that knocked him off his pinnacle? Was it the vague nihilism of "modern life" that deposed modernism's prophet? Was Eliot shrugged off because his pessimistic longings were ultimately judged to be beside the point? The answer may not be as clearcut as any of that. The changes that occurred in the forty years be-tween the Nobel award in 1948 and Eliot's centennial in 1988 have still not been assimilated or even remotely understood. The Wordsworth of the "Ode to Duty" (composed the same year as "Intimations of Immortality") has more in common with the Eliot of *Four Quartets*—the differing idioms of the poetry aside—than Eliot has with Allen Ginsberg. And yet Ginsberg's "Howl," the sin-gle poem most representative of the break with Eliot, may owe as much, thematically, to *The Waste Land* as it does to the bardic Whitman, or to the opening of the era of anything-goes. Ginsberg belongs to the generation that knew Eliot as sanctified, and, de-spite every irruption into indiscipline, Eliot continues alive in Ginsberg's ear. For the rest, a look at the condition of most poetry in America today will disclose how far behind we have left Eliot. William Carlos Williams, a rival of Eliot's engaged in another vein of diction and committed to sharply contrasting aesthetic goals ("no ideas but in things"), said of the publication of *The Waste Land* that he "felt at once it had set me back twenty years," largely be-cause of its European gravity of erudition. The newest generation in the line of descent from Williams, though hardly aware of its own ancestry, follows Williams in repudiating Eliot: music is not wanted, history is not wanted, idea is not wanted. Even literature is not much wanted. What *is* wanted is a sort of verbal snapshot: the quick impression, the short flat snippet that sounds cut from a sentence in a letter to a friend, the casual and scanty "revela-tion." As Eliot in his time spurned Milton's exalted epic line as too sublime for his need, so now Eliot's elegiac fragments appear too arcane, too aristocratic, and too difficult, for contemporary ambi-tion. Ironic allusiveness—Eliot's inspired borrowing—is out of the question: there is nothing in stock to allude to. Now and then there are signs—critical complaints and boredom—that the school of pedestrian verse-making is nearly exhausted, and more and more there are poets who are venturing into the longer line, the denser stanza, a more intense if not a heightened diction.

But the chief elements of the Age of Eliot are no longer with us, and may never return: the belief that poetry can be redemptive, the conviction that history underlies poetry. Such notions may still be intrinsic to the work of Joseph Brodsky and Czeslaw Milosz—Europeans resident in America. Eliot was an American resident in Europe. Even as he was exacting from both poetry and life a perfected impersonation of the European model, he was signing himself, in letters, *Metoikos*, the Greek word for resident alien. He knew he was a contradiction. And it may simply be that it is in the renunciatory grain of America to resist the hierarchical and the traditional. Eliot's "high culture" and its regnancy in and beyond the American university may have been an unsuccessful transplant that "took" temporarily, but in the end would be rejected by the formation of natural tissue. Or, as Eliot himself predicted in the "Dry Salvages" section of *Four Quartets*,

We had the experience but missed the meaning.

For the generation for whom Eliot was once a god (my own), the truth is that we had the experience and were irradiated by the meaning. Looking back over the last forty years, it is now our unsparing obligation to disclaim the reactionary Eliot. What we will probably go on missing forever is that golden cape of our youth, the power and prestige of high art.

ALFRED
CHESTER'S
WIG

*Images Standing
Fast*

The other day I received in the mail a card announcing the retirement of an old friend, not an intimate, but an editor with whom, over the years, I have occasionally been entangled, sometimes in rapport, sometimes in antagonism. The news that a man almost exactly my contemporary could be considered ready to retire struck me as one more disconcerting symptom of a progressive unreality. I say "one more" because there have been so many others. Passing my reflection in a shop window, for instance, I am taken by surprise by a striding woman with white hair. She is still wearing the bangs of her late youth, but there are shocking pockets and trenches in her face; she has a preposterous dewlap; she is no one I can recognize. Or I discover that the most able and arresting intellects currently engaging my attention were, when I was myself first possessed by the passions of mind they have brilliantly mastered, little children.

All the same, whatever assertively supplanting waves may lap around me—signals of redundancy, or of superannuation—I know I am held fast. Or, rather, it is not so much a fixity of self as it is

of certain exactnesses, neither lost nor forgotten: a phrase, a
scene, a voice, a moment. These exactnesses do not count as
memory, and even more surely escape the net of nostalgia or
memoir. They are platonic enclosures, or islands, independent of
time, though not of place—in short, they irrevocably *are*. Nothing
can snuff them. They are not like candle flames, liable to waver or
sputter, and not like windows or looking glasses that streak or
cloud. They have the quality of clear photographs, or of stone
friezes, or of the living eyes in ancient portraits. They are not subject to erasure or dimming.

Upon one of these impermeable platonic islands, the image of
Alfred Chester stands firm. It is likely that this name—Alfred
Chester—is no longer resonant in literary circles. As it happens,
the editor in question—the one who is now retiring—was among
the first to publish Chester. And Chester had his heyday. He knew
Truman Capote, or said he did, and Susan Sontag and Paul Bowles
and Princess Marguerite Caetani, the legendary aristocrat who
sponsored a magazine called *Botteghe Oscure*. He wrote energetically snotty reviews that swaggered and intimidated—the kind of
reviews that many young men (and very few young women) in
the Fifties and Sixties wrote, in order to found a reputation. But
his real calling was for fiction; and anyhow it was a time when
reputations were mainly sought through the writing of stories and
novels.

There is, by the way, another reason these reflections cannot be
shrugged off simply as a "memoir," that souvenir elevation of tri-
fles. A memoir, even at its best, is a recollection of what once was:
distance and old-fashionedness are taken for granted. But who and
what Chester was, long ago, and who and what I was, have neither
vanished nor grown quaint. Every new half-decade sprouts a fresh
harvesting of literary writers, equally soaked in the lust of ambition, equally sickened (or galvanized) by envy. There is something
natural in all this—something of nature, that is. The snows of yesteryear may be the nostalgic confetti of memoir, but last year's
writers are routinely replaced by this year's: the baby carriages are
brimming over with poets and novelists. Chester, though, has the
sorrowful advantage of being irreplaceable, not so much because

of his portion of genius (he may not, when all is said and done, deserve this term), as because he was cut down in the middle of the trajectory of his literary growth—so there is no suitable measure, really, by which to judge what he might have been in full maturity. He never came to fruition. He died young.

Or relatively young. He was forty-two. Well, Keats was twenty-five, Kafka forty, and, in truth, we are satisfied: no one feels a need for more Keats or more Kafka. What is there is prodigy enough. It might be argued that Chester had plenty of time to achieve his masterpieces, if he was going to achieve them at all—and yet it is difficult, with Chester, to assent to this. He rarely sat still. Time ran away with him, and hauled him from America to Europe to North Africa, and muddled him, and got in his way. His dogs—repulsive wild things he kept as pets—got in his way. His impatient and exotic loves got in his way. His fears and imaginings got in his way. Finally—the most dangerous condition for any writer—it was the desolation of life itself that got in his way: moral anguish, illness, helpless and aimless wanting, relentless loneliness, decline.

All this I know from the hearsay of that small accumulation of letters and essays and other testimony by witnesses to his latterday bitterness, and the suffering it led to. By then, Chester and I were long since estranged—or merely, on my part, out of touch. I am as certain as I can be of anything that I was never in Chester's mind in the last decade of his life; but he was always in mine. He was a figure, a presence, a regret, a light, an ache. And no matter how remote he became, geographically or psychologically, he always retained the power to wound. He wounded me when he was in Paris. He wounded me when, in 1970, we were both in Jerusalem. And once—much, much earlier—in an epistolary discussion of what we both termed "the nature of love," I wounded him terribly: so terribly that, after those letters were irretrievably written, and read, and answered, our friendship deteriorated. Paris, Tangier, Jerusalem. He lived in all these fabled cities, but I knew him only in New York. I knew him only at—so to speak—the beginning. "In my beginning is my end" was not true for Chester; and having been there at the beginning, I am convinced that he was intended for an end utterly unlike the one he had. I have always believed this—that his life as he was driven to conduct it was a distortion, not a destiny. I even believed that if Chester and I had not been so severely separated, I might have persuaded him (how he would have scoffed at such arrogance) away from what was never, in my view, inevitable.

Unless you count the wig. Chester was the wig's guardian. He was fanatically careful of it in the rain—he wore a rain hat if rain was expected, or, if it was not, covered his head with his coat. He was also the wig's prisoner and puppet: it gave him the life he had, and perhaps the life he eventually chose.

So it is possible, even likely, that I am wrong in my belief—a conviction four decades old—that Chester was not meant to die drugged, drunken, desolate, in the company of a pair of famished wild dogs. It may be—if you count the wig as the beginning—that his end *was* in his beginning, after all. It may be that that orange-yellow wig he so meticulously kept from being rained on determined Chester's solitary death.

Most people called him "Al," and, later, "Alfred." As far as I can tell, except for Mr. Emerson I am the only one who ever called him "Chester," and of course I still call him that. "Chester" has a casual and natural sound to it, and not merely because it can pass as a given name. I go on saying "Chester" because that is how I first heard him referred to. Mr. Emerson regularly said "Chester." Me he called, according to the manners of the time, "miss." On the other hand, it was not quite the manners of the time; it was a parody of the time before our time; sarcasm and parody and a kind of thrillingly sardonic spite were what Mr. Emerson specialized in. Mr. Emerson's own first name was not accessible to us; in any case, I cannot recollect it. Like Chester in Jerusalem a quarter of a century on, Mr. Emerson either was or was not a suicide. In the summer following our semester with him, the story went, Mr. Emerson stepped into a wood and shot himself. The wood, the shotgun, the acid torque of Mr. Emerson's mouth at the moment of extinction—they all scattered into chill drops of conjecture, drowned in the roil of the thousands of ex-soldiers who were flooding New York University that year. The only thing verifiable in the rumor of Mr. Emerson's suicide was the certainty of his absence: he never came back to teach in the fall.

Mr. Emerson's class was freshman composition, and it was in this class, in 1946, that Chester and I first met. We were starting college immediately after the war—the Second World War, which my generation, despite Korea and Vietnam, will always call, plainly and unqualifiedly, "the war." The G.I. Bill was in full steam, and Washington Square College—a former factory building that housed the downtown liberal arts branch of N.Y.U.—had reverted to assembly-line procedures for the returning swarms of serious men still in army jackets and boots, many of them New Yorkers, but many of them not: diffident Midwesterners with names like Vernon and Wendell, wretchedly quartered in Long Island Quonset huts together with old-fashioned wives and quantities of babies. To the local teen-agers just out of high school, they seemed unimpassioned and literal-minded—grave, patient, humorless old men. Some of them actually *were* old: twenty-seven, thirty-two, even thirty-five. The government, in a historic act of public gratitude, was footing the bill for the higher education of veterans; the veterans, for their part, were intent on getting through and getting jobs. They were nothing if not pragmatic. They wanted to know what poetry and history were *for*.

The truth is, I despised these anxious grownups, in their seasoned khaki, with their sticky domestic worries and ugly practical needs. I felt them to be intruders, or obstacles, or something worse: contaminants. Their massive presence was an affront to literature, to the classical vision, to the purity of awe and reverence, to *mind*. They had an indolent contempt for contemplation, for philosophy, for beauty. There were so many of them that the unventilated lecture halls, thronged, smelled of old shoes, stale flatulence, boredom. The younger students sprawled or squatted in the aisles while the veterans took mechanical notes in childishly slanted handwriting. Their gaze was thickened, dense, as if in trance, exhausted: when, in the first session of the term, a professor of Government (a required course), quoting Aristotle, startled the air with the words "Man is by nature a political animal," they never looked up—as if "animal," used like that, were not the most amazing syllables in the world. Nothing struck them as new, nothing enchanted them, nothing could astonish them. They were a mob of sleepwalkers, heating up the packed corridors and crammed staircases with their sluggish breath and the perpetual fog of their cigarette smoke, inching like a languid deluge from one overcrowded classroom to another. They were too old, too enervated, too indifferent. In the commons I would hear them comparing used cars. They were despoiling my youth.

And youth was what I was jealous of: youth in combination with literary passion. Nowadays one can hardly set down this phrase—"literary passion"—without the teasing irony of quotation marks representing abashed self-mockery: the silly laughter of old shame. Of course the veterans were, in their sensible fashion, right: they had survived the battlegrounds of catastrophic Europe, had seen mortal fragility and burned human flesh up close, and were preparing for the restoration of their lives—whereas I, lately besotted by the *Aeneid*, by "Christabel," by Shelley's cloud and Keats's nightingale, was an adolescent of seventeen. Chester, though, was not. He was not, as I was, heading for eighteen. He was sixteen still; I envied him for belonging to the other side of the divide. He had the face of a very young child. His skin was as pure and unmarked as a three-year-old's, and he had a little rosy mouth, with small rosy lips. His lips were as beautifully formed as a doll's. His pretty nose was the least noticeable element of his pretty face; the most noticeable was the eyelids, which seemed oddly fat. It took some time—weeks or perhaps months—to fathom that what distinguished these eyelids, what gave them their strangeness, was that they were altogether bald. Chester had neither eyebrows nor eyelashes. He was a completely hairless boy.

He was, besides, short and ovoid, with short active fingers like working pencil erasers. His pale eyes were small and shy; but they had a rapid look, akin to hiding—a kind of skip, a quickstep of momentary caution. We stood at the blackboard in a mostly empty classroom, doodling with the chalk. The veterans, those wearily cynical old men, began straggling in, swallowing up the rows of chairs, while Chester and I made tentative tugs at each other's credentials. He identified himself as a writer. Ordinarily I was skeptical about such claims; high school had already proved the limitations of the so-called "flair." He told me the name of his high school. I told him the name of mine. I knew without his mentioning it that he had arrived by subway from Brooklyn: I knew it because he had one of the two varieties of Brooklyn speech I could recognize. The first was exceedingly quick; the other was exceedingly slow, dragging out the vowels. Chester's talk sped, the toe of the next sentence stumbling over the heel of the last. A flying fleck of spittle landed on my chin: he was an engine of eagerness. I was, in those days, priggishly speech-conscious, having been subdued by the Shavian Pygmalions of my high school Speech Department, under whose fierce eyes, only a couple of weeks earlier, I had delivered the graduating address. These zealous teachers, missionaries of the glottis and diaphragm, had effectively suppressed the miscreant Northeast Bronx dentalizations of Pelham Bay—a fragrant nook of meadows and vacant lots overgrown with cattails and wild flowers, archaeologically pocked with the ruins of old foundations: building starts cut off by the Depression, and rotting now into mossy caverns. I lived at the subway's lowest vertebra— the end of the Pelham Bay line; but the ladies of the Speech Department (all three of whom had nineteenth-century literary names, Ruby, Olive, Evangeline) had turned me into a lady, and severed me forever from the hot notes of New York. Chester, rapidfire, slid up and down those notes—not brashly, but minstrel-like, ardent, pizzicato. I saw into him then—a tender, sheltered, eager child. And also: an envious hungry writing beast, and not in embryo. In short, he was myself, though mine was the heavier envy, the envy that stung all the more, because Chester was sixteen and I was not.

The veterans were invisible. We dismissed them as not pertinent. What *was* pertinent was this room and what would happen in it. Here were the veterans, who were invisible; here was a resentful young woman who was to vanish within the week; here was Chester; and Mr. Emerson; and myself, the only surviving female. The young woman who deserted complained that Mr.

Emerson never acknowledged her, never called on her to speak, even when her hand was conspicuously up. "Woman hater," she spat out, and ran off to another course section. What it came to, then, when you subtracted the veterans, was three. But since Mr. Emerson was what he was—a force of nature, a geological fault, a gorge, a thunderstorm—what it came to, in reality, was two. For Chester and for me, whatever it might have been for the veterans in their tedious hordes, there was no "freshman composition." A cauldron, perhaps; a cockpit. Chester and I were roped-off roosters; or a pair of dogs set against each other—pitbulls; or gladiators obliged to fight to the death. All this was Mr. Emerson's scheme—or call it his vise or toy—arbitrarily settled on after the first assignment: a character study, in five hundred words.

On the day the papers were returned, Mr. Emerson ordered me to stand in front of the class—in front of Chester, in effect—and read aloud what I had written. There was an explicit format for these essays: an official tablet had to be purchased at the university book store, with blanks to fill in. Then the sheets had to be folded in half, to make a rectangle. The face of the rectangle was for the instructor's grade and comment.

"Read that first sentence!" Mr. Emerson bawled.

I looked down at my paper. There was no grade and no comment.

" 'Gifford was a taciturn man,' " I read.

"Louder! Wake up those sleeping soldiers back there! And keep in mind that I'm a man who's deaf in one ear. What's that goddamn adjective?"

"Taciturn."

"Where'd you swipe it from?"

"I guess I just thought of it," I said.

"Picked it up someplace, hah? Well, what in hell's it *mean*?"

It was true that I had only recently learned this word, and was putting it to use for the first time.

"Does it mean quiet?" I choked out.

"Don't ask *me*, miss. I'm the one that's supposed to do the goddamn asking."

"I think it means quiet."

"You think! *I* think you got it out of some trash heap. Read on," he commanded.

He let me continue, quavering, for another paragraph or so. Then his arm shot out like a Mussolini salute.

"All right, miss. Sit! Now you! Chester!"

Chester stood. The somnolent veterans were surprised into alertness: they stared across at the ringmaster and his livestock. Now the rapid Brooklyn voice began—a boy's voice, a boy's throat. The little pink lips—that rosy bouquet—stretched and pursed, looped and flattened. Chester read almost to the end; Mr. Emerson never interrupted. Humiliated, concentrating, I knew what I was hearing. Behind that fragile mouth, dangerous fires curled: a furnace, a burning bush. The coarse cap of false orange-yellow hair shook—it narrowed Chester's forehead, lifted itself off his nape, wobbled along the tops of his ears. He was bold, he was rousing, he was loud enough for a man deaf in one ear. It was ambition. It was my secret self.

"That's enough. Sit, Chester!" Mr. Emerson yelled. "Gentlemen, you'll never find a woman who can write. The ladies can't do it. They don't have what it takes, that's well known. It's universal wisdom, and I believe in it. All the same," he said, "these two, Chester and the lady, I'm not the fool that's going to let them drop back into the pond with the catfish."

After that Chester and I had separate writing assignments—separate, that is, from the rest of the class. Mr. Emerson may have been a woman hater, but it was the veterans he declined to notice and looked to snub. His teaching (if that is what it was) was exclusively for the two of us. It was for our sakes—"that plumber," he sneered—that he disparaged Walt Whitman. It was for our sakes that he devoted minutes every day—irascible still, yet reverential—to praising *Brideshead Revisited*, the Evelyn Waugh bestseller he was reading between classes. And sometimes *in* class: while the veterans slid down in their seats like a silent communal pudding, Mr. Emerson opened to where he had left off and fell into a dry recital:

I was always given the room I had on my first visit; it was next to Sebastian's, and we shared what had once been a dressing-room and had been changed to a bathroom twenty years back by the substitution for the bed of a deep, copper, mahogany-framed bath, that was filled by pulling a brass lever heavy as a piece of marine engineering; the rest of the room remained unchanged; a coal fire always burned there in winter. I often think of that bathroom—the water colours dimmed by steam and the huge towel warming on the back of the chintz armchair—and contrast it with the uniform, clinical little chambers, glittering with chromium plate and looking-glass, which pass for luxury in the modern world.

Dry, but there was a suppressed rapture in it—rapture for the brass lever, for the water colours (in their transporting British spelling) dimmed by steam. It was clear that Mr. Emerson himself, an unhappy man with tired eyes—they often teared—did not like the modern world; perhaps he would not have liked any world, even one with picturesque coal fires. In the grip of some defenseless fatigue, he gave way to fits of yawning. His snarl was inexhaustible; also comically unpredictable. He took a sardonic pleasure in shock. Certainly he shocked me, newly hatched out of the decorous claims of Hunter High (finishing-school-cum-Latin-prep), where civilization hung on the position of a consonant struck upon the upper gums (never against the teeth), and mastery of the ablative absolute marked one out for higher things. Mr. Emerson said "God damn," he said "hell," he even alluded, now and then, to what I took to be sexual heat.

It was not that I was ignorant of sexual heat: I had already come upon it in the *Aeneid*; there it was, in Dido and Aeneas. Dido on her pyre, burning for love! And here it was again, between Agnes and Gerald in the dell, in *The Longest Journey*, the early E. M. Forster novel that was included in our freshman composition curriculum. The first paragraphs alone—well before sexual heat made its appearance—were undiluted pleasure:

"The cow is there," said Ansell, lighting a match and holding it out over the carpet. No one spoke. He waited till the end of the match fell off. Then he said again, "She is there, the cow. There, now."

"You have not proved it," said a voice.

"I have proved it to myself."

"I have proved to myself that she isn't," said the voice. "The cow is *not* there." Ansell frowned and lit another match.

"She's there for me," he declared. "I don't care whether she's there for you or not. Whether I'm in Cambridge or Iceland or dead, the cow will be there."

It was philosophy. They were discussing the existence of objects. Do they exist only when there is someone to look at them? or have they a real existence of their own? It is all very interesting, but at the same time it is difficult. Hence the cow. She seemed to make things easier. She was so familiar, so solid.

None of this was familiar in the spring of 1946; E. M. Forster was an unknown name, at least to me; philosophy lay ahead; nothing was solid. Rickie and Ansell were lost in Mr. Emerson's mercurial derisions. For years afterward I remembered only Rickie's limp. Much later I began to read *The Longest Journey* over and over again, until ultimately I had certain passages by heart. In class it was hardly discussed at all. It appeared to hold no interest for Mr. Emerson, and Chester and I never spoke of it. It was not what we read that counted for Mr. Emerson, anyhow; it was what we wrote. Chester and I wrote—were intended to write—as rivals, as yoked competitors under the whip. "Got you that time, didn't she? Made you look small, didn't she?" he chortled at Chester; and, the following week, to me: "Males beat females, it's in the nature of things. He's got the stuff, the genuine shout. He's wiped you out to an echo, miss, believe me." Sometimes he made no comment at all, and gave back our papers, along with the weekly work of the rest of the class, with no more than a cocky glare. That left us stymied; there was no way to find out who had won over the other. Since Mr. Emerson never graded what Chester and I turned in (he routinely graded the others), the only conclusion was that we were both unworthy. And the next week he would be at it again: "She knocked you off your high horse, hah, Chester?" Or: "You'd better quit, miss. You'll never be in the running." All that term we were—Chester and I—a pair of cymbals, ringing and striking in midair; or two panting hares, flanks heaving, in a mad marathon; or a couple of legs-entangled wrestlers in a fevered embrace. It was as if—for whatever obscure reason—Mr. Emerson were some sly, languid, and vainglorious Roman emperor presiding over the bloody goings-on in the Colosseum of his classroom, with the little green buds of Washington Square Park just beginning to unfold below the college windows.

What came out of it, beside a conflagration of jealousy, was fraternity. I loved Chester; he was my brother; he was the first real writer of my generation I had ever met, a thing I knew immediately—it was evident in the increasingly rococo noise of his language, and in Mr. Emerson's retributive glee. If promoting envy was Mr. Emerson's hidden object in instigating the savagery of Chester's competitiveness with me, and mine with him, it is conceivable that it was his own envy Mr. Emerson suffered from, and was picking at. It is not unheard-of for older would-be writers to be enraged by younger would-be writers. The economy of writing always operates according to a feudal logic: the aristocracy blots out all the rest. There is no, so to speak, middle class. The heights belong, at most, to four or five writers, a princely crew; the remainder are invisible, or else have the partial, now-and-then visibility that attaches to minor status. Every young writer imagines only the heights; no one aspires to be minor or invisible, and when, finally, the recognition of where one stands arrives, as it must, in maturity, one either accepts the limitations of fate or talent, or surrenders to sour cynicism. Whether Mr. Emerson was embittered by chances lost or hope denied, or by some sorrowful secret narrowing of his private life, it was impossible to tell. Whichever it was, it threw Chester and me, red in tooth and claw, into each other's arms. It also made us proud: we had been set aside and declared to be of noble blood. (All this, of course, may be retrospective hubris. Perhaps Mr. Emerson saw us as no more than what we were: a couple of literary-minded freshmen whose strenuousness an attentive teacher was generously serving and cultivating.)

We took to walking up and down Fourth Avenue in the afternoons, the two of us, darting into one after another of those rows and rows of second-hand book stores the long straight street was famous for. The cheapest books were crammed into sidewalk racks under awnings, to protect them from the rain. It seemed always to be raining that spring, a tenderly fickle drizzle and fizz that first speckled and then darkened the pavement and made Chester hood the crown of his head with his jacket. We drilled into back rooms and creaked down wooden basement steps; everywhere those thousands of books had the sewery smell of cellar—repellent, earthen, heart-catching. In these dank crypts, with their dim electric bulbs hanging low on wires over tables heaped with comatose and forgotten volumes, and an infinity of collapsing shelves along broken-plastered brick walls labeled "THEOSOPHY," "HISTORY," "POETRY" (signs nailed up decades back, faded and curled by dampness), one could loiter uninterrupted forever. The proprietor was somewhere above, most likely on a folding chair in the doorway, hunched over a book of his own, cozily insulated from the intrusions of customers, bothering nobody and hoping not to be bothered himself. Gradually the cellar smells would be converted, or consecrated, into a sort of blissful incense; nostrils that flinched in retreat opened to the tremulous savor of books waiting to be aroused, and to arouse. Meandering in the skinny aisles of these seductive cellars, Chester and I talked of our childhoods, and of our noses. I admired Chester's nose and deplored my own. "Yours isn't so bad, just a little wide," he said kindly. He told me of his long-ago childhood disease; he did not name it, though he explained that because of it he had lost all his hair. He did not say that he wore a wig.

There was something Hansel-and-Gretelish about our excursions, so brotherly and sisterly, so childlike and intimate, yet prickly in their newness. Fresh from an all-girls high school, I had never before conversed with a boy about books and life. I had never before gone anywhere with a boy. Boys were strangers, and also—in my experience, if not in principle—as biologically unfathomable as extraterrestrials. Though I had a brother, there was a divide between us: he had ascended to college when I was in grade school, and at this hour was still in the army. At home, with my parents at work in their pharmacy, I had the house to myself: I sat at my little wooden Sears, Roebuck desk (a hand-me-down from my brother, the very desk I am using right now), and fearfully pressed out my five hundred words for Mr. Emerson, jealous of what I imagined Chester might be contriving on the same subject, and burning against him with a wild will. I wanted more than anything to beat him; I was afraid he would beat me. When I listened to him read his paper aloud, as Mr. Emerson occasionally had us do even well into the semester, a shrewdly hooked narrative turn or an ingenious figure of speech or some turbulently reckless flash of power would afflict me like a wound. Chester was startling, he was robust, he was lyrical, he was wry, he was psychological, he was playful, he was scandalous. He was better than I was! In one respect, though, I began to think I was stronger. We were equally attracted to the usual adolescent literary moonings: to loneliness, morbidity, a certain freakishness of personality. But I felt in myself stirrings of history, of idea, something beyond the senses; I was infatuated with German and Latin, I exulted over the Reformation. I supposed it meant I was more *serious* than Chester—more serious, I presumed, about the courses we were enrolled in. Chester was indifferent to all that. Except for English classes, he was careless, unexcited. He was already on his way to bohemianism (a term then still in its flower). I, more naively, more conventionally, valued getting an A; I pressed to excel, and to be seen to excel. I thought of myself as a neophyte, a beginner, an apprentice—it would be years and years (decades, aeons) before I could accomplish anything worth noticing. I regarded my teachers not as gods, but as those who wore the garments of the gods. I was as conscious of my youth as if it were a sealed envelope, and myself a coded message inside it, indefinitely encased, arrested, waiting. But Chester was poking through that envelope with an impatient fist. He was becoming gregarious. He was putting his noisiness to use.

And still he was soft, susceptible. He was easily emotional. I saw him as sentimental, too quickly inflamed. He fell soppily in love at a moment's glance. And because we were brother and sister, I was his çonfidante; he would tell me his loves, and afterward leave me feeling resentful and deserted. I was not one of the pretty girls; boys ignored me. Their habitual reconnoitering wheeled right over me and ran to the beauties. And here was Chester, no different from the others, with an eye out for looks—flirting, teasing, chasing. Nearly all young women seemed extraordinary that spring: archaic, Ewardian. The postwar fashion revolution, appropriately called the New Look, had descended, literally descended, in the form of long skirts curling around ankles. All at once half the population appeared to be in costume. Only a few months earlier there had been a rigid measure for the length of a skirt: hems were obliged to reach precisely, uncompromisingly, to the lower part of the knee. What else had that meant but an irreversible modernity? Now the girls were all trailing yards and yards of bright or sober stuff, tripping over themselves, delightedly conspicuous, enchanted with their own clear absurdity. Chester chased after them; more often they chased after Chester. When I came to meet him in the commons nowadays, he had a retinue. The girls moved in on him; so did the incipient bohemians; he was more and more in the center of a raucous crowd. He was beginning to display himself—to accept or define himself—as a wit, and his wit, kamikaze assaults of paradox or shock, caught on. In no time at all he had made himself famous in the commons—a businesslike place, where the resolute veterans, grinding away, ate their sandwiches with their elbows in their accounting texts. Chester's success was mine. He was my conduit and guide. Without him I would have been buried alive in Washington Square, consumed by timidity.

He journeyed out to visit me twice—a tediously endless subway trip from the bowels of Brooklyn to Pelham Bay. We walked in the barren park, along untenanted crisscross paths, down the hill through the big meadow to the beach. I was proud of this cat-tailed scene—it was mine, it was my childhood, it was my Brontëan heath. Untrammelled grasses, the gray keen water knocking against mossy stones. Here I was master. Now that Chester was celebrated at school, I warmed to the privilege of having him to myself, steering him from prospect to prospect, until we were light-headed with the drizzly air. At the end of the day, at the foot of the high stair that led to the train, we said goodbye. He bent toward me—he was taller than I, though not by much—and kissed me. The pale perfect lips and their cold spittle rested on my mouth; it was all new. It had never happened before, not with any other boy. I was bewildered, wildly uncertain; I shrank back, and told him I could not think of him like that—he was my brother. (Ah, to retrieve that instant, that movietone remark learned from the silver screen of the Pilgrim Theater, half a mile down the tracks! To retrieve it, to undo it, to wipe it out!) He wormed his blunt white fingers into his jacket pockets and stood for a while. The el's stanchions shook. Overhead the train growled and headed downtown. Two puddles lay against his lower eyelids, unstanched by the missing lashes. It was the same, he said, with Diana; it was just the same, though Diana wasn't a brute, she hadn't said it outright. He didn't want to be anyone's brother—mine, maybe, but not Diana's. I knew Diana, a brilliant streak in the commons excitements: in those newfangled long skirts she had a fleet, flashing step, and she wore postwar nylons and neat formal pumps (unrenovated, I was still in my high school sloppy Joes and saddle shoes). Diana was one of the beauties, among the loveliest of all, with a last name that sounded as if it had fallen out of a Trollope novel, but was actually Lebanese. In after years I happened on a replica of her face on the salvaged wall of an ancient Roman villa, with its crimson tones preserved indelibly: black-rimmed Mediterranean eyes fixed in intelligence, blackly lit; round cheeks and chin, all creamy pink. An exquisite ur-Madonna. Diana had a generous heart, she was vastly kind and a little shy, with a penetrating attentiveness untypical of the young. Like many in Chester's crew, she was single-mindedly literary. (She is a poet of reputation now.) Chester yearned; and more than anyone, Diana was the object and representation of his yearning.

But I yearned, too. The word itself—soaked in dream and Poesy—pretty well embodies what we were, Chester and I, in a time when there was no ostensible sex, only romance, and the erotic habits of the urban bookish young were confined to daring cafeteria discussions of the orgone box (a contrivance touted by Wilhelm Reich), and severely limited gropings at parties in the parental domicile. One of these parties drew me to Brooklyn—it was my first look at this fabled place. The suburban atmosphere of Flatbush took me by surprise—wide streets and tall brick Tudor-style houses flawed only by being set too closely together. The party, though given by a girl I will call Carla Baumblatt, was altogether Chester's: he had chosen all the guests. Carla would not allow us to enter through the front door. Instead, she herded us toward the back yard and into the kitchen. She had managed to persuade her parents to leave the house, but her mother's admonishments were all around: Carla worried about cigarette ashes, about food spilling, about muddy shoes. She especially worried about the condition of the living room rug; someone whispered to me that she was terribly afraid of her mother. And soon enough her mother came home: a tough, thin, tight little woman, with black hair tightly curled. Carla was big and matronly, twice her mother's size. She had capacious breasts that rode before her, and a homely mouth like a twist of wax, and springy brown hair, which she hated and attempted to squash down. She was dissatisfied with herself and with her life; there was no movie rhapsody in it. An argument began in the kitchen, and there was Carla, cowed by her tiny mother. Curiously, a kitchen scene turns up in Chester's first novel, *Jamie Is My Heart's Desire*, published in England in 1956, a decade after Carla's party—the last time she ever tried to give a party at home. The narrator describes a young woman's "largeness": "I have always felt that her body was the wrong one, that it was an exaggerated contrast with her personality, and that one must disregard it in order to know Emily at all. It is her fault I have believed this so long, for in all her ways she had negated the strength and bigness her figure shows, and substituted weakness and dependency and fright, so that one imagines Emily within as a small powerless girl." When Carla reappeared in the living room after quarreling with her mother, she seemed, despite her largeness, a small powerless girl; she was as pale as if she had been beaten, and again warned about dirtying the carpet.

In the middle of that carpet a young woman lay in a mustard glow. Her head was on a fat cushion. Her mustard-colored hair flowed out over the floor. Her mustard-colored New Look skirt was flung into folds all around. She was sprawled there like an indolent cat. Now and again she sat up and perched her chin on her elbow—then the dark trough between her breasts filled with lamplight. She had tiger's eyes, greenly chiaroscuro, dappled with unexpected tinsel flecks. Her name was Tatyana; she gave out the urgency of theater, of Dostoyevsky, of sea gulls. A circle of chairs had somehow grouped in front of her; she had us all as audience, or as a body of travelers stung by a spell into fixity. Carla, stumbling in from the kitchen, seemed devoured by the sight: it was the majesty of pure sexuality. It was animal beauty. Carla's plump stooped shoulders and plump homely nose fell into humility. She called to Chester—they were old neighborhood friends, affectionate old school friends. The familial currents that passed between them had the unearned rhythms of priority. I resented Carla: she had earlier claims than I, almost the earliest of all. I thought of her as a leftover from Chester's former life—the life before Mr. Emerson. It was only sentimentality that continued to bind him to her. She was a blot on his escutcheon. She had no talents other than easy sociability; away from home, in the commons, she was freely companionable and hospitable: she would catch hold of me in the incoming lunch crowd and wave me over to her table. But we did not like each other. On Chester's account we pretended congeniality. Worse yet, Carla dissembled bookishness; it was an attempt to keep up. In April, on my eighteenth birthday, she astonished me with a present: it was Proust, *Cities of the Plain,* in the Modern Library edition. Carla was so far from actual good will that her gift struck me as an intrusion, or an act of hollow flattery, or an appeasement. I owned few books (like everyone else, I frequented the public library), and wanted to love with a body-love the volumes that came permanently into my hands. I could not love a book from Carla. When I eventually undertook to read *Cities of the Plain,* it was not the copy she had given me. I have Carla's copy in front of me now, still unfondled, and inscribed as follows: "*Ma chère—c'est domage que ce livre n'est pas dans l'originale—mais vous devriez être une si marveilleuse linguiste comme moi pour lire cela—Amour toujours—*" Carla's English was equally breezy and misspelled. Her handwriting was a super-legible series of girlish loops. Chester had inherited her along with other remnants of his younger experience. He rested in Carla's sympathy. I imagined she knew the secret of the yellow wig.

Because of Tatyana—the mustard glow on Carla's mother's carpet—Chester was undistractable. When Carla tried to get his attention, he threw out some mockery, but it was to Tatyana. He was a man in a trance of adoration; he was illuminated. Tatyana stretched her catlike flanks and laughed her mermaid's laughter. She was woman, cat, fish—silvery, slithery, mustard-colored. She spread her hair and whirled it. She teased, turned, played, parried, flirted. The room swam with jealousy—not simply Carla's, or mine, or the other girls'. Call it the jealousy of the gods: Tatyana, a mortal young woman, was in the seizure of an unearthly instant. The engines of her eyeballs moved all around with the holy power of their femaleness.

The second and last time Chester came to Pelham Bay, it was in the company of Ben Solomons. Ben had become Chester's unlikely sidekick. Together they were Mutt and Jeff, squat pepperpot and tall broom, Arthur's handsomest knight and Humpty Dumpty. Ben was nicely dressed and not very talkative (taciturn!). He was a little older than I (even weeks counted), and had the well-polished shoes of a serious pre-med student. (When I heard, decades later, that he was Dr. Solomons, the psychiatrist, I was surprised. Not urology? Not gastroenterology?) Since he did not say much, it was hard to assess his intelligence. What mattered to me, though, was his breath, his tallness, his nearness. I had been sickened, that afternoon, by infatuation: out of the blue I was in love with Ben. The lunch my mother had left us had been mysteriously unsatisfactory; it lacked some bourgeois quality I was growing aware of—the plates, the tablecloth, the dining room chairs. It was only food. All my tries at entertainment were a nervous failure. At three o'clock we walked, in the eternal rain (Chester's jacket up over his head), to the next el station to see a movie at the Pilgrim Theater—called, in the neighborhood, the Pillbox, because it was so cramped. In the middle of the day the theater was desolate. I was self-conscious, guilty, embarrassed. It was as if I had dragged us to a pointless moonscape. We settled into the center of the house—myself, Ben, and Chester, in that order, along the row of vacant seats. The movie came on; I suffered. Next to me Ben was bored. Chester tossed out cracks about the dialogue; I laughed, miserably; Ben was silent. Then I shut my eyes, and kept them shut. It was a wall against tears. It was to fabricate boredom and flatter Ben's judgment. It was to get Ben to notice. His big hand on his left knee, with his gold high school graduation ring pressed against the knuckle, drew me into teary desire. I unsealed an eye to be sure that they were still there—the hand, the ring, the knuckle. Ben was sedate, waiting out the hours.

At the time it seemed a long friendship—Chester's with Ben—and, except for that single aching afternoon in Pelham Bay, which came like a fever and passed like a fever, I was as wary of Ben as I was of Carla, as I was of Chester's entrance into Tatyana's apotheosis. Like Byron's sister, I wanted Chester for myself. I soon understood that it was useless: he was a public magnet. Everyone was his straight man and acolyte. To be with Chester was to join his gang at the edge of bohemia, or what was imagined to be bohemia, since all the would-be bohemians went home every night, by subway, to their fathers and mothers in their Bronx and Brooklyn apartments. In our little house in Pelham Bay, I had my own tiny room, flowery with the do-it-yourself yellow wallpaper my mother had put up as a surprise. Onto this surface I pasted, with Scotch tape, a disjointed Picasso woman, cut out from *Life* magazine. She was all bright whorls and stripes and misplaced eyes and ears. She had whirligig breasts. She gave me pride but no pleasure. She stood for eccentricity, for the Unconventional—she was an inkling of what Chester was more consciously heading for. There was nothing of any of this in Ben—no scrambled testing-grounds, no pugnacity, no recklessness, no longing for the inchoate, no unconventionality. No intimations of unknown realms. He was a solid student, with inconspicuous notions; he was conspicuously good-looking, in the style of the familiar hero of a 1940's B movie: broad-shouldered, square-chinned, long-lashed. His chief attraction was the velvety plenitude of his deeply black hair: one wavy lock dropped in a scallop on his forehead, like Superman's. Ben was rarely seen in the commons. He was not one of Chester's cosmopolitan hangers-on; he was too businesslike, too intent on propriety. But he represented for Chester what my Picasso woman represented for me: the thing closed off, the thing I could not become. I could not become one of the bohemians: I was diffident and too earnest, too "inhibited." I was considered "naive," I was not daring enough. When Chester's gang began to meet in Village bars after classes, I envied but could not follow.

Yellowing on the yellow walls, my cut-out Picasso lingered for years. Chester's attachment to Ben was, by contrast, brief, though while it lasted it was a stretched-out, slow-motion sequence—the stages of a laboratory experiment requiring watchful patience. Ben had the glamorous long torso Chester would have liked to have. He had, especially, the hair. Ben was a surrogate body, a surrogate head of hair. Girls were smitten by him. He was an ambassador from the nation of the normal and the ordinary. When Chester cast off Ben, it was his farewell to the normal and the ordinary. It was the beginning of the voyage out. In the commons one day, not long after Ben was jettisoned, coming on Chester surrounded by his gang and dangling, between third finger and thumb, a single hair, I asked (the innocent candor of an assistant clown) what it was. "A pubic hair," he retorted.

He was never again not outrageous; he was never again soft. He had determined to shut down the dreamy boy who mooned over girls. Either they rebuffed him, or, worse, embraced him as a friendly pet, good for banter or hilarity. He was nobody's serious boyfriend. Tatyana, after Carla's party, had gone on cosseting him as a plaything to tantalize. Diana, always empathic, withheld the recesses of her heart. I was a literary rival, a puritan and a bluestocking. Carla was an old shoe. What, after having been so much crushed, was left for Chester's moist sensibility? It dried into celebrity. It dried into insolence and caprice. Chester's college fame depended—was founded—on the acid riposte, the quick sting; on anything implausible. He flung out the unexpected, the grotesque, the abnormal. Truman Capote's short stories were in vogue then, miniature Gothic concoctions specializing in weird little girls, in clairvoyance, in the uncanny. Chester began modeling his own stories on these. He committed to memory long passages from an eerie narrative called "Miriam"; he was bewitched by Truman Capote's lushness, mystery, baroque style. In his own writing he was gradually melting into Truman Capote. He opened his wallet and pulled out an address book: that number there, he bragged, was Truman Capote's unlisted telephone, set down by the polished little master himself.

All this while Chester was wearing the yellow wig. He wore it more and more carelessly. It was as curly as a sheep's belly, and now took on a ragged, neglected look, grimy. It hardly mattered to him if it went askew, lifting from his ears or pressing too far down over where the absent eyebrows should have been.

In 1966 he published a portion of "The Foot," an abandoned novel that is more diary and memoir than fiction. By then his style was entering its last phase, disjointed, arbitrary, surreal— deliberately beautiful for a phrase or two, then deliberately un-beautiful, then dissolved into sloth. The characters are mercurial fragments or shadowless ghosts, wrested out of exhaustion by a drugged and disintegrating will: Mary Monday and her double, also named Mary Monday; Peter Plate, standing for Paul Bowles, whom Chester knew in Morocco; Larbi ("the Arab"), Chester's cook, servant, and sexual companion. All changing themes and short takes, "The Foot" is part travelogue (portraits of Morocco and of New York), part writhing confession ("my long idle life, always occupied by suffering," "I am afraid of who I am behind my own impersonations"), and part portentous pointless fantasy. The effect is of a home slide-show in a blackened room: the slides click by, mainly of gargoyles, and then, without warning, a series of recognizable family shots flashes out—but even these responsible, ordinary people are engaging in gargoylish activity. In this way one impressionist sketch after another jumps into the light, interrupted by satiric riffs—satiric even when mildly pornographic—until five heartbreaking pages of suffering recollected without tranquility all at once break out of their frames of dread, cry their child's cry, and fall back into the blackness. "Do you let a book like this, this book, go back into the world just as it is—with its wounds and blemishes, its bald head and lashless eyes, exposed to the light?" the section starts off, and darkens into a melancholy unburdening:

I was fourteen when I put on my first wig. It was, I believe, my sister's idea. So she and my mother and I went—I forget where . . . Simmons & Co?—some elegantish salon with gold lamé drapes where they did not do such splendid work.

I sat and accepted the wig. It was like having an ax driven straight down the middle of my body. Beginning at the head. Whack! Hacked in two with one blow like a dry little tree. Like a sad little New York tree.

I wore it to school only. Every morning my mother put it on for me in front of the mirror in the kitchen and carefully combed it and puffed it and fluffed it and pasted it down. Then, before going out of the house, I would jam a hat on top of it, a brown fedora, and flatten the wig into a kind of matting. I hated it and was ashamed of it, and it made me feel guilty.

And so to school. The Abraham Lincoln High School.

Up until then I'd gone to a Yeshiva where all the boys wore hats, little black yarmulkas. I too wore a hat, though not a yarmulka, which only covered the tip of the head. I wore a variety of caps. I'd wear a cap to shreds before getting a new one, since I felt any change at all focused more attention on my head. . . .

Coming home from school was a problem. As once the world had been divided for me into Jews and Italians, it was now divided between those who could see me with the wig [and hat] and those who could see me [only] with a hat. Only my most immediate family—mother, father, sister, brother—could see me with both, and only they could see me bald.

Hat people and wig people. Wig people at school. Hat people at home. The wig people could see me with both wig *and* hat (hat-on-top-of-wig, that is). But the hat people must never see me with wig, or even with wig and hat.

This went on for years, decades.

The terror of encountering one side in the camp of the other. Of the wig people catching me without the wig. Of the hat people catching me with it. Terror . . .

And then, there from the corner where the trolley stopped, if it was a fair day, I would see my mother and maybe an aunt or two or a neighbor sitting on our porch in the sun.

Hat people.

Horrible, unbearable, the thought of walking past those ladies to get into the house. . . . Sometimes I would go around corners, down alleys, through other people's gardens to reach our back fence. I'd climb over the back fence so I could get into the house via the door which was usually open.

A thief! Just like a thief I'd have to sneak through the side lanes, unseen across backyards. . . .

I could bear no references to the wig. If I had to wear it, all right. But I wasn't going to talk about it. It was like some obscenity, some desperate crime on my head. It was hot coals in my mouth, steel claws gripping my heart, etc. I didn't want to recognize the wig . . . or even my baldness. It just wasn't there. Nothing was there. It was just something that didn't exist, like a third arm, so how could you talk about it? But it hurt, it hurt. . . .

My second wig was a much fancier job than the first. An old Alsatian couple made it; I think they were anti-Semitic, she out of tradition, he out of fidelity to her.

When the wig was ready, my father and mother and I went to collect it. Evening. I wish I could remember my father's reaction. Mama probably fussed and complained. I imagine Papa, though, like me, simply pretending that the whole thing didn't exist, wasn't even happening. . . .

Anyway, most likely, he said something polite like—how nice it looks! . . .

But the evening of the new wig we went to a restaurant, me wearing the wig. A white-tiled Jewish restaurant. Vegetarian. . . . With fluorescent lights . . .

I just want you to see the three of us—even at home we never ate together—at that white-linened, white-tiled, blue-white-lighted restaurant. . . .

I wonder what we ate that night or why the evening took place at all. It is such a strange thing for Papa to have done. Gone to the wigmakers at all. Met me and Mama in the city. Taken us out to supper.

Perhaps there were a lot of mirrors in that restaurant. Catching a glimpse of myself, wig or no, is dreadful for me. I have to approach a mirror fully prepared, with all my armor on.

But I have a turn-off mechanism for mirrors as well. The glimpse-mirrors, I mean. I simply go blind.

When Chester set down these afflicted paragraphs, he was thirty-seven years old. He had long ago discarded the wig. He had long ago discarded our friendship. He had ascended into the hanging gardens of literary celebrity: *Esquire* included him in its annual Red Hot Center of American writing, and he was a prolific and provocative reviewer in periodicals such as *Partisan Review* and *Commentary*. He had lived in Paris, close to the founding circle of *Paris Review*; at parties he drank with Jimmy Baldwin and George Plimpton. He had been drawn to Morocco by Paul Bowles, the novelist and composer who, according to legend, ruled in Tangier like a foreign mandarin ringed by respectful disciples and vaguely literary satellites devoted to smoking hemp. In Tangier Chester finally took off the wig for good; I, who had known him only when he was still at home with his family in Brooklyn, never saw him without it. His anguish was an undisclosable secret. The wig could not be mentioned, neither by wig-wearer nor by wig-watcher. No one dared any kind of comment or gesture. Yet there were hints—protective inklings—that Ben Solomons had somehow passed through this taboo: on the rainy day Chester brought him to Pelham Bay, it was Ben who, with a sheltering sweep around Chester's shoulders, made the first move to raise Chester's jacket up over his matted crown.

Gore Vidal, in his introduction to a posthumous collection, including "The Foot," of Chester's fiction (*Head of a Sad Angel: Stories 1953–1966*, edited by Edward Field and published by Black Sparrow Press in 1990), speaks of Chester's life as "a fascinating black comedy." "Drink and drugs, paranoia and sinister pieces of trade did him in early," he concludes. I suppose he is not wrong. Yet "sinister pieces of trade" is an odious locution and a hard judgment, even if one lacks, as I confess I do, the wherewithal—the plain data—to see into its unreachable recesses. Vidal calls Chester "Genet with a brain." But if Vidal is alluding to the bleaker side of homosexual mores, Chester himself can be neither his source nor his guide; Chester's breezy erotic spirit has more in common with the goat-god Pan at play than with Genet in prison, scratching a recording pencil across brown paper bags. (Genet's portraits of homosexuals were anyhow tantamount to heartbreak for Chester. "The naked truth of Genet's writing," he remarked in a 1964 review of *Our Lady of the Flowers*, "continues to be unbearable." And he noted that even "the ecstatic whole of [a] masterpiece" is "cold comfort to a man in agony.")

Except for that single passage in "The Foot," nothing in Chester's mind was not literary. His life, nearly all of it, was a lyrical, satirical, or theatrical mirage. In the end the mirage hardened into a looking glass. But what was not strained through literary affectation or imitation or dreamscape, what it would be crueler than cruel to think of as black comedy, is the child's shame, the child's naked truth, that hits out like a blast of lightning in the middle of "The Foot." The child is set apart as a freak. And then the bald boy grows into a bold man; but inside the unfinished man—unfinished because the boy has still not been exorcised—the hairless child goes on suffering, the harried boy runs. "I did have the great good luck never to have so much as glimpsed Alfred Chester," Vidal admits; nevertheless he does not hesitate to name him "a genuine monster." It may require a worldly imagination of a certain toughened particularity—a temperament familiar with kinkiness and hospitable to it—to follow Vidal into his conjectures concerning Chester's sexual practices ("sinister pieces of trade"), but one must leave all heartlessness behind in order to enter the terrors of the man, or the child, who believes he is a monster.

And it was only baldness. Or it was not so much baldness as wig. From any common-sense point of view, baldness is not a significant abnormality, and in the adult male is no anomaly at all. But the child felt himself to be abnormal, monstrous; the child was stricken, the child saw himself a frenzied freak tearing down lane after lane in search of a path of escape.

That path of escape (I was sure of this four decades ago, and am partly persuaded of it even now) was homosexuality—implying an alternative community, an alternative ethos, an alternative system of getting and receiving attention. Chester loved women; women would not love him back; Q.E.D. They would not love him back because, by his own reckoning, he was abnormal, monstrous, freakish. He was too horrifically ugly. With this gruesome impetus, he turned his hairless, beardless, lashless countenance to the alternative world, a world without women, where no woman could wound him because no woman belonged.

All this—folded invisibly, or not so invisibly, into notions of "the nature of love"—I wrote to Chester, in a letter sent to Paris. I had heard that he had "become homosexual." (A term learned at Washington Square College—not from Mr. Emerson—at eighteen. "Gay" had not yet come into general use.) We had been corresponding, not without acrimony, about Thomas Mann. Chester was contemptuous. "Middlebrow," he growled from across the sea, "Somerset Maugham in German," though he had so far not approached a word of anything by Mann. I urged him to read *Death in Venice*. He wrote back, exalted. It was, he said, among the great works of literature; he declared himself converted. By then we had been separated for two or three years. He had gone off to be an expatriate in the second Parisian wave—modeled on Hemingway and Gertrude Stein in the first—and I, returning from graduate school in the Midwest, had settled back into my tiny yellow bedroom in Pelham Bay to become a writer. My idea was to produce a long philosophical novel that would combine the attributes of André Gide, Henry James, George Eliot, Graham Greene, and Santayana's *The Last Puritan*; it was an awkward and juvenile sort of thing, and kept me in the dark for years. Chester, meanwhile, was writing and actually publishing short stories in newly established postwar periodicals—*Merlin, Botteghe Oscure, Paris Review, Proefschrift*. It was the era of the little magazines: these, springing up in Europe, had a luster beyond the merely contemporary. They smacked of old literary capitals, of Americans abroad (Scott and Zelda), of bistros, of Sartre and Simone de Beauvoir, of existentialist ennui. They were as intellectually distant from my little desk in Pelham Bay as it was possible to be. The Scotch tape that held my Picasso woman on the wall turned brittle; superannuated, she fell to pieces and was put in the trash. Chester in Paris was well into the beginnings of an international reputation—he was brilliantly in the world—while I, stuck in the same room where I had fussed over Mr. Emerson's assignments, was only another tormented inky cipher. I had nothing of the literary life but my trips on the bus to the Westchester Square Public Library, and the changing heaps of books these occasioned.

The letters from Paris crowed. Chester made it plain that he had arrived, and that I had been left behind. He condescended, I smarted. *Death in Venice* brought him up short. Literature—its beauty and humanity—had nothing to do with the literary barometer, with ambition and rivalry and the red hot center. Only the comely sentence mattered. The sentence!

> Aschenbach noted with astonishment the lad's perfect beauty. His face recalled the noblest moment of Greek sculpture— pale, with a sweet reserve, with clustering honey-colored ringlets, the brow and nose descending in one line, the winning mouth, the expression of pure and godlike serenity. Yet with all this chaste perfection of form it was of such unique personal charm that the observer thought he had never seen, either in nature or art, anything so utterly happy and consummate.

We began to talk, as we never had before, of the varieties of human attraction. He was not "naturally" homosexual, I insisted; I *knew* he was not; he knew it himself. I reminded him of his old stirrings and infatuations. I made no mention of the old rebuffs. I felt a large, earnest, and intimate freedom to say what I thought—we had between us, after all, a history of undisguised tenderness. And had he not yearned after Diana? He was not obliged, or destined, to be homosexual; he had chosen dramatic adaptation over honest appetite.

His reply was a savage bellow. The French stamps running helter-skelter on the envelope had been licked into displacement by a wild tongue, and pounded down by a furious fist. He roared back at me, in capital letters, "YOU KNOW NOTHING ABOUT LOVE!"

He broke with me then, and I saw how I had transgressed. Privately I took virulence to be confirmation. He was protesting too much. His rage was an admission that he had followed the path of escape rather than the promptings of his own nature. He was not what he seemed; he was an injured boy absurdly compelled to wear a yellow wig. Shame gave him the power of sham—an outrageously idiosyncratic, if illusional, negation of his heart's truth. He could, as it were, hallucinate in life as vividly as on a page of fiction; he had license now for anything.

Chester is long dead, and though I speak retrospectively about the letter that exasperated him and put an end to our friendship, there are living voices much like his own, and probably just as exasperated. They will claim I am simple-minded in theorizing that Chester's self-revulsion (sad little New York tree grown into blindness before mirrors) was the true engine of his turning from women. Psychologists and psychoanalysts will know better than I, bisexual men will know better, gay men will know better (and will reprimand me for overlooking the importance of physical loveliness to the homosexual sensibility). And yes, I know nothing about it. Or, rather, I know that no one knows anything about it: about the real sources of homosexuality. Besides, not every boy who supposes himself unattractive to girls will become a man who courts men. No doubt hundreds, if not thousands, of young men unhappy with their looks and their lives have moved on to conventionally heterosexual arrangements, including marriage. A wig is above all superficial: its site is on top of the head, not inside it. Proclivities are likely innate, not pasted on to accommodate circumstance. The homoerotic matrix may inhabit the neural system.

These are fair objections. But how can I surrender what I genuinely saw? I saw that Chester had once loved, and had wanted to be loved by, women. Believing himself radically unfit, he sought an anodyne. Homosexuality was, at least initially, a kind of literary elixir. It brought him apparitions. Who does not recall, on the dust jacket of *Other Voices, Other Rooms*, the photograph of the beautiful young Truman Capote in a tattersall vest, reclining on a sofa, indolent as an odalisque, with lucent galactic eyes? And what of those luring draughts of Paris and North Africa—brilliant Proustian scenes, Durrellian sweeps of albino light? Anodyne; elixir; apparition. Beyond this, my understanding dims. I cannot pursue Chester into his future; I was not witness to it.

After our last exchange, I never expected to hear from him again. I recognized that I had inflicted a violent hurt—though I had no accurate measure of that violence, or violation, until long afterward, when I came on "The Foot" and the "ax driven straight down the middle of my body."

But Chester had his revenge: he repaid me wound for wound.

If I had intruded on his erotic turf, he, it developed, would tread on ground equally unnameable—our rivalry, or what was left of it. Nothing, in fact, was left of it. Chester was publishing, and being talked of, in Paris and New York. I was still futilely mired in my "ambitious first novel," which reached three hundred thousand words before I had the sense to give up on it. Mr. Emerson had pushed us into a race, and Chester had indisputably won.

About two years after I had lectured him on love, I took the bus to the post office and mailed a short story to Italy—to *Botteghe Oscure*, at an address in Rome. It had already been submitted to the *New Yorker*, for which I had hungrily but mistakenly designed it, relying on some imitative notion of what "a *New Yorker* story" was in those days reputed to be. The story was a failure—the characters were artificial and brittle, the theme absurd. When it was rejected, instead of disposing of my folly, with the recklessness of envy I thought of Chester's dazzlements in *Botteghe Oscure*. He had matured quickly. Whereas I was still writing what I would eventually classify as juvenilia, Chester's Paris stories were exquisite, and more—focused and given over to high diction, they seemed the work of an old hand. They had the tone and weight of translations from this or that renowned classical European author whose name you could not quite put your finger on: Colette, or Lampedusa, or the author of *Death in Venice*. Their worked and burnished openings were redolent of delectable old library books: "Once, in autumn, I sat all night beside the immense stone wall that surrounds the ancient cemetery of Père Lachaise." Or: "Our appointment was for after lunch, down the street from my house in a little formal park full of trees and flowers called the Garden of the Frog." When I reread these early stories now, they sometimes have, here and there, a poison drop of archaism—as if the 1950's had all collapsed into the very, very long ago. And I am startled to notice that we were writing then—both of us—in what from this distance begins to look like the same style, possessed, in the manner of the young, by the ravishments of other voices.

Several months went by. A letter from Paris! But Chester and I had stopped corresponding. He had cut me off and thrown me out. It was a period, I discovered later, when he was writing hundreds of letters, a number of them to new friends made at Columbia University, where, after college, he was briefly enrolled as a graduate student. When his father died and left him a little money, he escaped courses and schedules and headed for Mexico, and then on to Paris. With no constraints now, he was fashioning a nonconformist life for himself—partly out of books, but mainly inspired by the self-proclaimed expatriate nonconformists who were doing exactly the same. He had made it plain that there was no place in that life for me. Impossible, after our rupture, that I would hear from him; yet I knew no one else in Paris. I looked again at the letter. In the upper left-hand corner, in faint green rubber-stamped print, were two intoxicating words: *Botteghe Oscure*. The big manila envelope with my story in it, containing another big manila envelope for its return, had been addressed to Rome. This was not a big manila envelope; no manuscript was being returned; it was a thin small letter. Why from Paris, why not from Rome? *Botteghe Oscure* had its headquarters, whatever they might be (a row of dark shops), in Rome. Princess Marguerite Caetani, the founder, sponsor, and deep pockets of *Botteghe Oscure*, was a princess of Italy; but ah, nobility travels glitteringly from capital to capital. Princess Caetani—it must be she—was writing not from Rome, where the season had ended, but from a grand apartment in Paris, in the grandest arrondissement of all, not far from a little formal park full of trees and flowers. She had put aside her gold-embossed lorgnette to pick up a silver-nibbed pen. A thin green sheet peeped from the thin small envelope. I drew the paper out in a strange kind of jubilation, half-regretful—it was late, nearly too late, for this glimmer of good fortune. It was years after Chester's success, though we had set out together. I had been writing seriously since the age of twenty-two, and had never yet been published—all my literary eggs, so far, were in that dubious basket of an unfinished, unfinishable novel.

I recognized the handwriting in an instant. The letter was not from the Princess. Chester was reading for the Princess, he explained, winnowing, going through the pile of awful things the mail habitually brought—the Princess sent everything over from Rome. You wouldn't believe what awful things he was obliged to slog through. Well, here was my story. It wasn't all that good, he liked a few things in it, they weren't completely awful—he would make sure the Princess got his recommendation anyhow.

Chester on Mount Olympus, tossing crumbs. Humiliation: my story was published in *Botteghe Oscure*. He had won, he had won.

What happened afterward I gathered from rumor and report. Chester left Paris in 1959. Between 1959 and 1963 he lived in New York, and so did I. We never met, spoke, or wrote. As always, he was noisily surrounded, prodding to get a rise out of people, on the lookout for adventures, upheavals, darkening mischiefs. His reviews, of books and theater, were as ubiquitous as sky-writing: you looked up, and there he was. For a while he abandoned the wig, then put it on again. Edmund Wilson, notorious for crusty reclusiveness, sent him a fan letter. But he was restless and ambitious for more, especially for fame of the right sort. He wanted to be writing stories and novels. In 1960 he went off to the perilously companionable isolation of the MacDowell Colony—a retreat in rural New Hampshire for writers, artists, and composers—and stumbled into a private loneliness so absolute that he was beginning to populate it with phantom voices. Unable to sustain his own company, he took on the more engaging job of busybody and troublemaker, begging for attention by riling everyone in sight. In letters that have since been published (how this would have delighted him: he did nothing not for dissemination), he complained to a pair of friends back in New York:

> They all have cars and seem rich. Except some of the painters. They see me walking into town and wave to me as they fly by in their convertibles on their way to lakes and cookouts. They are mainly dumb. They are very square. Nobody's queer, not even me anymore. Besides I hate myself too. I can't stand it anymore not having any stable I. It is too much. Thrust into a totally new situation, here, I don't know who I am. My neighbor Hortense Powdermaker walks by and I feel some creature in me rise. I just want to scream fuck I am alfred chester who? But no one will believe me, not even me. who is writing this now? . . . And the voices in my head go on and on. As there is no me except situationally, I have to have mental conversation in order

to be. . . . Ugh. It's to die. . . . WRITE TO ME WRITE TO ME WRITE TO ME AS I FADE AWAY WITH LONELINESS.

I have had a blowout with Mme. Powdermaker at breakfast this morning and am still quivering. I come to the table, at which she, Ernst Bacon, Leon Hartl (a French painter I adore), and Panos, a Greek, sit. Morning, Powdie, say I, for I have been shaking since last night, aching to give it to her. Aching to give it to most of them in fact, this rude, ungenerous, terrified, ungiving teaparty group who preserve nothing but the surface, so illmannered and illbred, so lacking in spirit. . . . Last night I decided I was no longer going to submit, but to rebel against every act of unkindness. The colony is in an uproar. . . . First of all I have been persona non grata since last Saturday night when I danced with Gus the cook at the MacDowell version of wild party in Savidge Library. . . . Gus wanted to fuck me but I wouldn't let him because of his wife. There has been a party every day since, sometimes twice a day, to which I have been cordially uninvited by the wild young set. I don't mind. It is all like a tea party with the people made of china. But what I do mind is their hypocrisy, the extreme courtesy toward someone they can't bear: me. I also mind their bad manners, like leaving me to put away the pieces in the scrabble board, or Powdie saying yes, very snidely, yes she'd guessed I was a Russian Jew.

There followed a dustup over Chester's having requested Hortense Powdermaker for a lift in her car, which, according to Chester's account, she refused, deliberately allowing him to stand futilely in the road in the dark on a summer's night.

It got pretty hysterical after this and the other tables as well as the kitchen staff were hysterical.

She: (to Ernst Bacon) As head of the house committee, I wish you would take the matter up with this young man. I'm not obliged to be anyone's chauffeur. It is customary to wait to be offered something. Not to ask for it. You're a brash young man. You don't know anything about communal living. You have no place in this colony.

After an official dressing-down, he was asked to leave MacDowell. He was, as he put it in a telegram, "flung out." He announced that Gus, the cook, and Gus's wife, were departing with him, along with Chester's two rambunctious dogs, Columbine and Skoura, who had sunk their teeth into assorted mattresses and the body parts of other residents. (He had been given special permission to bring the dogs with him to MacDowell. He was also supplied with a new typewriter and "a full-length mirror for my yoga.") "And he is lovely," he said of himself. "I love him. He is sweet and cute. . . . O I'm so much gladder to be me than all these pathetic silly other people."

Half a decade later, he was similarly flung out of Morocco, where he had been living since 1963, invited there by Paul Bowles. A young Arab fisherman named Dris, who practiced sympathetic witchcraft and genial conning—the Larbi of "The Foot"—became his lover, factotum, and dependent. "It is traditional in Morocco," Chester remarks in a story ("Glory Hole," subtitled "Nickel Views of the Infidel in Tangier"), "to pay for sex. There are nicer, but not truer, ways of putting it. The lover gives a gift to the beloved: food, clothing, cash. The older pays the younger." It was not because of his sexual conduct that Chester was expelled from Morocco. Tangier was, one might say, a mecca for "Nazarene" homosexuals from the States, who were as officially welcome as any other dollar-bearing visitors. As far as anyone can make out, Chester's landlord complained to the authorities about the savagery of Chester's dogs, and of Chester's own furies, his fits of quarreling with the neighbors over the racket their numerous children made. At MacDowell he had brought in booze to supplement the bland fare in the dining room. In Tangier he turned to pills and kif, a local hallucinogen, and fell into spells of madness. Bounced out of Morocco, he fled to New York and then to London, where he was deranged enough to be tended by a psychiatric social worker. He repeatedly attempted to be allowed back in, enlisting Paul Bowles to intervene for him. Morocco remained obdurate.

In 1970 I was in Jerusalem for the first time, to read a literary paper at a conference. I had published, four years earlier, a very long "first" novel that was really a third novel. It was sparsely reviewed, and dropped, as first novels are wont to do, into a ready oblivion. In Jerusalem, though, I was surprised by a fleeting celebrity: my essay—many thousands of words, which had taken nearly two hours to deliver—was reprinted almost in its entirety, along with my picture, in the weekend book section of the English-language *Jerusalem Post*. All this I saw as fortuitous and happy bait.

Chester was now living in Jerusalem. The moment I arrived in Israel I tried to find him. I had been given the address of a poet who might know how to reach him, but the poet was himself inaccessible—he was sick and in the hospital. I waited for Chester to come to me. I felt hugely *there*; you couldn't miss me. The *Post* had published, gratuitously, the biggest "personals" ad imaginable. Every day I expected Chester's telephone call. It had now been fourteen years since he had winnowed on behalf of the Princess, and more than two decades since I had looked into his bleached and lashless eyes. I longed for a reunion; I thought of him with all the old baby tenderness. I wanted to be forgiven, and to forgive. In contemplating the journey to Israel, my secret, nearly single-minded, hope had been to track him down. In New York his reputation had dwindled; his name was no longer scrawled across the sky. An episodic "experimental" novel, *The Exquisite Corpse* (horrific phantasmagoria bathed in picture-book prose that Chester himself called "delicious"), appearing three years before, had left no mark. Even rumors of Chester's travels had eluded me: I had heard nothing about the life in Morocco, or of his meanderings in Spain and Greece and Sicily; I had no idea of any of it. Jealousy, of Chester or anyone, had long ago burned itself out. It was an emotion I could not recognize in myself. I was clear of it—cured. The ember deposited on the cold hearth of Mr. Emerson's ancient conflagration was of a different nature altogether: call it love's cinder. It lay there, black and gray, of a certain remembered configuration, not yet disintegrated. Chester did not turn up to collect it.

He did not turn up at all. He was already dead, or dying, or close to dying—perhaps even while I was walking the curved and flowering streets of Jerusalem, searching for the ailing poet's house, the poet who was to supply the clue to Chester's whereabouts.

Why had Chester come to Jerusalem? In 1967, back in Paris

again, he put on a new English fedora over his now exposed and glossy scalp, and plunged into the byways of the Marais to seek out a synagogue. Not since his boyhood in the yeshiva had he approached the Hebrew liturgy. Despite this singular visit, his habits continued unrestrained and impenitent. He drank vodka and bourbon and cognac by the quart, smoked kif and hashish, took barbiturates and tranquilizers, and was unrelentingly, profoundly, mercilessly unhappy.

In Jerusalem he set to work on a travel report, never published, called "Letter from the Wandering Jew"—a record, really, of personal affronts, most of them provoked by loneliness in quest of sensationalism. In it he purports to explain why he had left Europe for Israel. "No roads lead to Israel," the manuscript begins. A parenthesis about the opening of a "sex-aids" shop in Tel Aviv follows. And then:

> Why I came is a very long story, a couple of thousand years long, I suppose. I'd been living unhappily in France since May, I and my two dogs Momzer [Hebrew for "bastard"] and Towzer who are Arabs, having been born in Morocco. The idea of Israel had been with me for some time, a kind of latent half-hearted hope that there was a place on this planet where people who had suffered had come together to shelter each other from pain and persecution: a place of lovingkindness. Besides, does a Jew ever stop being a Jew? Especially one like me whose parents had fled the Russian pogroms for the subtler barbarisms of New York? Yiddish was as much my first language as English, and Hebrew came soon after, for [since I was his] youngest and belated child, my father was determined that at least one of his sons would be a good Jew.

This faintly sentimental opening (not counting the sex-shop parenthesis) misrepresents. The rest is bitter stuff, bitter against father and mother, against going to school, against childhood and children, against teachers and rabbis and restaurants and waiters, against God ("that pig called Jehovah"), against France and the French, against Arab hotels and Jewish hotels, against Arabs, against Jews, against traffic noise, even against the scenery. Once again there are the rows over the dogs, flocks of urchins teasing, exasperated neighbors, bewildered policemen. There are forays after eccentric houses to rent; unreasonable landlords; opportunistic taxi drivers. There are rages and aggression and digression and jokes in the mode of sarcasm and jokes in the mode of nihilism. Satire wears out and reverts to snideness, and snideness to open fury. Eventually vodka and Nembutal and little blue Israeli tranquilizers take charge of the language—now gripping, now banal, now thrilling, now deteriorated, now manic, now shocking. At moments it is no more than pretty, a make-do remnant of what was once a literary style:

> The neighborhood was quiet, the house pleasant and sunny; the dogs had a great garden to run around in and there was a pack of ferocious Airedales next door to bark at all the time. Flowers grew all through the winter—roses, narcissi, pansies, and lots of others whose names I don't know—and when spring came, virtually on the heels of [winter], the roof of the house went absolutely crazy with those gorgeous Mediterranean lilacs that have hardly any smell but almost make up for it by the tidal madness of their bloom.

"Letter from the Wandering Jew" was Chester's last performance. A paranoid document, it is not without self-understanding. The Promised Land is always over the crest of the hill, and then, when you have surmounted the hill and stepped into the lovely garden on the other side, you look around and in ten minutes discover that everything has been corrupted. The truth is that the traveler himself, arriving, is the corrupter. Chester, in his last words, fathomed all this to the lees:

> Aren't you tired of listening to me? I am. If I had any tears left, I would cry myself to sleep each night. But I haven't, so I don't. Besides, it is *morning* that comes twisting and torturing my spirit, not nights of dreamless sleep. Morning, another day. I open the shutters and am assailed by the long day unstretching itself like a hideous snake. Does hope spring eternal? Is there still within me the inane dream that somewhere, sometime, will be better?
>
> A few wild poppies are blooming in my littered weedy garden. When I walk out with the dogs I see the poppies opening

here and there among the weeds, and here and there a few sickly wilting narcissi. Surely death is no dream, and that being the case, there is then in truth a homeland, a nowhere, a notime, noiseless and peaceful, the ultimate utopia, the eternal freedom, the end to all hunting for goodness and home.

Chester wrote these sad cadences, I learned afterward, less than a block from my Jerusalem hotel. He never looked for me; I never found him. I never saw him alive again. (His dogs, I heard, were discovered locked in a closet, ravenous.)

He lives in my mind, a brilliant boy in a wig.

VERY FEW are familiar with Chester's work or name nowadays, not even bookish people of his own generation. He counts, I suppose, as a "neglected" writer; or perhaps, more to the point, as a minor one. To be able to say what a minor writer is—if it could be done at all—would bring us a little nearer to defining a culture. The tone of a culture cannot depend only on the occasional genius, or the illusion of one; the prevailing temper of a society and a time is situated in its minor voices, in their variegated chorus, but above all in the certainty of their collective presence. There can be no major work, in fact, without the screen, or ground, of lesser artists against whom the major figure is illuminated. Or put it that minor writers are the armature onto which the clay of greatness is thrown, pressed, prodded. If we looked to see who headed the bestseller list the year *The Golden Bowl* came out, the likelihood is that not a single name or title would be recognizable. Minor writers are mainly dead writers who do not rise again, who depend on research projects—often on behalf of this ideology or that movement—to dig up their forgotten influence. Minor writers are the objects of literary scholarship—who else, if not the scholars, will creep through archives in search of the most popular novelists of 1904?

Quantity is not irrelevant. A minor writer may own an electrifying gift, but a trickle of work reduces power. In the absence of a surrounding forest of similar evidences, one book, no matter how striking, will diminish even an extraordinary pen to minor status. There are, to be sure, certain blazing exceptions—think, for example, of *Wuthering Heights*, a solo masterwork that descends to us unaccompanied but consummate. By and large, though, abundance counts. Balzac is Balzac because of the vast thick row of novel after novel, shelf upon shelf. Imagine Balzac as the author only of *Lost Illusions*, say, a remarkable work in itself. Or imagine James as having written *The Golden Bowl* and nothing else. If *Lost Illusions* were to stand alone, if *The Golden Bowl* were to stand alone, if there were no others, would Balzac be Balzac and James James?

Sectarianism also touches on minorness. There is nothing in the human predicament, of course, that is truly sectarian, parochial, narrow, foreign, of "special" or "limited" or "minority" interest; all subjects are universal. That is the convenience—for writers, anyhow—of monotheism, which, envisioning one Creator, posits the unity of humankind. Trollope, writing about nineteenth-century small-town parish politics, exactly describes my local synagogue, and, no doubt, an ashram along the Ganges. All "parochialisms" are inclusive. Sholem Aleichem's, Jane Austen's, Faulkner's, García Márquez's villages have a census of millions. By sectarianism, for want of a better term, I intend something like monomania—which is different from obsessiveness. Geniuses are obsessive. Kafka is obsessive, Melville is obsessive. Obsessiveness belongs to ultimate meaning; it is a category of metaphysics. But a minor writer will show you a barroom, or a murder victim, or a sexual occasion, relentlessly, monomaniacally. Nothing displays minorness so much as the "genre" novel, however brilliantly turned out, whether it is a Western or a detective story or *The Story of O*, even when it is being deliberately parodied as a postmodernist conceit.

Yet minor status is not always the same as oblivion. A delectable preciousness (not inevitably a pejorative, if you consider Max Beerbohm), or a calculated smallness, or an unstoppable scheme of idiosyncrasy, comic or otherwise—or simply the persnickety insistence on *being* minor—can claim permanence as easily as the more capacious qualities of a Proust or a Joyce. The names of such self-circumscribed indelibles rush in: Christina Rossetti, Edward Lear, and W. S. Gilbert out of the past, and, near our own period,

Ronald Firbank, Ivy Compton-Burnett, A. M. Klein, Edward Dahlberg, S. J. Perelman, James Thurber. Perhaps Beerbohm above all. (There are a handful more among the living.) Minor art is incontrovertibly art, and minor artists, like major ones, can live on and on. Who can tell if Alfred Chester—whose fiction and essays are currently tunneling out into the world again via new editions—will carry on among the minor who are designed to survive, or among those others who will be lost because, beyond their given moment, they speak to no one?

The question leads once more to sectarianism and its dooms. It may be that Chester is a sectarian writer in a mode far subtler than genre writing (he once published a pornographic novel under a pseudonym, but let that pass) or monomania. Homosexual life, insofar as he made it his subject, was never, for Chester, a one-note monody: what moved him was the loneliness and the longing, not the mechanics. His sectarianism, if I am on the right track, took the form of what is sometimes called, unkindly and imprecisely, ventriloquism. It is a romantic, even a sentimental, vice that only unusually talented writers can excel at—the vice, to say it quickly, of excessive love of literature; of the *sound* of certain literatures. Ventriloquist writers reject what they have in common with their time and place, including its ordinary talk, and are so permeated with the redolence of Elsewhere that their work, even if it is naturally robust, is plagued by wistfulness. I am not speaking of nostalgia alone, the desire to revisit old scenes and old moods. Nor am I speaking of the concerns of "mandarin" writers, those who are pointedly out of tune with the vernacular, who heighten and burnish language in order to pry out of it judgments and ironies beyond the imagination of the colloquial. Ventriloquist writers may or may not be nostalgic, they may or may not be drawn to the mandarin voice. What ventriloquist writers want is to live inside *other literatures.*

Chester, I believe, was one of these. It made him seem a poseur to some, a madman to others; and he was probably a little of both. He drove himself from continent to continent, trying out the Moroccan sunlight as he had read of it, Malcolm Cowley's Paris as the garden of liberating "exile," the isles of Greece for the poetry of the words, Jerusalem for the eternal dream. Literature was a costume, or at any rate a garment: he hardly ever went naked. He saw landscapes and cities through a veil of bookish imaginings. Inexorably, they failed him. The Greek island had unworkable plumbing. Jerusalem had traffic noise. Paris turned out to be exile in earnest. The Moroccan sunlight came through as promised, but so did human nature. Wherever he ran, the nimbus grew tattered, there were quotidian holes in the literary gauze.

This is not to say that Chester was not an original, or that he had a second-hand imagination. Who is more original than a man who fears he is not there? "And I would watch myself, mistrustful of my presence . . . I want to be *real*," he wrote in an early story. (Its title, "As I Was Going Up the Stair," echoes the nursery chant: "I met a man who wasn't there.") For the tormented who blind themselves before mirrors, a wash of hallucination will fill the screen of sight. Woody Allen's Zelig falls into old newsreels, his Kugelmass into a chapter of *Madame Bovary.* Chester allowed himself to become, or to struggle to become, if not a character in fiction, then someone who tilted at life in order to transmogrify it into fiction. He is remembered now less as the vividly endowed writer he was born to be than as an eccentric ruin in the comical or sorrowing anecdotes of a tiny circle of aging scribblers.

Most of the writers who on occasion reminisce about Chester have by now lived long enough to confirm their own minor status. If he was in a gladiatorial contest, and not only from the perspective of Mr. Emerson's adolescent amphitheater, but with all of his literary generation, then it is clear that Chester has lost. In 1962, commenting on a first collection of short stories by John Updike, he was caustic and flashy: ". . . a God who has allowed a writer to lavish such craft upon these worthless tales is capable of anything." A reviewer's callow mistake, yes. Updike has gone from augmentation to augmentation, and nobody can so much as recognize Chester's name. It is common enough that immediately after writers die, their reputations plummet into ferocious eclipse: all at once, and unaccountably, a formerly zealous constituency will stop reading and teaching and talking about the books that only a short while before were objects of excitement and gossip. It is as if, for writers, vengeful mortality erases not only the woman or the man but the page, the paragraph, the sentence—pages, paragraphs, and sentences that were pressed out precisely in order to spite mortality. Writers, major or minor, may covet fame, but what they really *work* for is that transient little daily illusion—phrase by phrase, comma after comma—of the stay against erasure.

I sometimes try to imagine Chester alive, my own age (well, a few months younger), still ambitiously turning out novels, stories, essays. No white hair for Chester; he would be perfectly bald, and, given his seniority, perfectly undistinguished by his baldness. I see him as tamed though not restrained, a practiced intellectual by now; industrious; all craziness spent. Instead of those barbaric dogs, he owns a pair of civilized cats. If I cannot untangle the sex life of his later years, I also know that it is none of my business. (In "The Foot" he speaks glancingly of having had sexual relations with a woman for the first time, at thirty-seven.) His ambition, industry, and cantankerous wit have brought him a quizzical new celebrity; he is often on television. In degree of attention-getting he is somewhere between Norman Mailer and Allen Ginsberg, though less political than either. He avoids old friends, or, if not, he anyhow avoids me; my visits with him take place in front of the television set. There he is, talking speedy Brooklynese, on a literary panel together with Joyce Carol Oates and E. L. Doctorow.

I look into the bright tube at those small, suffering, dangerous eyes under the shining scalp and think: *You've won, Chester, you've won.*

OUR
KINSMAN,
MR.
TROLLOPE

T HREE-QUARTERS of a century have slipped away since
Bloomsbury last sneered at the British Victorians; fiction's new career, in the form of *Ulysses*, began over seventy years ago. We post-
moderns are by now so far from the modernist repudiation of
Victorian influence that we can look with an unembarrassed
eye—an eye of one's own, we might say—at the three-decker Victorian novel's subplots and coincidences, its bloated serializations,
its unnaturally heightened and speechifying dialogue. We can see
past their potboiler mechanisms into what these baggy old novelists humanly, and sometimes half-divinely, *knew*.

Anthony Trollope has long been excluded from this percipient,
and undeceived, reassessment. He is nearly the only Victorian
novelist who has been critically doomed to remain a Victorian. He
alone appears to be unforgiven. Dickens and Henry James and
George Eliot and Thackeray—even the colonialist-imperialist
Kipling!—are permitted, and sometimes prodded, to transcend
the accident of their chronology and the confines of their mores.
Only Trollope is regarded as still mired in his devices—devices

that are, in their pre-video yet cinematic way, archetypes of our present-day story-machines, glowing like colored apothecary globes in rooms where pianos used to stand. Trollope, in brief, is dismissed as a kind of antiquated television set; he is said to be "undemanding." Dickens, by contrast, survives in all his greatness as caricaturist; George Eliot as moralist; Thackeray as ironist; Hardy as determinist. (Shorthand, it goes without saying, for the orchestrally manifold.)

But there is no organizing epithet or central insight for Trollope. He is all those sharp-edged things: caricaturist, moralist, ironist (very strong here), determinist (to a degree). And still he is flicked off as shallow. So he is left behind among the unemerged Victorians, deprived of the stature of transcendence. Much of the fault is extrinsic: a case can be made that the blame falls on those preening bands of Trollope cultists, farflung votaries in Papua, Tel Aviv, and Hay-on-Wye (not to mention certain pockets of the Upper West Side)—coterie enthusiasts and credit-seekers who suppose that to esteem a writer is to take on some of that writer's cachet. Trollope's reputation has rested (or foundered) too long and too stickily on the self-congratulation and misdirection of Trollopean zealots. These, like the even more notorious Janeites, or like the pious devotees of an apotheosized George Eliot, are misled in assuming that their hero is all tea-cozies and country comforts, in the style of *Masterpiece Theater's* bright palette. Worse, single-author addicts have the naive habit of equating literature with the easy pleasures of self-approval.

But there is, I think, a more significant reason for the omission of Trollope from most contemporary reappraisals. It isn't only that serious readers will run from what the zealots praise. The truth is that Trollope is more *ours* than any of those honored others (Dickens, for instance)—which may be why the current generation has the instinct to undervalue him. Writers who describe for us precisely the way we live now tend to be scorned—a single glance at how the so-called multiculturalists and other politico-literary trendists have slighted Saul Bellow is a sufficient sampling. Trollope is ten times slyer than his adorers (adorers of village parsonages) can dream—slyer and colder, with a brainy analytic laughter so remote it can register nearly as indifference. Trollope, like Bellow, is a meticulous and often ferocious anatomizer of character and society. His hand can be both light and weighty; he gets to the bottom of vileness, and also of decency; he is magisterially shrewd—shrewd in the manner of Cervantes; he likes to write about churchmen but is easy on belief; nothing in the pragmatic workings of worldliness escapes him.

Henry James complained early and nastily about Trollope's "devotion to little things," and charged him with "the virtues of the photograph." "Mr. Trollope is a good observer," James said, "but he is literally nothing else." A surprisingly grudging comment from the novelist whose most celebrated dictum is "Try to be one of the people on whom nothing is lost," and who was himself possessed by the voyeurism of the ardent observer. Well, yes, there *is* in Trollope something of a camera mounted on a helicopter—the Olympian looking down at a wide map strewn with wriggling mortals and their hungers; I mean by this that Trollope is at heart a cynic. But a cynic is a great deal more than an observer; a cynic is a metaphysical necessity. Trollope is not much concerned with retributive justice: his comeuppances come and go. He accepts and will not judge; or, if he judges, he will not invest his soul in the judgment. He may be a moralist—he certainly responds to the discriminations of the moral life—but he is too dispassionate to jubilate or grieve. Whatever is is exactly what one might expect.

"Cynic" commonly suggests a detached pessimism, a pessimism sans bitterness—but a cynic is acutely alert to an element of strangeness in the way matters fall out. From the Olympian's view, everything is strange—love, hate, religion, skepticism, exultation, apathy, domesticity, class, greed, infatuation, mercilessness, godliness. That may be why, having witnessed in our own century the strangest and the worst, we seem finally to be disconnected from the impersonal though earnest virtues of the photograph. What is a photograph if not a stimulus to the most deliberate attentiveness: time held motionless in a vise of profound concentration, so that every inch of the seized moment can be examined? Bellow, in his own version of James's exhortation, adds it all up as follows: "Writers are naturally attentive; they are trained in attentiveness, and they adduce attentiveness in their readers (without a high degree of attentiveness, aesthetic bliss is an impossibility)." The term "aesthetic bliss" Bellow borrows from Nabokov, linking it to the "recognition or rediscovery of certain essences permanently associated with human life" by "artists who write novels or stories." The notion of the photograph as one likely key to (or recognizer of) human essence is useful enough; though we know the camera can be made to lie, we also know it as reality's aperture. We say we are in earnest about the importance of being earnest, but we frequently choose (it is the way we live now) social superstition over social truth; or the partisan simulacrum over historical reality; or furry pointillism over the unrelenting snapshot; or sentimental distortion over exact measure. All of this is just what Trollope will *not* do; it takes a peculiar literary nerve to admit to the way we live now. And nerve (or call it courage) is the foundation of the aesthetic (or call it, more plainly, art).

Anthony Trollope wrote forty-seven novels. Out of that bottomless inkpot flowed, besides, biographies, histories, travel books, sketches, and five collections of short stories. There is a tradition that Trollope damaged his own reputation by revealing, in his *Autobiography*, how he daily sat with his pocket watch before him on his writing table. This is presumed to be a confession that the Trollopean Muse is mainly and merely mundane diligence (as if diligence were not the only reliable means of securing the Muse's descent); but industry of this kind is itself the artist's portion, indistinguishable from literary passion. There is no question that quantity—added, of course, to genius—is what separates major writers from minor ones. (If only E. M. Forster had written forty-seven—or even fourteen—novels to accompany *A Passage to India*!) Yet Trollope, for all his abundance, is somehow still relegated among the minor.

Restitution is necessary. Trollope's recognition of certain perilous human essences lifts him out of the Victorian minor. Let beginners who have never before read Trollope test this thesis— genuine readers not susceptible to cultism. The cultists, proselytizers all, will usually send novices to *The Warden*, or else to

Barchester Towers. I would recommend *The Way We Live Now*—Trollope's thirty-third novel, written in 1873 and set in that same year. I would recommend it because it is very long (Trollope's longest) and very contemporary, despite its baronets and squires and rustics, and despite its penniless young women whose chief employment is husband-seeking, and its penniless young lords whose chief employment is heiress-hunting. If all this sounds as far as possible from the way *we* live now, think again; or else wait and see. As for length: *The Way We Live Now* is nine hundred and fifty-two pages in the orange-framed Penguin softcover edition, and therefore will take longer to disappoint. What disappoints in any novel by Trollope is the visible approach of its end: when more has been read than remains to be read.

The Way We Live Now is best described as a business novel; it is above all about deal-making, and about how power can be nudged to tip, and about taking advantage. It is about all these market-place things even when what is at issue is romance, or marriage, or religion, or law, or book reviewing, or gambling, or property, or altruism, or running for office. There is almost no character who does not have an eye out for the main chance, whether it is a London millionaire or an American frontierswoman, a raffish solicitor or an unmarried elder sister worried about being left on the shelf.

In the very first chapter, called "Three Editors," we come upon Lady Carbury in the act of insuring a fraudulent reception for work she knows is shoddy; she is a hack writer in urgent need of financial rescue via bestsellerdom. (Nothing dated in that. Ambitious mediocrities nowadays chase after blurbs with equal oil and chutzpah.) Lady Carbury is a widow supporting a reprobate son whom she coddles and a neglected daughter too love-struck, and too recalcitrant, to yield to a sensible marriage. Marriage—or, rather, matchmaking—is the center, and not only because it is the late nineteenth century, when few women have careers (though Lady Carbury herself surely does, and tends it assiduously), but because a perspicacious match is, then and now, the nexus of every business deal. Exploitation, after all, signifies a contract between two parties: the greed of the exploiter is ideally met by the need of the exploited. Trollope's great theme is people making use of other people, especially in the accumulation of money, and who can doubt the contemporaneity of a novel about money?

The commanding money-man who is, so to speak, the lubricant of *The Way We Live Now*, greasing its wheelings and dealings with promises and promissory notes, is Augustus Melmotte, a foreigner arrived in London with his daughter and his cowed Bohemian Jewish wife to become the City's most powerful financier. Now and again Trollope will play the game of giveaway names, so we may look into "Melmotte" and see a Latinic glimmer of "honey-word." Melmotte is, in short, a mighty con artist: we are on to him almost instantly. Our interest is not in finding out his scam, but in watching him inveigle and enmesh the gullible. What he has to offer is air—the South Central Pacific and Mexican Railway, "which was to run from the Salt Lake City, thus branching off from the San Francisco and Chicago line, and pass down through the fertile lands of New Mexico and Arizona, into the territory of the Mexican Republic, run by the city of Mexico, and come out on the gulf at the port of Vera Cruz," a distance of more than two thousand miles. As for the probable cost of this grand undertaking, and the actual laying of track, "no computation had or perhaps could be made."

In fact, there will never be a railway to Vera Cruz. Melmotte and his several shady sidekicks (one of whom is named Cohenlupe—ancient priestly honorific joined to the wolfish) are successfully engaged in selling shares in a phantom project. It is a ruse—a Ponzi scheme—to attract investors. Melmotte's prestige and influence are themselves phantoms, seductive constructs in the minds of the ignorant young dupes invited to serve on his board of directors. These are aristocratic wastrels, gamblers and boozers, some good-natured enough, one or two of them actual louts, many bearing hereditary titles. Lady Carbury's son, Sir Felix, a baronet, is certainly among the louts. The search for respectability is double-edged: Melmotte requires the presence of titles to legitimate and adorn—and Anglicize—his imperfect status, and the raw young nobles, glad to take on the appearance of being seriously occupied, are hoping for quick and lavish returns. The clever business buccaneer may be a commonplace of public ambition (and not only in novels: Melmotte's uncannily exact real-life counterpart is the notorious late tycoon Robert Maxwell), but Trollope's high-flying swindler is one of those masterly figures who break through the membrane of invention to go on electrifying the living imagination ever after.

Melmotte at the pinnacle of his London fame takes everyone's measure, mentally auditing the value of properties, titles, inherited wealth: his aim is to find footholds on an ascent to the loftiest plane of London society. Having himself no claim to English blood, he means to attain it through his only daughter, the unprepossessing Marie Melmotte. Marie is up for sale in a marriage of mutual service: the asking price is the best available title. A bargain is to be struck: the rich foreign intruder with no background (or, as the rumors have it, a soiled and possibly crooked history in far-off places) will negotiate hard for a visibly aristocratic son-in-law. Gold in exchange for the bluest blood.

Sir Felix Carbury, at his mother's urging, is enlisted as suitor; he botches the job through drunkenness and half-hearted dallying with a brash country girl. But Marie is not the only young woman who is buffeted and thwarted by matrimonial opportunism: there is Hetta, Sir Felix's sister, maternally pressed toward marriage with her propertied older cousin Roger; and Georgiana Longestaffe, desperate to marry anyone who can supply a house in London during the high season; and Ruby Ruggles of Sheep's Acre Farm, shoved into taking a husband for the sake of a dry roof over her head. Not all these coercions are conceived in unkindness; some, in fact, are rooted in sense and solicitude; but they *are* coercions.

Still, in the company of Trollope, let no one pity the condition of nineteenth-century women! Trollope's young marriageables are not so vulnerable, and not so easily crushed, as their dependent circumstances would lead us to think. Apart from Melmotte's mammoth grip (both as charmer and as bully), all the sexual force and aggressive scheming are, in this novel, the province of women. The older men, the men of position, are mainly fools and bigots; the younger men are fools, too, and also idle and enervated. But the women are robust, demanding, driven, resolute, erotically insistent. Even Melmotte's mousy daughter turns dangerously headstrong. And the remarkable Mrs. Hurtle of San Francisco, sophisticated, compassionate, ingratiating, yet a woman who can shoot to kill, is a dozen times sturdier than the wan and useless young lords who exchange empty IOU's and cheat at cards. She is undoubtedly more authoritative than her erstwhile fiancé, the always equivocating Paul Montague, Hetta Carbury's lover, whom Mrs. Hurtle pursues with a torrent of contrivance so single-minded that it nearly exhausts the narrative around her.

Yet nothing can really exhaust any part of this narrative; it is alive and stingingly provocative at every turn. The grotesquely overblown dinner party Melmotte gives for the Emperor of China, an elephantiasis of self-advertisement (Trollope based its braggadocio splendors on the royal visit of the Shah of Persia in June of 1873), is as baleful as it is comic: Melmotte here becomes a parodic Lear of the banquet hall, too much accommodated by unregarded luster. And always Trollope is after the clamor and confusions of temperament. An argument between an Anglican bishop and a Roman Catholic priest reflects their theological differences far less than it does the divide between tractable and intractable spirits. The fanatical priest lives humbly, the tolerant bishop in conspicuous luxury; and it is the recurrent scramble and contradiction of variable traits that seize the novelist's relentless eye.

A trace of that scramble may be in Trollope himself: the inventor of the gaudily offensive Cohenlupe is also a furious satirist of antisemitism—there is no noisier Jew-hater than Trollope's Mr. Longestaffe, and no more telling vindication of ethical nicety than Trollope's Mr. Brehgert, a Jew. Melmotte, forger as well as swindler, is suspected all around of being a Jew, and is revealed in the novel's last pages to be the son of "a noted coiner in New York—an Irishman of the name of Melmody"—i.e., an American adventurer. (A query. Did Melmotte become Melmody only after Trollope's own exposure to the rantings of Mr. Longestaffe? Novels do frequently influence their authors.)

The Way We Live Now ends in four sensible weddings, the traditional signal that we have been present at a comedy, and one sensible exile. There is in Trollope a clear pull toward reasonableness; toward moderation; toward reason itself, in language precise, exuberant, substantive—in spite of which, the comic cannot suppress the grievous, and a naturalist's brew of so many botches and blotches sends up its tragical fumes. Suicide, malice, stupidity, greed, manipulativeness, fakery, cowardice, dissoluteness, deceit, prejudice without pride, pretension, ambitiousness, even pathological self-abnegation—excess of every kind—dominate Trollope's scrutiny of his "now." If our now departs a little from his, it is only because we have augmented our human matériel with heightened technological debris. All the same, there is the impress of grandeur in Trollope's account—or call it, with James, his photography. What James missed was the peculiarly elusive quality of a poetry akin to his own. Like it or not, Trollope is the poet of anti-poetry. His lens is wide, extraordinarily so: wide enough to let in, finally, a slim ghost of the prophetic.

WHAT
HENRY JAMES
KNEW

I. THE HORRIBLE HOURS

A S MODERNISM sinks in, or fades out—as it recedes into a kind of latterday archaism, Cubism turned antiquated, the old literary avant-garde looking convincingly moth-eaten—certain writers become easier to live with. It is not only that they seem more accessible, less impenetrable, simpler to engage with, after decades of familiarity: the quality of mystery has (mysteriously) been drained out of them. Joyce, Proust, Woolf, surely Pound and Eliot—from all of these, and from others as well, the veil draws back. One might almost say, as the twentieth century shuts down, that they are objectively less "modern" than they once were. Their techniques have been absorbed for generations. Their idiosyncrasies may not pall, but neither do they startle. Their pleasures and their stings, while far from humdrum, nevertheless open out into psychological references that are largely recognizable. What used to be revelation (Proust's madeleine, the world that ends not with a bang but a whimper) is reduced to reflex. One reads these masters now with satisfaction—they have been ingested—but without the fury of early avarice.

Yet one of the great avatars of modernism remains immune to this curious attrition: in the ripened Henry James, and in him almost alone, the sensation of mysteriousness does not attenuate; it thickens. As the years accumulate, James becomes, more and more compellingly, our contemporary, our urgency.

The author of *Daisy Miller* (1878), and of *Washington Square* (1880), and even of *The Portrait of a Lady* (1881), was a nineteenth-century writer of felicitous nuance and breadth. The earlier stories and novels are meant to be rooms with a view, thrown open to the light. If mysteries are gathered there, they are gathered to be dispelled. The entanglements of human nature, buffeted by accident, contingency, mistaken judgment, the jarrings of the social web, the devisings of the sly or the cruel, are in any event finally transparent, rational. Isabel Archer's long meditation, in *The Portrait of a Lady*, on her marriage to Gilbert Osmond leads her to the unraveling—the clarification—of her predicament. "They were strangely married," she perceives, "and it was a horrible life"— directly seen, understood, stated, in the manner of the fiction of realism. Like Catherine Sloper, the heroine of *Washington Square*, Isabel has known too little and now knows more. For the James of this mainly realist period, it is almost never a case of knowing too much.

After 1895, the veil thickens. Probably the most celebrated example of a darkening texture is the interpretive history of "The Turn of the Screw" (1898); what was once read wholly in the light of its surfaces can no longer sustain the innocence, or the obtuseness, of its original environment. The tale's first readers, and James himself, regarded this narrative of a frightened governess and her unusual young charges as primarily a ghost story, suitably shadowed in eerie riddle. In his Notebook sketch of 1895, James speaks of "apparitions," of "evil presences," of hauntings and their "strangely gruesome effect." In the Preface to "The Turn of the Screw" for the 1906 New York Edition of his work, he appears light-handedly to toss out the most conventional of these rumblings. "I cast my lot with pure romance," he insists, and calls "this so full-blown flower of high fancy" a "fairy-tale pure and simple." But also, and contradictorily, he assigns his apparitions "the dire duty of causing the situation to reek with the air of Evil," the specifications of which James admits he has left it to the reader to supply. "Make him *think* the evil, make him think it for himself," he asserts.

Since then, under the tutelage of Freud, later readers *have* thought it for themselves, and have named, on James's behalf, a type of horror he could not or would not have brought to his lips. What was implicit in James became overt in Freud. With time, and with renewed critical speculation, James's ghosts in "The Turn of the Screw" have swollen into the even more hideous menace of eros corrupted, including the forbidden, or hidden, sexuality of children. Whether James might have conceived explicitly of these images and hints of molestation is beside the point. There is, he contends in the Preface, "from beginning to end of the matter not an inch of expatiation," and evil's particulars are, on purpose, "positively all blanks," the better to delegate the imagination of terror to anyone but the author himself. Still, is it likely that the privacy of James's own imagination can be said to hold positively all blanks? Imagination works through exactitudes of detail, not through the abdication of its own authority. Whatever it was James thought, he thought *some*thing. Or, rather, he felt something: that gauzy wing that brushes the very pit of the mind even as the mind declares nothing is there. James is one of that handful of literary proto-inventors—ingenious intuiters—of the unconscious; it is the chief reason we count him among the imperial moderns.

The pivotal truth about the later Henry James is not that he chooses to tell too little—that now and then he deliberately fires blanks—but that he knows too much, and much more than we, or he, can possibly take in. It is as if the inklings, inferences, and mystifications he releases in his maturest fictions (little by little, like those medicinal pellets that themselves contain tinier pellets) await an undiscovered science to meet and articulate them. The Freud we already have may be insufficient to the James who, after 1895, became the recondite conjurer whom the author of *Daisy Miller* might not have recognized as himself.

In the fiction of realism—in the Jamesian tale before the 1895 crux—knowledge is the measure of what can be rationally ascertained, and it is almost never a case of knowing too much—i.e., of a knowledge beyond the reach not only of a narrative's dramatis personae but also of the author himself. The masterworks of modernism, however, nearly always point to something far more subterranean than simple ascertainment. *The Castle,* for example, appears to know more than Kafka himself knows—more about its own matter and mood, more about its remonstrances and motives, more about the thread of Kafka's mind. In the same way, "The Turn of the Screw" and other Jamesian works of this period and afterward—*The Awkward Age* above all, as we shall see— vibrate with cognitions that are ultimately not submissive to their creator. It is as if from this time forward, James will write nothing but ghost stories—with the ghosts, those shadows of the unconscious, at the controls. Joyce in particular sought to delineate whatever demons beat below, to bring them into the light of day—to explain them by playing them out, to incarnate them in recognizable forms, or (as in *Finnegans Wake*) to re-incubate them in the cauldron of language. This was what the modernists did, and it is because they succeeded so well in teaching us about the presence of the unconscious that we find them more and more accessible today. But the later James—like Kafka, a writer seemingly as different from James as it is possible to be—is overridden by a strangeness that is beyond his capacity to domesticate or explicate. James, like Kafka, enters mazes and penetrates into the vortex of spirals; and, again like Kafka, the ghost in the vortex sometimes wears his own face.

The 1895 crux, as I have called it, was James's descent into failure and public humiliation. The story of that humiliation—a type of exposure that damaged James perhaps lastingly, and certainly darkened his perspectives—is brilliantly told in Leon Edel's consummate biography: a biography so psychologically discriminating that it has drawn generations of its readers into a powerful but curious sympathy with James. Curious, because an admirable genius is not nearly the same as a sympathetic one, an instruction James himself gives us in, to choose only two, Hugh Vereker and Henry St. George, the literary luminaries of a pair of tales ("The

Figure in the Carpet," "The Lesson of the Master") bent on revealing the arrogance of art. Yet to approach James through Edel is, if not practically to fall in love with James, to feel the exhilarations of genius virtually without flaw. James, for Edel, is sympathetic and more; he is unfailingly and heroically civilized, selfless for art, gifted with an acuity of insight bordering on omniscience. He is—in James's own celebrated words—one of those upon whom nothing is lost. Edel's is a portrait that breaks through the frame of immaculate scholarship into generous devotion, a devotion that in the end turns on a poignant theory of James's fragility of temperament—and never so much as on the night of January 5, 1895, when James's play, *Guy Domville,* opening that evening, was jeered at and its author hissed.

Too nervous to sit through the rise of the curtain, James had gone down the street to attend Oscar Wilde's new work, *An Ideal Husband.* When it was over, scorning Wilde as puerile even as he made his way out through a wash of delighted applause, he returned to *Guy Domville* just as the closing lines were being spoken. Though the clapping that followed was perilously mixed with catcalls, the theater manager, misjudging, brought James out on the stage. "All the forces of civilization in the house," James described it afterward, "waged a battle of the most gallant, prolonged and sustained applause with the hoots and jeers and catcalls of the roughs, whose roars (like those of a cage of beasts at some infernal zoo) were only exacerbated by the conflict." George Bernard Shaw, who was in the audience as a reviewer, wrote of the "handful of rowdies" and "dunces" who sent out "a derisive howl from the gallery." James stumbled off the stage and walked home alone, brooding on "the most horrible hours of my life." The catastrophe of public rejection, James's biographer concludes, "struck at the very heart of his self-esteem, his pride and sovereignty as an artist."

It *had* been a sovereignty. In fact it had been an impregnability. He would not have been so damaged had he not had so far to fall. Literary embarrassment, to be sure, was familiar enough to James; it depressed him, as he grew older, that his novels were no longer widely read, and that his sales were often distressingly puny. But the assault on *amour-propre* that rocked James in the wake of his theater debacle was something else. It was a vulnerability as unprecedented as it was real—feelings of jeopardy, the first faint cracks of existential dread, the self's enfeeblement. He was unused to any of that; he had never been fragile, he had never been without the confidence of the self-assured artist, he had never been mistrustful. What he had been all along was magisterial. Admirers of Leon Edel's James may be misled by Edel's tenderness into imagining that some psychological frailty in James himself is what solicits that tenderness—but sovereign writers are not commonly both artistically vulnerable *and* sovereign.

And James's record of sovereignty—of tough impregnability—was long. He was fifty-two when the rowdies hissed him; he was twenty-one when he began publishing his Olympian reviews. To read these early essays is to dispel any notion of endemic hesitancy or perplexity. In 1866, at twenty-three, reviewing a translation of Epictetus, he speculates on the character of this philosopher of Stoicism with oracular force: "He must have been a wholesome spectacle in that diseased age, this free-thinking, plain-speaking old man, a slave and a cripple, sturdily scornful of idleness, luxury, timidity, false philosophy, and all power and pride of place, and sternly reverent of purity, temperance, and piety,—one of the few upright figures in the general decline." This has the tone not simply of a prodigy of letters, but of large command, of one who knows the completeness of his powers. If anything can be said to be implicit in such a voice, it is the certainty of success; success on its own terms—those terms being the highest imaginable exchange between an elite artist and his elite readership. And the earlier these strenuous yet ultimately serene expectations can be established, the stronger the shield against vulnerability; mastery in youth arms one for life.

Or nearly so. On the night of January 5, 1895, when the virtuoso's offering was received like a fizzled vaudeville turn, the progress of unquestioned fame came to a halt. What was delicacy, what was wit, what was ardor, what was scrupulous insight? What, in brief, was the struggle for art if its object could be so readily blown away and trodden on? James might wrestle with these terrors till dawn, like that other Jacob, but his antagonist was more likely a messenger from Beelzebub than an angel of the Lord. Failure was an ambush, and the shock of it led him into an inescapable darkness.

He emerged from it—if he ever emerged from it at all—a different kind of writer. Defensively, he began to see in doubles. There was drama, and there was theater. And by venturing into the theater, he had to live up to—or down to—the theater's standards and assumptions. "I may have been meant for the Drama—God knows!—but I certainly wasn't meant for the Theater," he complained. And another time: "Forget not that you write for the stupid—that is, that your maximum of refinement must meet the minimum of intelligence of the audience—the intelligence, in other words, of the biggest ass it may contain. It is a most unholy trade!" Yet in 1875, twenty years before the *Guy Domville* calamity, he exalted what had then seemed the holiest of trades, one that "makes a demand upon an artist's rarest gifts." "To work successfully beneath a few grave, rigid laws," he reflected, "is always a strong man's highest ideal of success." In 1881 he confided to his journal that "beginning to work for the stage" was "the most cherished of my projects."

The drama's attraction—its seductiveness—had its origin in childhood theater-going; the James children were introduced first to the New York stage, and then to the playhouses of London and Paris, of which they became habitués. But the idea of the *scene*—a passion for structure, trajectory, and revelation that possessed James all his life—broke on him from still another early source: the transforming ecstasy of a single word. On a summer night in 1854, in the young Henry's presence, a small cousin his own age (he was then eleven) was admonished by her father that it was time to go to bed, and ran crying to her mother for a reprieve. "Come now, my dear; don't make a scene—I *insist* on your not making a scene," the mother reproved, and at that moment James, rapturously taking in the sweep of the phrase, fell irrevocably in love with the "witchcraft," as he called it, of the scene's plenitude and allure. "The expression, so vivid, so portentous," he said in old age, "was one I had never heard—it had never been addressed to us at home. . . . Life at these intensities clearly became 'scenes'; but the great thing, the immense illumination, was that we could make them or not as we chose."

That, however, was the illumination of drama, not the actuality of theater managers, actors, audiences. The ideal of the stage—as a making, a kneading, a medium wholly subject to the artist's will—had become infected by its exterior mechanisms. "The dramatic form," he wrote in 1882, "seems to me the most beautiful thing possible; the misery of the thing is that the baseness of the English-speaking stage affords no setting for it." By 1886 he was driven to confess that the "very dear dream . . . had faded away," and that he now thought "less highly of the drama, as a form, a vehicle, than I did—compared with the novel which can do and say so much more." In James's novel of the theater, *The Tragic Muse,* begun in 1888, a character bursts out, "What crudity compared to what the novelist does!" And in 1894, in a letter to his brother William, James speculated that "unless the victory and the spoils have not . . . become more proportionate than hitherto to the humiliations and vulgarities and disgusts, all the dishonor and chronic insult," he intended "to 'chuck' the whole intolerable experiment and return to more elevated and independent courses. I have come to *hate* the whole theatrical subject."

It was a gradual but steady repudiation, repeatedly contradicted by James's continuing and zigzag pursuit of managers and productions. In the end, the theater repudiated *him*; but the distinction he insisted on between theater, that low endeavor, and drama, that "highest ideal," went on to serve him in what would become one of his strangest fictions. After *Guy Domville*, he undertook to imagine a novel which would have all the attributes of a theatrical production. The reader would be supplied with dialogue, sets, grand and ingenious costuming, gestures of the head and hand; there would be entrances and exits; there would be drawings rooms and wit. The "few grave, rigid laws" of the drama would wash away all the expository freedoms and flexibilities of the traditional novel—above all the chance to explain the action, to comment and interpret, to speak in metaphor. Narrative, and the narrator's guiding hum, would give way to the bareness of talk unaccoutered and unconstrued, talk deprived of authorial amplification; talk as *clue*.

The work that was to carry the burden of this lucidly calculated experiment was conceived on March 4, 1895, three months after the failure of *Guy Domville*. On that day James entered into his Notebook "the idea of the little London girl who grows up to 'sit with' the free-talking modern young mother . . . and, though the conversation is supposed to be expurgated for her, inevitably hears, overhears, guesses, follows, takes in, becomes acquainted with, horrors." The Notebook recorded nothing about any intention to mimic the form of a play. But in his Preface to the New York Edition (1908) of *The Awkward Age*, James stressed that, from the start, the story and its situation had presented itself to him "on absolutely scenic lines, and that each of these scenes in itself . . . abides without a moment's deflexion by the principle of the stage-play." Speaking of the "technical amusement" and "bitter-sweetness" arising from this principle, he reflected on the rich novelistic discursiveness he had early determined to do without: "Exhibition may mean in a 'story' twenty different ways, fifty excursions, alternatives, excrescences, and the novel, as largely practiced in English, is the perfect paradise of the loose end." The play, by contrast, "consents to the logic of but one way, mathematically right, and with the loose end as gross an impertinence on its surface, and as grave a dishonour, as the dangle of a snippet of silk or wool on the right side of a tapestry." Moreover, he pointed out, the play is committed to "objectivity," to the "imposed absence of that 'going behind,' " to eschewing the "storyteller's great property-shop of aids to illusion."

In choosing to write a novel confined to dialogue and scene; in deciding to shape *The Awkward Age* according to self-limiting rules of suppression and omission; in giving up the brilliant variety of the English novel's widest and lushest potential, an art of abundance that he had long ago splendidly perfected—what was James up to? What system of psychological opposition had he fallen into? On the one hand, a play in the form of a novel, or a novel in the form of a play, was a response to "the most horrible hours of my life." What the stage would not let him do, he would do in any case—on his own venerable turf, with no possibility of catcalls. An act of triumph, or contempt, or revenge; perhaps a reward for having endured so much shame. And on the other hand, a kind of penance: he was stripping himself clean, reducing a luxuriant craft to a monkish surrender of its most capacious instruments.

But penance for what? *The Awkward Age* represents an enigma. Though it intends unquestionably to be a comedy—a social comedy, a comedy of manners (as "The Turn of the Screw" unquestionably sets out to be a ghost story)—some enormous grotesquerie, or some grotesque enormity, insinuates itself into this ultimately mysterious work. Having straitjacketed his tale with the "few grave, rigid laws" of the stage, James resolved not to "go behind" its scenes with all those dozens of canny analyses and asides that are possible for the novel; yet on the whole it is as if proscenium and backdrop, and all the accouterments between them, have melted away, and nothing is left but what is "behind"—a "behind" any ordinary novelistic explication would not be equal to and could not touch. Paradoxically, the decision *not* to "go behind" put James squarely backstage, in the dark of the wings, in ill-lit and untidy dressing rooms among discarded makeup jars and their sticky filth—in the very place where there can be no explanation of the world on stage, because the world on stage is an invention and an untruth. James descended, in short, into an interior chaos; or to say it otherwise, with the composition of *The Awkward Age* he became, finally and incontrovertibly, a modernist. Like the modernists, he swept past the outer skin (the theater and its stage, the chatter of counterfeit drawing rooms, the comings and goings of actors and audiences, the coherent conscious machinery of things) to the secret life behind—glimmers of buried truths, the undisclosed drama of hint and inference.

The façade of comedy and the horror behind. And the penalty for "going behind"—while rigging up, via those "few grave, rigid laws," every obstacle to it—was the impenetrable blackness, the blankness, the *nox perpetua*, that gathered there, among the ropes and pulleys, where it is inevitable that one "hears, overhears, guesses, follows, takes in, becomes acquainted with, horrors." (The condition, one might note, of K. in *The Castle*.) And the horrors themselves? They cannot be named. It is their namelessness that defines them as horrors.

Yet James did give them a name—amorphous, suggestive, darkened by its imperial Roman origins, reminiscent of ancient clerical pageantry, more a riddle than a name: "the sacred terror." A translation, or, more likely a transmutation, of *sacro terrore*: the awe one feels in the presence of sacred or exalted personages, pope or emperor, before whom one may not speak; the dread one feels before the divine mysteries, or the head of Medusa. The face of a knowledge that is beyond our knowledge—intimations that cannot be borne. In the Preface to "The Turn of the Screw," James referred (handling it lightly so as not to be burned) to "the dear old sacred terror" as "the withheld glimpse" of "dreadful matter." The glimpse is withheld; to be permitted more than the glimpse would be to know too much. The sacred terror is, in fact, the sensation— not simply fright, but a kind of revulsion—that comes when glimpse perilously lengthens into gaze.

II. THE SACRED TERROR

IN 1894, the year before the idea of *The Awkward Age* materialized in his Notebook, and not long before *Guy Domville* went into rehearsals, two electrifying personal events brought James close to the sacred terror, far closer than he wished to be. In both instances he stopped at glimpse and contrived to shut himself away from gaze. The first event was the suicide, in Italy, of Constance Fenimore Woolson. A relation of James Fenimore Cooper, Fenimore (as she was called) was an American novelist who settled successively in Florence, Venice, and Rome. Bent on homage, she had first approached James in 1880, in Florence, with a letter of introduction from America. James found her intelligent and moderately engaging, and offered his assistance as an acutely sophisticated guide to Florentine art. But what was a cautious friendship on his part became, on hers, a worshipful love. James could not reciprocate. She was middle-aged, unmarried, deaf in one ear—an admirable companion whom he was learning to be wary of. He worried that she might mistake occasional camaraderie for an encouragement of the affections. The news of her death in 1894, after nearly a decade and a half of correspondence (her letters were very long, his very short) bewildered and initially misled him. He had the impression she had died of "pneumonia supervening on influenza," and prepared to journey from London to her funeral in Rome. "Poor isolated and fundamentally tragic being!" he summed her up. "She was intrinsically one of the saddest and least happy natures I have ever met; and when I ask myself what I *feel* about her death the only answer that comes to me is from what I felt about the melancholy, the limitations and the touching loneliness of her life. I was greatly attached to her and valued exceedingly her friendship." All that, however, was glimpse, not gaze. The moment James learned it was suicide that had removed Fenimore—she had leaped from a second-story window—he retreated quickly and decided against attending her burial. Leon Edel speculates that James felt some responsibility for the hopelessness that had led to what James termed her "suicidal mania." Whether that is so or not, it is certainly true that James came to rest in a conventional, and distancing, judgment—"fundamentally tragic being!"—and averted his eyes from any connection he might have had with Fenimore's dread, or her destruction. He would not seek to know too much. He would evade the sacred terror. He would not "go behind": the preparation for going behind—the horrible hours—had not yet occurred.

Two years before Fenimore's death, James's sister Alice died in London. The cause was breast cancer, but she had been strangely invalided since girlhood, and was in the care of a young woman companion, Katharine Loring. Alice had followed James to London, or had at least followed his inclination to extract himself from America. Hers was an activist temperament (she interested herself in the hot politics of Irish Home Rule) that had chosen, for reasons neither her physicians nor her family could fathom, to go to bed for life. An 1889 photograph of her lodgings at Leamington—a health resort outside of London—survives: a capacious sick-room, high-ceilinged, with a single vast window, curtained and draperied; pictures dropped on long wires from the wainscoting; a chandelier sprouting fat globes; a tall carved mirror over a black fireplace; a round table with lamp, vase, flowers, books, magnifying glass. The effect is of Victorian swathing—layers of cloth over every flat and vertical surface: the mantel hung with cloth, the table, the back of a chair. Lamps, jugs, flowers, photos parade across the mantel. The Persian hearthrug smothers still another carpet, splotched with large flowers. Alice James herself seems swathed, almost swaddled, half-erect on a kind of sofa muffled in voluminously sprawling bedclothes, pillows propping her shoulder and neck. Next to her, nearer the window, holding a book, sits Miss Loring, her throat and bosom lost in a flurry of scarves. Both women are severely buttoned to the chin. It is a photograph that incites the lungs to gulp air; if it were possible to step into this scene, though the looking glass is polished and clear, one might feel choked by too many flower-patterns, the mistiness of light incarcerated, the stale smells of unrelieved enclosure.

William James, in his farewell letter to his sister, wrote that "if the tumor should turn out to be cancerous, . . . then goodbye to neurasthenia and neuralgia and headache, and weariness and palpitation and disgust all at one stroke." To this physician brother, Alice had all along suffered from "the inscrutable and mysterious character of the doom of nervous weakness which has chained you down for all these years." Alice's illness, in short, was—until the advent of cancer—what we nowadays call "psychological." The genius sister of two genius brothers, she was self-imprisoned, self-restricted. Engulfed by cushions and shawls and wrappings at Leamington, in 1889 she began a diary: "I think that if I get into the habit of writing a bit about what happens, or rather what doesn't happen, I may lose a little of the sense of loneliness and desolation which abides with me."

She had had a history of terrors and nightmares. At twenty she had her first nervous breakdown (if that is what it was), at thirty her second, whereupon she was launched into an infinite series of undiagnosable ailments and their dubious, sometimes bizarre, remedies. She talked of suicide, and kept lists of contemporary suicides. She struggled for intellectual autonomy in an age when young women submitted, through marriage or otherwise, to the limitations of the domestic. Invalidism was, obliquely, one manner of solution: it yielded up an escape from ordinary female roles and contexts. At rest on her sofa, surrounded by heaps of books on every table-top, Alice lived in her head.

In her head she fought for Irish liberation; in her head she fought for her own. A famous sentence in her diary records a passionate revolution, in fantasy, of body and soul against a ruling class of one: "As I used to sit immovable reading in the library with waves of violent inclination suddenly invading my muscles, taking some one of their myriad forms such as throwing myself out of the window or knocking off the head of the benignant pater as he sat with his silver locks, writing at his table, it used to seem to me that the only difference between me and the insane was that I had not only all the horrors and suffering of insanity but the duties of doctor, nurse, and straitjacket upon me too."

In contrast to these dark recollections, Alice's diary offers a mellow view of Henry James, who often came to divert her and Miss Loring, bringing catty news and speculative gossip from his broader social world. "I have given him endless care and anxiety but notwithstanding this and the fantastic nature of my troubles I have never seen an impatient look upon his face or heard an unsympathetic or misunderstanding sound cross his lips. He comes at my slightest sign," she wrote, and spoke of a "pitch of brotherly devotion never before approached by the race." After Alice's death in 1892, Katharine Loring took away with her to Boston an urn containing Alice's ashes, and two thick notebooks; the latter were the pages of the diary. Two years later—in 1894, the year of Fenimore's suicide—Miss Loring arranged for the diary to be privately printed, and dispatched one copy to Henry, and another to William. Both brothers were impressed. Henry described his sister's literary claim—he recognized that the diary *was* a literary work—as "heroic in its individuality, its independence—its face-to-face with the universe for and by herself," and praised the "beauty and eloquence," the "rich irony and humor," of Alice's pen. William's own high pleasure—"a leaf in the family laurel crown"— was tempered by a graver evaluation: "personal power venting itself on no opportunity," he concluded.

But it was Henry who backed away from the diary—much as

he had had second thoughts about going to Fenimore's funeral. To begin with, he insisted that the diary not be published in his lifetime; and then he burned his copy—motivated, he said, by Alice's habit of setting down his sometimes unseemly accounts of friends and acquaintances. (Years later he made a bonfire of all the thousands of letters in his possession, obliterating the revelations of decades.) Amusement had become, in his sister's hands, document. James found himself shaken by "so many names, personalities, hearsays (usually, on Alice's part, through *me!*)"; he informed William that Alice's exposures made him "intensely nervous and almost sick with terror about possible publicity, possible accidents, reverberation etc.," and that he "used to say everything to Alice (on system) that could *égayer* [entertain] her bedside and many things in confidence. I didn't dream she wrote them down. . . . It is a 'surprise' that is too much of a surprise." There was more for James to grapple with, though, than the mortification of stumbling on his own remarks. It might be disconcerting that Alice had mentioned a certain essayist's "self-satisfied smirk." Yet something else lay coiled at the bottom of his sister's diary, and James was unequipped to live with it.

He met there, in fact—side by side with the bits of raillery and the vehement Irish nationalism—terrifying resonances and reminiscent apparitions. After the death of the James paterfamilias at home in Massachusetts, the diary disclosed, Alice, desolate in an empty house, was assaulted by the vibrations of a voice: "In those ghastly days, when I was by myself in the little house on Mt. Vernon Street, how I longed to flee . . . and escape from the 'Alone, Alone!' that echoed thro' the house, rustled down the stairs, whispered from the walls, and confronted me, like a material presence, as I sat waiting, counting the moments." James himself, five years after the undoing of *Guy Domville*, grieved over *"the essential loneliness of my life"* (the emphasis is his own). "This loneliness," he put it, "what is it still but the deepest thing about one? Deeper, about *me*, at any rate, than anything else; deeper than my 'genius,' deeper than my 'discipline,' deeper than my pride, deeper, above all, than the deep counterminings of art."

Alice James's "Alone!" and Henry James's "deepest thing" had their antecedents in a phantasmagorical visitation endured by their father fifty years before. It was a vision, or a phantom, or an omen, so paralyzing to the spirit, so shocking in its horror, that Henry James Senior was compelled to give it a name (seemingly a fusion of "devastation," "visitation," "vast") out of Swedenborgian metaphysics: *vastation*. One spring day after dinner, he testified, "feeling only the exhilaration incident to a good digestion," he was all at once flooded by panic: "To all appearance it was a perfectly insane and abject terror, without ostensible cause, and only to be accounted for, to my perplexed imagination, by some damnèd shape squatting invisible to me within the precincts of the room, and raying out from his fetid personality influences fatal to life. The thing had not lasted ten seconds before I felt myself a wreck; that is, reduced from a state of firm, vigorous, joyful manhood to one of almost helpless infancy." And another time he described himself as "inwardly shriveled to a cinder," altered to a "literal nest of hell within my own entrails."

The younger Henry James had turned away from Fenimore's suicide. In nearly the same moment he had turned away from his sister's diary. The suicide intimated influences fatal to life from a fetid personality. The diary was fundamentally a portrait of infantile helplessness, a shriveled soul, hell within the entrails. The elder James, with his damnèd shape; Fenimore, flinging herself to the pavement; Alice, listening to the ghostly susurrations of her abandonment—each had dared to look into the abyss of knowing-too-much; James would not look with them. It was not until he had himself succumbed to his own vastation—eye to eye with the sacred terror on the stage of the St. James Theater in 1895—that he was ready to exchange glimpse for gaze. The brawling pandemonium (it continued, in fact, for fifteen minutes) had not lasted ten seconds before he felt himself a wreck, reduced from a state of firm, vigorous, sovereign artistry to one of almost helpless infancy. Everything he had thought himself to be—a personage of majestic achievement—disintegrated in an instant. He could not go on as he had. Simply, he lost his nerve.

But he found, in the next work he put his hand to, not only a new way of imagining himself, but a new world of art. By paring away narrative rumination and exposition—by treating the novel as if it were as stark as a play-script—he uncovered (or invented) a host of labyrinthine depths and devices that have since been signally associated with literary modernism. For one thing, representation, while seeming to keep to its accustomed forms, took on a surreal quality, inscrutably off-center. For another, intent, or reason, gave way to the inchoate, the inexpressible. The narrative no longer sought to make a case for its characterizations; indirection, deduction, detection, inference proliferated. An unaccountable presence, wholly unseen, was at last let in, even if kept in the tale's dark cellar: the damnèd shape, the sacred terror. The tale began to know more than the teller, the dream more than the dreamer; and Henry James began his approach to the Kafkan. In those "most horrible hours of my life" after his inward collapse on the stage of the St. James, the curtain was being raised for *The Awkward Age*.

III. *The Awkward Age*

The Awkward Age is, ostensibly, a comedy of manners, and resembles its populous class in that it concerns itself with the marriageability of a young woman. Nearly a hundred years after James wrote, no theme may appear so moribund, so obsolete, as the notion of "marrying off" a daughter. Contemporary daughters (and contemporary wives) enter the professions or have jobs, and do not sit on sofas, month after month, to be inspected by possibly suitable young men who are themselves to be inspected for their incomes. The difference between late-Victorian mores and our own lies in female opportunity and female initiative, with freedom of dress and education not far behind. Yet the similarities may be stronger than the differences. It is still true that the term of marital eligibility for young women is restricted to a clearly specified span of years; it is still true that a now-or-never mentality prevails, and that young women (and often their mothers) continue to be stung by the risks of time. The gloves, parasols, boas, corsets, feathered hats, and floor-sweeping hems have vanished; the anxiety remains. A century ago, getting one's daughter appropriately married was a central social preoccupation, and, though marriage is nowadays not a young woman's only prescribed course in life, it is as much a gnawing preoccupation as it ever was. In this respect, no one can call the conditions of *The Awkward Age* dated.

In respect of sexual activity, those conditions are equally "modern." If sexual activity, in habit and prospect, defines manners, then—as a comedy of manners—*The Awkward Age* is plainly not a period piece. To be sure, society no longer pretends, as the Victorians did, to an ideal of young virgins kept from all normal understanding until the postnuptial deflowering; but in *The Awkward Age*, which depicts a public standard of ineffable purity not our own, that standard is mocked with bawdy zest. (Henry James bawdy? Consider the scuffle during which little Aggie sets her bottom firmly down upon a salacious French novel.) *The Awkward Age,* as a matter of fact, teems with adultery and emblems of incest; what appears to be wholesome finally suggests the soiled and the despoiled.

Still, it is not sexual standards and their flouting that move this novel from its opening lightness toward the shadowed distortions that are its destination. Rather, it is the unpredictable allegiances of probity. Probity arrives in the shape of Mr. Longdon, who "would never again see fifty-five" but is rendered as an aged, even antediluvian, gentleman, complete with pince-nez, old-fashioned reticences, and touchy memories of his prime. In his prime, in a moral atmosphere he judges to be superior to that of the present, he (long ago) loved and lost Lady Julia. He has never married, and for years has lived away from London, in the country, in a house poignantly similar to James's own Lamb House in Rye. He is a meticulous watcher and silent critic, sensitive, upright, certainly elderly in his perception of himself; a man of the past. One might imagine at first that Mr. Longdon (he is always called "Mr.") is yet another incarnation of James's eager old gentlemen—the life-seeker Strether who, in *The Ambassadors*, opens himself to the seductions of Paris, or the thrill-thirsty John Marcher of "The Beast in the Jungle," who waits for some grand sensation or happening to befall him. Mr. Longdon, by contrast, is a backward-looker. Lady Julia was his Eden, and the world will never again be so bright or so right. "The more one thinks of it," he remarks, "the more one seems to see that society . . . can never have been anything but increasingly vulgar. The point is that in the twilight of time—and I belong, you see, to the twilight—it had made out much less how vulgar it *could* be."

He has come to London, then, as a kind of anthropologist (though his motives are never clarified), on the trail of Lady Julia's descendants, and is welcomed into the culture of the natives: the chief of the natives being Mrs. Brookenham, Lady Julia's daughter, who is at the hub of a fevered salon. All roads lead to Mrs. Brook's, and the travelers are encrusted with bizarre trappings. The Duchess, a callously opportunistic Englishwoman who is the widow of a minor Italian aristocrat, is rearing her Neapolitan ward, Agnesina ("little Aggie"), as a snow-white slate on which "the figures were yet to be written." The hugely rich Mr. Mitchett, known as Mitchy, rigged out in unmatched merry-andrew gear and tolerant to the point of nihilism, is the zany but good-hearted son of a shoemaker become shoe mogul. Vanderbank, or Van—a handsome, winning, self-protective, evasive young man of thirty-five, impecunious on a mediocre salary, whom Mr. Longdon befriends—is Mrs. Brook's (relatively) secret lover. In and out of Mrs. Brook's salon flow schemers, snobs, faithless wives and husbands, jesters, idlers, fantastic gossips; even a petty thief, who happens to be Mrs. Brook's own son, Harold. And at the tea table in the center of it all sits (now and then) her daughter, Lady Julia's granddaughter, Fernanda—Nanda—who smokes, runs around London "squeezing up and down no matter whose staircase," and chooses as an intimate a married woman with an absent husband.

Nanda is fully aware of the corrupted lives of her mother's circle. Her father is indifferent, negligent, a cipher; her brother sponges on everyone who enters the house, and on every house he enters; her parents live enormously beyond their means; all relationships are measured by what can be gotten out of them. "Edward and I," Mrs. Brook declares to the Duchess, "work it out between us to show off as tender parents and yet to get from you everything you'll give. I do the sentimental and he the practical." With her "lovely, silly eyes," Mrs. Brook at forty-one is youthfully attractive, but cuts two years off her daughter's age in order to

snip two years from her own. There is no shame, no guilt, no conscience; the intrinsic has no value.

All these people (but for the blunt Duchess, who is plain Jane)
have names that are cursory, like their lives: Mrs. Brook, Van,
Mitchy, Aggie, Tishy, Carrie, even Nanda; it is as if only Mr.
Longdon troubles to take a long breath. "I've been seeing, feeling, thinking," he admits. He understands himself to be "a man of
imagination," an observer, with a "habit of not privately depreci-
ating those to whom he was publicly civil." (A habit that James
himself, on the evidence of the embarrassments of Alice's diary,
did not always live up to.) Mrs. Brook's salon, by contrast, feeds on
conspiracy, on sublimely clever talk, on plots and outrageous cal-
culations, on malice and manipulation, on exploitation, on matchmaking both licit and illicit; everyone is weighed for cash worth.
Mitchy rates high on the money scale, low on social background.
Vanderbank, with his beauty and cultivated charm, is the reverse. Mr. Longdon has money, judiciousness, and an unappeased
and unfinished love for Lady Julia, whose memory serves as a
standard for fastidious decorum and civilized reciprocity—none of
it to be found in present-day London, least of all in Mrs. Brook's
drawing room. Mr. Longdon despises Mrs. Brook and is almost
preternaturally drawn to Nanda. Though Lady Julia was beautiful
and Nanda is not, he is overcome by what he takes to be a magical
likeness. In Nanda, Lady Julia is nearly restored for him—except
that Nanda is a modern young woman with access to the great
world; she knows what Lady Julia in her girlhood would never
have been permitted (or perhaps would never have wished) to
know.

The ground on which *The Awkward Age* is spread—and woven,
and bound, and mercilessly knotted—is precisely this: what a
young woman ought or ought not to know, in a new London that
"doesn't love the latent or the lurking, had neither time nor sense
for anything less discernible than the red flag in front of the steam-
roller," as Vanderbank cautions Mr. Longdon. "It wants cash over
the counter and letters ten feet high. Therefore you see it's all as
yet rather a dark question for poor Nanda—a question that in a
way quite occupies the foreground of her mother's earnest little

life. How *will* she look, what will be thought of her and what will she be able to do for herself?" Nanda at eighteen, having come of age (Mrs. Brook, for all her shaving of years, can no longer suppress this news), is ready to be brought down—from the schoolroom, so to speak—to mingle among the denizens and fumes of Mrs. Brook's nether realm. "I seem to see," James complained in his Notebook, ". . . English society before one's eyes—the great modern collapse of all the forms and 'superstitions' and respects, good and bad, and restraints and mysteries . . . decadences and vulgarities and confusions and masculinizations and femininizations—the materializations and abdications and intrusions, and Americanizations, the lost sense, the brutalized manner . . . the general revolution, the failure of fastidiousness." And he mourned the forfeiture "of nobleness, of delicacy, of the exquisite"—losses he connected with "the non-marrying of girls, the desperation of mothers, the whole alteration of manners . . . and tone, while our theory of the participation, the *presence* of the young, remains unaffected by it."

Nanda, in brief, still unmarried at twenty, becomes, by virtue (or, one might say, by vice) of her saturation in her mother's circle, unmarriageable. The Duchess has reared little Aggie on a different scheme—the strict continental preservation of her purity, mental and other. Little Aggie is consequently a marvel of protected innocence and ignorance, decorative and inutile, "like some wonderful piece of stitching." She is "really the sort of creature," Vanderbank offers, that Nanda "would have liked to be able to be." And Mrs. Brook lightly yet chillingly notes, "She couldn't possibly have been able . . . with so loose—or, rather, to express it more properly, so perverse—a mother."

Nanda's mother's looseness and perverseness is pointed enough: she knows her daughter is in love with Vanderbank, but means to keep hold of him for herself. Vanderbank, in any event, is useless as a potential husband—he has no money. Mitchy has both money and hope, and is perpetually in pursuit of Nanda. But fond though she is of him, Mitchy—a free balloon, a whimsical cynic, dotingly unconcerned, endlessly kind, all without being rooted in serious discrimination—is for Nanda literally untouchable. She will not so much as allow him to kiss her hand. Mitchy, she tells Mr. Longdon, is "impossible." Whom, then, will Nanda marry? In surroundings thickened by innuendo and conspiracy, Mr. Longdon, man of probity, himself descends to insinuation and plot—though he might think of these as inference and discretion. In combination with the Duchess, he cooks up the idea of inducing Vanderbank to marry Nanda. Despite the delicacy that veils his intent, it crudely comes down to money: Mr. Longdon will make it worth Vanderbank's while to propose to Nanda. After which, hearing of Mr. Longdon's scheme, Mitchy will relinquish Nanda (Nanda has herself urged Mitchy on Aggie), and the Duchess, finally, will have a clear field to sweep him up for her immaculate little ward. Shoemaker's offspring or no, Mitchy is a prize promising strings of pearls.

Aggie, wed to Mitchy, turns instantly wild. What was yesterday a *tabula rasa* grows hectic overnight with prurient scribblings. But under Mrs. Brook's reign (and London practice), a sullied Aggie is acceptable, predictable, even conventional. The Duchess is not simply calm. She is smug. Aggie, married, is promptly expected to know whatever there is to know of sexual heat, deceit, the denigration of husbands, the taking of lovers, the scufflings of wives. There is no surprise in any of it. English rules apply: abdications and intrusions, revolution and the failure of fastidiousness—as long as the wedding is past. Postnuptial contamination troubles no one.

Nanda's is a different case. She is tainted and unmarried. "If Nanda doesn't get a husband early in the business," the Duchess advises Mr. Longdon, "she won't get one at all. One, I mean, of the kind she'll take. She'll have been in it over-long for *their* taste." "Been in what?" Mr. Longdon asks. "Why in the air they themselves have infected for her!" the Duchess retorts. The infection is carried by the clever young men who, "with intellectual elbow-room, with freedom of talk," hang about Mrs. Brook's drawing room, putting their hostess "in a prodigious fix—she must sacrifice either her daughter or . . . her intellectual habits." And the Duchess crows: "You'll tell me we go farther in Italy, and I won't deny it, but in Italy we have the common sense not to have little girls in the room." Yet Nanda is far from being a little girl. "Of course she's supposedly young," the Duchess pursues, "but she's really any age you like: your London world so fearfully batters and bruises them."

In the end Vanderbank declines to marry Nanda, not even for profit. She delights him; he admires her; he may even adore her; and he is certainly not in love with her mother. Nanda, on her side, seemingly ignorant of Mr. Longdon's bribe (though she is ignorant of nothing else), longs for Vanderbank's proposal. On a lyrical summer afternoon, it appears about to come; finally it does not. Nanda is "infected": she knows too much. Superficially, one may protest fashionable London's double standard—excessive worldliness does not interfere, after all, with the marital eligibility of young men. And the argument can be made—it *is* made—that if Vanderbank cannot marry without money, he cannot marry with it either: perhaps he scruples to wed on means not his own. But it is not Mr. Longdon's bribe that Vanderbank finds impossible. It is Nanda herself, Nanda in her contamination. Nor is the infection he intuits in her merely social worldliness, however alarming that worldliness may be.

Nanda's infection is more serious than that. Her knowing pestilential things heard and seen in her mother's salon is not the whole source and sum of her malady. What might have stopped at taintedness through oversophistication has, since the arrival of Mr. Longdon—to whom she has passionately attached herself— deepened into another order of contagion. Behind the comedy, a seal lifts from over the void; the sacred terror is seeping into the tale. A gentleman of integrity, universally understood as such, Mr. Longdon begins to draw after him a gradual toxicity, screened by benevolence. Nanda speaks affectionately of his "curious infatuation." She is herself curiously infatuated: "I set him off—what do you call it?—I show him off," she tells Vanderbank, "by his going round and round as the acrobat on the horse in the circle goes round the clown." And she acknowledges that her conversations with Mr. Longdon explore "as far as a man and a woman can together." To her mother she explains, "I really think we're good friends enough for anything." "What do you call that then," Mrs.

Brook inquires, "but his adopting you?" And another time Mrs. Brook wonders whether this "little fussy ancient man" is attempting to "make up to" her daughter.

But the bond between Mr. Longdon and Nanda is more mysterious than any December–May flirtation, and it is assuredly not an adoption. It is true that Mr. Longdon pursues, he courts, he possesses. He takes Nanda away to his country house for a long stay. And finally he takes her to live with him permanently. Still, it is not an adoption, not a liaison, not anything like a marriage. It may be intended as a salvation: Nanda must be removed from Mrs. Brook's polluting household; Nanda, infected, is not marriageable. Mrs. Brook is privy to the fact of Mr. Longdon's bribe (Vanderbank has tattled to her), and though it may (or may not) portend her losing Vanderbank as lover, nothing could gratify her more. "I can't help feeling," she observes, "that something possibly big will come of Mr. Longdon." "Big" means, in this lexicon, money; and when the bribe to Vanderbank fails, Nanda, for want of an alternative falling under Mr. Longdon's protection, decidedly *does* fall into money.

She also falls into a peculiar aura: the aura of James's post-*Guy Domville* mood. James endowed Mr. Longdon not only with his own house, but with his own age, and with his own intimations of mortality and loss. To Nanda Mr. Longdon bursts out: "Oh, you've got time—you can come round again; you've a margin for accidents, for disappointments and recoveries: you can take one thing with another. But I've only my last little scrap." Mr. Longdon, one surmises, is here a mirror for certain darkening aspects of James himself. And so, interestingly, is Nanda, whose early self-recognition—"I shall never marry"—is a version of James's own youthful announcement: "I am too good a bachelor to spoil." The price of being so good a bachelor was a latterday profundity of loneliness, and in his later years—though there was no Lady Julia in James's past on which to hang a present attachment—there were sentimental yearnings toward a whole series of engaging and gifted young men. The journalist Morton Fullerton (who became Edith Wharton's lover for a time) was one of them; Hendrik Andersen, a sculptor, was another. A third, who struck James as especially endearing, was Jonathan Sturges. Sturges, crippled by polio in childhood, was an American residing in England, "full of talk and intelligence, and of the absence of prejudice, . . . saturated with London, and with all sorts of contrasted elements in it, to which he has given himself up." This account of Sturges, appearing in one of James's letters, might easily be a portrait of Nanda. During the course of composition of *The Awkward Age*, which James was just then serializing for *Harper's*, Sturges was received with tender hospitality in Lamb House, and remained for many weeks. Nanda's visit to Mr. Longdon in his house in Suffolk (Lamb House is in Sussex) similarly lasts a number of weeks. The charming young men who so much appealed to James in this desolate period may have turned up, in Nanda, as a kind of imagined solution to isolation and despair. In real life, the charming young men came and went. In the novel, Nanda will move in and stay forever.

But *The Awkward Age* offers no solution after all. Nanda's ultimately going to live with Mr. Longdon is—for James's time and for our own—a serious anomaly. Nanda has twice been the subject of a bribe—once with Vanderbank, and again with her parents, who are only too glad to see that Mr. Longdon, by taking her in, really *is* doing something "big" for her. There is nothing honorable in Vanderbank's refusal of Mr. Longdon's bribe, and there is nothing straightforward in that refusal, which is never directly spoken. Vanderbank, pleasing everyone and no one, simply drifts away. He has the carelessness of consummate indifference; what is too tangled, or too demanding, can have no claim on him. He will never come through. "There are things I ought to have done that I haven't," he reluctantly tells Nanda in their brief last meeting. "I've been a brute and I didn't mean it and I couldn't help it." Moments before this admission, he sums it all up: "The thing is, you see, that *I* haven't a conscience. I only want my fun."

Mr. Longdon himself, presumably a man of acute conscience, does not escape corruption. Entering a corrupt community—a bribable community—he uncovers in himself an inclination to offer bribes. For Nanda's parents, the thing is more flagrant than a bribe. Mrs. Brook has, beyond question, sold her daughter to a rich man who will undoubtedly make her his heir. Mrs. Brook's acquiescence in Nanda's removal confirms the smell of the marketplace: plainly she would have declared against Nanda's going off with a "little fussy ancient man" who was poor. Mr. Longdon, in consequence, has succeeded in buying for his empty house a young woman nearly a third his age—and no matter how benign, or rescuing, or salvational this arrangement may appear to him, it is at bottom a purchase transaction, intended to assuage his lonely need. The young woman he purposes to protect will be sequestered from society on the premise that she is anyhow unmarriageable; on his account (even if he supposes it to be on *her* account) she will be foreclosed from the turnings and chances of a life beyond his own elderly precincts.

But Nanda has been brought to Mr. Longdon's house for still another reason: the revenge of love and the revenge of hate. Love of Lady Julia, hatred of Mrs. Brook. If Lady Julia in all her loveliness once passed him by, two generations afterward he is in possession of her grandchild. "I'm a hater," he says bluntly, reflecting on the decline of the standard that once made a "lady." In secluding Nanda from her mother's reach, he is trumpeting his contempt for Mrs. Brook: private hatred becomes public scorn. Nanda, for her part, goes with him willingly. She is complicit in the anomaly of their connection; she is the instrument of her own retreat. It is not the money—the being provided for—that lures Nanda; it is the strangeness, and, above all, the surrender.

For Nanda, Mr. Longdon's house holds out a suicidal peace: renunciation, a radical swerving from hope. Agreeing to enter that house of relinquishment (and moribund refinement)—this time never again to leave it—she is hurtled into a final storm of grief. Long ago, Mr. Longdon lost Lady Julia. Now Nanda has lost Vanderbank. They are matched in desolation.

It burst from her, flaring up in a queer quaver that ended in something queerer still—in her abrupt collapse, on the spot, into the nearest chair, where she choked with a torrent of tears. Her buried face could only after a moment give way to the flood, and she sobbed in a passion as sharp and brief as the flurry of a wild thing for an instant uncaged; her old friend meantime keeping his place in the silence broken by her sound and distantly—across the room—closing his eyes to his help-lessness and her shame. Thus they sat together while their trouble both conjoined and divided them.

Here James, in suddenly "going behind," momentarily abandons his "few grave, rigid laws" of dramatic restraint. It is as if, in this outburst of bereavement, the idea of helplessness and shame cannot be prevented from pressing forward, willy-nilly, from the cobwebbed backstage dark. The sacred terror is at last flung straight in the face of the tale. Not only helplessness and shame, but corruption; callousness; revenge; sexual displacement. Nanda displaces (or replaces) Lady Julia; beyond the novel's enclosure she may displace—or mask—James's endearing young men who come and go. There are, besides, incestuous hints: the young woman who might have been her protector's grandchild is intimately absorbed into the days and nights of his house. Her parents have abdicated. Her mother has sold her. The man she hoped to marry will not have her, even for a fortune. The man who takes her in, troubled by secret fevers and unthreshed motives, is sunk in a web of confusion; the young woman represents for him half a dozen identities, relations, unwholesome resolutions. And she, in joining him, has gone to bed, in effect, for life—as a penalty, or perhaps in penance, for knowing too much.

A panicked scenario. How much of it did James know? Did the teller penetrate to the bowels of the tale? The tale, in any case, penetrates—or decodes—the teller. The mosaic fly-eye of the narrative assembles all the shards and particles of James's chronicle of crisis, glimpse after glimpse, and sweeps them up, and compiles and conflates them into one horrendous *seeing*—James in his aging forlornness, in a house devoid of companionship and echoing with his sister's "Alone!"; Fenimore's wild crash; Alice's burial-in-life; the return of his father's "damnèd shape" and its fatal influences. And what was that shape if not James himself, at the crest of a life delivered over wholly to art, helpless on the stage on the evening of January 5, 1895, the crown of his genius thrown brutally down? "Thus they sat together while their trouble both conjoined and divided them." Divided, because James in his domicile, unlike Mr. Longdon, is alone, and will always be alone. Conjoined, because James is at once both Mr. Longdon and Nanda. But surely more than either or both. These two have been dropped into a pit. James is the pit's master, its builder and evoker.

After the cataclysmic turning point of *Guy Domville*, hidden knowings are everywhere in James—notably in *What Maisie Knew* (1897) and "The Turn of the Screw," and culminating in the last great pair of conspiratorial works, *The Wings of the Dove* (1902) and *The Golden Bowl* (1904). The recurrence, in his own sensibility, of the paternal vastation, the recognition of an immutable deprivation *("the essential loneliness of my life")*, the nearby explosions of suicide and self-immolation, the "horrible hours" themselves—all these pitchforked James out of the Victorian and into the modern novel. He broke down both social and narrative forms and plummeted, sans the old fastidiousness (and optimism), into the smoldering detritus of exhausted ways. It is probable that *The Awkward Age* is a novel that knows far more than its author knew, and holds more secrets of panic, shame, helplessness, and chaos than James could candidly face. But it was this work that crucially and decisively pried open the inmost door to the void. After which, released from glimpse into gaze, James could dare as Conrad dared, and as Kafka dared.

At the climax of his powers Henry James looked freely into the Medusan truth, he snared the unconsciousness. "Make him *think* the evil," he said, soliciting the unprepared nineteenth-century reader as the twentieth came near (a century that was to supply unthinkable evil), "make him think it for himself." And in the end—anarchy loosed upon the world, and pitilessness slouching toward him—James thought it for himself.

ISAAC BABEL
AND THE
IDENTITY
QUESTION

Identity, at least, is prepared to ask questions.
                                        —Leon Wieseltier

A YEAR OR SO before the Soviet Union imploded, S.'s mother, my first cousin—whose existence until then had been no more than a distant legend—telephoned from Moscow. "Save my child!" she cried, in immemorial tones. So when S. arrived in New York, I expected a terrified refugee on the run from the intolerable exactions of popular antisemitism; at that time the press was filled with such dire reports. For months, preparing for her rescue, I had been hurtling from one agency to another, in search of official information on political asylum.

But when S. finally turned up, in black tights, a miniskirt, and the reddest lipstick, it was clear she was indifferent to all that. She didn't want to be saved; what she wanted was an American holiday, a fresh set of boyfriends, and a leather coat. She had brought with her a sizable cosmetics case, amply stocked, and a vast, rattling plastic bag stuffed with hundreds of cheap tin Komsomol medals depicting Lenin as a boy. She was scornful of these; they were worthless, she said; she had paid pennies for the lot. Within two weeks S., a natural entrepreneur, had established romantic relations with the handsome young manager of the local sports store and had got him to set up a table at Christmas in his heaviest traffic location. She sold the tin Lenin medals for three dollars each, made three hundred dollars in a day, and bought the leather coat.

Of course she was a great curiosity. Her English was acutely original, her green eyes gave out ravishing ironic lightnings, her voice was as dark as Garbo's in *Ninotchka*, and none of us had ever seen an actual Soviet citizen up close before. She thought the telephone was bugged. She thought the supermarket was a public exhibition. Any show of household shoddiness—a lamp, say, that came apart—would elicit from her a comical crow: "Like in Soviet!" She was, emphatically, no atheist: she had an affinity for the occult, believed that God could speak in dreams (she owned a dream book, through which Jesus often walked), adored the churches of old Russia, and lamented their destruction by the Bolsheviks. On the subject of current antisemitism she was mute; that was her mother's territory. Back in Moscow, her boyfriend, Gennadi, had picked her up in the subway *because* she was Jewish. He was in a hurry to marry her. "He want get out of Soviet," she explained.

At home she was a *Sportsdoktor*: she traveled with the Soviet teams, roughneck country boys, and daily tested their urine for steroids. (Was this to make sure her athletes were properly dosed?) She announced that *everybody* hated Gorbachev, only the gullible Americans liked him, he was a joke like all the others. A historically-minded friend approached S. with the earnest inquiry of an old-fashioned liberal idealist: "We all know, obviously, about the excesses of Stalinism," she said, "but what of the *beginning*? Wasn't Communism a truly beautiful hope at the start?" S. laughed her cynical laugh; she judged my friend profoundly stupid. "Communism," she scoffed, "what Communism? Naive! Fairy tale, always! No Communism, never! Naive!"

And leaving behind five devastated American-as-apple-pie boyfriends (and wearing her leather coat), S. returned to Moscow. She did not marry Gennadi. Her mother emigrated to Israel. The last I heard of S., she was in business in Sakhalin, buying and selling—

and passing off as the real thing—ersatz paleolithic mammoth tusks.

.

WELL, IT IS ALL over now—the Great Experiment, as the old brave voices used to call it—and S. is both symptom and proof of how thoroughly it is over. She represents the Soviet Union's final heave, its last generation. S. is the consummate New Soviet Man: the unfurled future of its seed. If there is an axiom here, it is that idealism squeezed into utopian channels will generate a cynicism so profound that no inch of human life—not youth, not art, not work, not romance, not introspection—is left untainted. The S. I briefly knew trusted nothing; in her world there was nothing to trust. The primal Communist fairy tale had cast its spell: a baba yaga's birth-curse.

In college I read the Communist Manifesto, a rapture-bringing psalm. I ought to have read Isaac Babel's *Red Cavalry* stories—if only as a corrective companion-text. Or antidote. "But what of the beginning?" my friend had asked. S. answered better than any historian, but no one will answer more terrifyingly than Isaac Babel. If S. is the last generation of New Soviet Man, he is the first—the Manifesto's primordial manifestation.

That Babel favored the fall of the Czarist regime is no anomaly. He was a Jew from Odessa, the child of an enlightened family, hungry for a European education; he was subject to the *numerus clausus*, the Czarist quota that kept Jews as a class out of the universities, and Babel in particular out of the University of Odessa. As a very young writer, he put himself at risk when—to be near Maxim Gorky, his literary hero—he went to live illegally in St. Petersburg, a city outside the Pale of Settlement (the area to which Jews were restricted). What Jew would not have welcomed the demise of a hostile and obscurantist polity that, as late as 1911, tried Mendel Beiliss in a Russian court on a fantastic blood libel charge, and what Jew in a time of government-sanctioned pogroms would not have turned with relief to forces promising to topple the oppressors? In attaching himself to the Bolshevik cause, Babel may have been more zealous than many, but far from aberrant. If the choice were either Czar or Bolshevism, what Jew could choose

Czar? (A third possibility, which scores of thousands sought, was escape to America.) But even if one were determined to throw one's lot in with the Revolution, what Jew would go riding with Cossacks?

In 1920 Isaac Babel went riding with Cossacks. It was the third year of the Civil War—Revolutionary Reds versus Czarist Whites; he was twenty-six. Babel was not new to the military. Two years earlier, during the First World War, he had been a volunteer—in the Czar's army—on the Romanian front, where he contracted malaria. In 1919 he fought with the Red Army to secure St. Petersburg against advancing government troops. And in 1920 he joined ROSTA, the Soviet wire service, as a war correspondent for the newspaper *Red Cavalryman*. Poland, newly independent, was pressing eastward, hoping to recover its eighteenth-century borders, while the Bolsheviks, moving west, were furiously promoting the Communist salvation of Polish peasants and workers. The Polish-Soviet War appeared to pit territory against ideology; in reality territory—or, more precisely, the conquest of impoverished villages and towns and their wretched inhabitants—was all that was at stake for either side. Though the Great War was over, the Allies, motivated by fear of the spread of Communism, went to the aid of Poland with equipment and volunteers. (Ultimately the Poles prevailed and the Bolsheviks retreated, between them despoiling whole populations.)

In an era of air battles, Babel was assigned to the First Cavalry Army, a Cossack division led by General Semyon Budyonny. The Cossack image—glinting sabers, pounding hooves—is indelibly fused with Czarist power, but the First Cavalry Army was, perversely, Bolshevik. Stalin was in command of the southern front—the region abutting Poland—and Budyonny was in league with Stalin. Ostensibly, then, Babel found himself among men sympathetic to Marxist doctrine; yet Red Cossacks were no different from White Cossacks: untamed riders, generally illiterate, boorish and brutish, suspicious of ideas of any kind, attracted only to horseflesh, rabid looting, and the quick satisfaction of hunger and lust. "This isn't a Marxist revolution," Babel privately noted; "it's a rebellion of Cossack wild men." Polish and Russian cavalrymen clashing in ditches while warplanes streaked overhead was no more incongruous than the raw sight of Isaac Babel—a writer who had already published short stories praised by Gorky— sleeping in mud with Cossacks.

Lionel Trilling, in a highly nuanced (though partially misinformed) landmark introduction to a 1955 edition of *The Collected Stories of Isaac Babel*—which included the *Red Cavalry* stories— speaks of "the joke of a Jew who is a member of a Cossack regiment." A joke, Trilling explains, because

> traditionally the Cossack was the feared and hated enemy of the Jew. . . . The principle of his existence stood in total antithesis to the principle of the Jew's existence. The Jew conceived of his own ideal character as being intellectual, pacific, humane. The Cossack was physical, violent, without mind or manners . . . the natural and appropriate instrument of ruthless oppression.

Yet Trilling supplies another, more glamorous, portrait of the Cossack, which he terms Tolstoyan: "He was the man as yet untrammeled by civilization, direct, immediate, fierce. He was the man of enviable simplicity, the man of the body—the man who moved with speed and grace." In short, "our fantasy of the noble savage." And he attributes this view to Babel.

As it turns out, Babel's tenure with Budyonny's men was more tangled, and more intricately psychological, than Trilling—for whom the problem was tangled and psychological enough—could have known or surmised. For one thing, Trilling mistakenly believed that Babel's job was that of a supply officer—i.e., that he was actually a member of the regiment. But as a correspondent for a news agency (which meant grinding out propaganda), Babel's position among the troops was from the start defined as an outsider's, Jew or no. He was there as a writer. Worse, in the absence of other sources, Trilling fell into a crucial—and surprisingly naive—second error: he supposed that the "autobiographical" tales were, in fact, autobiographical.

Babel, Trilling inferred from Babel's stories, "was a Jew of the ghetto" who "when he was nine years old had seen his father kneeling before a Cossack captain." He compares this (fictitious) event to Freud's contemplation of his father's "having accepted in a pacific way the insult of having his new fur cap knocked into the mud by a Gentile who shouted at him, 'Jew, get off the pavement.' " "We might put it," Trilling concludes, that Babel rode with Budyonny's troops because he had witnessed his father's humiliation by "a Cossack on a horse, who said, 'At your service,' and touched his fur cap with his yellow-gloved hand and politely paid no heed to the mob looting the Babel store."

There was no Babel store. This scene—the captain with the yellow glove, the Jew pleading on his knees while the pogrom rages—is culled from Babel's story "First Love." But it was reinforced for Trilling by a fragmentary memoir, published in 1924, wherein Babel calls himself "the son of a Jewish shopkeeper." The truth was that Babel was the son of the class enemy: a well-off family. His father sold agricultural machinery and owned a warehouse in a business section of Odessa where numerous import-export firms were located. In the same memoir Babel records that because he had no permit allowing him residence in St. Petersburg, he hid out "in a cellar on Pushkin Street which was the home of a tormented, drunken waiter." This was pure fabrication: in actuality Babel was taken in by a highly respectable engineer and his wife, with whom he was in correspondence. The first invention was to disavow a bourgeois background in order to satisfy Communist dogma. The second was a romantic imposture.

It did happen, nevertheless, that the young Babel was witness to a pogrom. He was in no way estranged from Jewish suffering or sensibility, or, conversely, from the seductive winds of contemporary Europe. Odessa was modern, bustling, diverse, cosmopolitan; its very capaciousness stimulated a certain worldliness and freedom of outlook. Jewish children were required to study the traditional texts and commentaries, but they were also sent to learn the violin. Babel was early on infatuated with Maupassant and Flaubert, and wrote his first stories in fluent literary French. In his native Russian he lashed himself mercilessly to the discipline of an original style, the credo of which was burnished brevity. At the time of his arrest by the NKVD in 1939—he had failed to conform to Socialist Realism—he was said to be at work on a Russian translation of Sholem Aleichem.

Given these manifold intertwinings, it remains odd that Trilling's phrase for Babel was "a Jew of the ghetto." Trilling himself had characterized Babel's Odessa as "an eastern Marseilles or Naples," observing that "in such cities the transient, heterogeneous population dilutes the force of law and tradition, for good as well as for bad." One may suspect that Trilling's cultural imagination (and perhaps his psyche as well) was circumscribed by a kind of either/or: *either* worldly sophistication *or* the ghetto; and that, in linking Jewish learning solely to the ghetto, he could not conceive of its association with a broad and complex civilization. This partial darkening of mind, it seems to me, limits Trilling's understanding of Babel. An intellectual who had mastered the essentials of rabbinic literature, Babel was an educated Jew not "of the ghetto," but of the world. And not "of both worlds," as the divisive expression has it, but of the great and variegated map of human thought and experience.

Trilling, after all, in his own youth had judged the world to be rigorously divided. In 1933, coming upon one of Hemingway's letters, he wrote in his notebook:

> [A] crazy letter, written when he was drunk—self-revealing, arrogant, scared, trivial, absurd; yet [I] felt from reading it how right such a man is compared to the 'good minds' of my university life—how he will produce and mean something to the world . . . how his life which he could expose without dignity and which is anarchic and 'childish' is a better life than anyone I know could live, and right for his job. And how far—far—far—I am going from being a writer.

Trilling envied but could not so much as dream himself into becoming a version of Hemingway—rifle in one hand and pen in the other, intellectual Jew taking on the strenuous life; how much less, then, could he fathom Babel as Cossack. Looking only to Jewish constriction, what Trilling vitally missed was this: coiled in the bottommost pit of every driven writer is an impersonator—protean, volatile, restless and relentless. Trilling saw only stasis, or, rather, an unalterable consistency of identity: either lucubrations or daring, never both. But Babel imagined for himself an identity so fluid that, having lodged with his civilized friend, the St. Petersburg engineer, it pleased him to invent a tougher Babel consorting underground with a "tormented, drunken waiter." A drunken waiter would have been adventure enough—but ah, that Dostoyevskian "tormented"!

"He loved to confuse and mystify people," his daughter Nathalie wrote of him, after decades spent in search of his character. Born in 1929, she lived with her mother in Paris, where her father was a frequent, if raffish, visitor. In 1935 Babel was barred from leaving the Soviet Union, and never again saw his wife and child. Nathalie Babel was ten when Babel was arrested. In 1961 she went to look for traces of her father in Moscow, "where one can still meet people who loved him and continue to speak of him with nostalgia. There, thousands of miles from my own home in Paris, sitting in his living room, in his own chair, drinking from his glass, I felt utterly baffled. Though in a sense I had tracked him down, he still eluded me. The void remained."

In a laudatory reminiscence published in a Soviet literary magazine in 1964—a time when Babel's reputation was undergoing a modicum of "rehabilitation"—Georgy Munblit, a writer who had known Babel as well as anyone, spoke of "this sly, unfaithful, eternally evasive and mysterious Babel"; and though much of this elusiveness was caution in the face of Soviet restriction, a good part of it nevertheless had to do with the thrill of dissimulation and concealment. In a mid-Sixties Moscow speech at a meeting championing Babel's work, Ilya Ehrenburg—the literary Houdini who managed to survive every shift of Stalinist whim—described Babel as liking to "play the fool and put on romantic airs. He liked to create an atmosphere of mystery about himself; he was secretive and never told anybody where he was going."

Other writers (all of whom had themselves escaped the purges) came forward with recollections of Babel's eccentricities in risky times: Babel as intrepid wanderer; as trickster, rapscallion, ironist; penniless, slippery, living on the edge, off the beaten track, down and out; seduced by the underlife of Paris, bars, whores, cabdrivers, jockeys—all this suggests Orwellian experiment and audacity. Babel relished Villon and Kipling, and was delighted to discover that Rimbaud too was an "adventurer." Amusing and mercurial, "he loved to play tricks on people," according to Lev Nikulin, who was at school with Babel and remembered him "as a bespectacled boy in a rather shabby school coat and a battered cap with a green band and badge depicting Mercury's staff."

Trilling, writing in 1955, had of course no access to observations such as these; and we are as much in need now as Trilling was of a valid biography of Babel. Yet it is clear even from such small evidences and quicksilver portraits that Babel's connection with the Cossacks was, if not inevitable, more natural than not; and that Trilling's Freudian notion of the humiliated ghetto child could not have been more off the mark. For Babel lamp-oil and fearlessness were not antithetical. He was a man with the bit of recklessness between his teeth. One might almost ask how a writer so given to disguises and role-playing could *not* have put on a Cossack uniform.

"The Rebbe's Son," one of the *Red Cavalry* tales, is explicit about this fusion of contemplative intellect and physical danger. Ilya, the son of the Zhitomir Rebbe, "the last prince of the dynasty," is a Red Army soldier killed in battle. The remnants of his possessions are laid out before the narrator:

> Here everything was dumped together—the warrants of the agitator and the commemorative booklets of the Jewish poet. Portraits of Lenin and Maimonides lay side by side. Lenin's nodulous skull and the tarnished silk of the portraits of Maimonides. A strand of female hair had been placed in a book of the resolutions of the Sixth Party Congress, and in the margins of Communist leaflets swarmed crooked lines of ancient Hebrew verse. In a sad and meager rain they fell on me—pages of the Song of Songs and revolver cartridges.

Babel was himself drawn to the spaciousness and elasticity of these unexpected combinations. They held no enigma for him. But while the Rebbe's son was a kind of double patriot—loyal to the God of Abraham, Isaac and Jacob, and loyal to a dream of the betterment of Russia—Babel tended toward both theological and (soon enough) political skepticism. His *amor patriae* was—passionately—for the Russian mother-tongue. Before the Stalinist prison clanged shut in 1935, Babel might easily have gone to live permanently in France, with his wife and daughter. Yet much as he reveled in French literature and language, he would not suffer exile from his native Russian. A family can be replaced, or duplicated; but who can replace or duplicate the syllables of Pushkin and Tolstoy? And, in fact (though his wife in Paris survived until 1957, and there was no divorce), Babel did take another wife in the Soviet Union, who gave birth to another daughter; a second family was possible. A second language was not. (Only consider what must be the intimate sorrows—even in the shelter of America, even after the demise of Communism—of Czeslaw Milosz, Joseph Brodksy, Norman Manea, and countless other less celebrated literary refugees.) By remaining in the Soviet Union, and refusing finally to bend his art to Soviet directives, Babel sacrificed his life to his language.

It was a language he did not allow to rest. He meant to put his spurs to it, and run it to unexampled leanness. He quoted Pushkin: "precision and brevity." "Superior craftsmanship," Babel told Munblit, "is the art of making your writing as unobtrusive as possible." Ehrenburg recalled a conversation in Madrid with Hemingway, who had just discovered Babel. "I find that Babel's style is even more concise than mine. . . . It shows what can be done," Hemingway marveled. "Even when you've got all the water out of them, you can still clot the curds a little more." Such idiosyncratic experiments in style were hardly congruent with official pressure to honor the ascent of socialism through prescriptive prose about the beauty of collective farming. Babel did not dissent from Party demands; instead he fell mainly into silence, writing in private and publishing almost nothing. His attempts at a play and a filmscript met convulsive Party criticism; the director of the film, an adaptation of a story by Turgenev, was forced into a public apology.

The *Red Cavalry* stories saw print, individually, before 1924. Soviet cultural policies in those years were not yet consolidated; it was a period of postrevolutionary leniency and ferment. Russian modernism was sprouting in the shape of formalism, acmeism, imagism, symbolism; an intellectual and artistic avant-garde flourished. Censorship, which had been endemic to the Czarist regime, was reintroduced in 1922, but the restraints were loose. Despite a program condemning elitism, the early Soviet leadership, comprising a number of intellectuals—Lenin, Bukharin, Trotsky—recognized that serious literature could not be wholly entrusted to the sensibilities of Party bureaucrats. By 1924, then, Babel found himself not only famous, but eligible eventually for Soviet rewards: an apartment in Moscow, a dacha in the country, a car and chauffeur.

Yet he was increasingly called on to perform (and conform) by the blunter rulers of a darkening repression: why was he not writing in praise of New Soviet Man? Little by little a perilous mist gathered around Babel's person: though his privileges were not revoked (he was at his dacha on the day of his arrest), he began to take on a certain pariah status. When a leftist Congress for the Defense of Culture and Peace met in Paris, for example, Babel was deliberately omitted from the Soviet delegation, and was grudgingly allowed to attend only after the French organizers brought their protests to the Soviet Embassy.

Certain manuscripts he was careful not to expose to anyone. Among these was the remarkable journal he had kept, from June to September 1920, of the actions of Budyonny's First Cavalry Army in eastern Poland. Because it was missing from the papers seized by the secret police at the dacha and in his Moscow flat, the manuscript escaped destruction, and came clandestinely into the possession of Babel's (second) wife only in the 1950's. Ehrenburg was apparently the journal's first influential reader, though very likely he did not see it until the 1960's, when he mentioned it publicly, and evidently spontaneously, in his rehabilitation speech:

> I have been comparing the diary of the Red Cavalry with the stories. He scarcely changed any names, the events are all practically the same, but everything is illuminated with a kind of wisdom. He is saying: this is how it was. This is how the people were—they did terrible things and they suffered, they played tricks on others and they died. He made his stories out of the facts and phrases hastily jotted down in his notebook.

It goes without saying that the flatness of this essentially evasive summary does almost no justice to an astonishing historical record set down with godlike prowess in a prose of frightening clarity. In Russia the complete text of the journal finally appeared in 1990. Yale University Press brings it to us now under the title *Isaac Babel: 1920 Diary*, in an electrifying translation, accompanied by a first-rate (and indispensable) introduction. (It ought to be added that an informative introduction can be found also in the Penguin *Collected Stories*; but the reader's dependence on such piecemeal discussions only underscores the irritating absence of a formal biography.) In 1975 Ardis Publishers, specialists in Russian studies, made available the first English translation of excerpts from the journal (*Isaac Babel: Forgotten Prose*). That such a manuscript existed had long been known in the Soviet Union, but there was plainly no chance of publication; Ehrenburg, in referring to it, was discreet about its contents.

The *Diary* may count, then, as a kind of secret document; certainly as a suppressed one. But it is "secret" in another sense as well. Though it served as raw material for the *Red Cavalry* stories, Babel himself, in transforming private notes into daring fiction, was less daring than he might have been. He was, in fact, circumspect and selective. One can move from the notes to the stories without surprise—or put it that the surprise is in the masterliness and shock of a ripe and radical style. Still, as Ehrenburg reported, "the events are all practically the same," and what is in the *Diary* is in the stories.

But one cannot begin with the stories and then move to the journal without the most acute recognition of what has been, substantively and for the most part, shut out of the fiction. And what has been shut out is the calamity (to say it in the most general way) of Jewish fate in Eastern Europe. The *Diary* records how the First Cavalry Army, and Babel with it, went storming through the little Jewish towns of Galicia, in Poland—towns that had endured the Great War, with many of their young men serving in the Polish army, only to be decimated by pogroms immediately afterward, at the hands of the Poles themselves. And immediately after *that*, the invasion of the Red Cossacks. The Yale edition of the *Diary* supplies maps showing the route of Budyonny's troops; the resonant names of these places, rendered half-romantic through the mystical tales of their legendary hasidic saints, rise up with the nauseous familiarity of their deaths: Brody, Dubno, Zhitomir, Belz, Chelm, Zamosc, etc. Only two decades after the Red Cossacks stampeded through them, their Jewish populations fell prey to the Germans and were destroyed. Riding and writing, writing and riding, Babel saw it all: saw it like a seer. "Ill-fated Galicia, ill-fated Jews," he wrote. "Can it be," he wrote, "that ours is the century in which they perish?"

True: everything that is in the stories is in the *Diary*—priest, painter, widow, guncart, soldier, prisoner; but the heart of the *Diary* remains secreted in the *Diary*. When all is said and done—and much is said and done in these blistering pages: pillaged churches, ruined synagogues, wild Russians, beaten Poles, mud, horses, hunger, looting, shooting—Babel's journal is a Jewish lamentation: a thing the Soviet system could not tolerate, and Ehrenburg was too prudent to reveal. The merciless minds that snuffed the identities of the murdered at Babi Yar would hardly sanction Babel's whole and bloody truths.

Nor did Babel himself publicly sanction them. The *Red Cavalry* narratives include six stories (out of thirty-five) that touch on the suffering of Jews; the headlong *Diary* contains scores. An act of authorial self-censorship, and not only because Babel was determined to be guarded. Impersonation, or call it reckless play, propelled him at all points. The *Diary* can muse: "The Slavs—the manure of history?"—but Babel came to the Cossacks disguised as a Slav, having assumed the name K. L. Lyutov, the name he assigns also to his narrator. And in the *Diary* itself, encountering terrified Polish Jews, he again and again steers them away from the knowledge that rides in his marrow, and fabricates deliberate Revolutionary fairy tales (his word): he tells his trembling listeners how "everything's changing for the better—my usual system—miraculous things are happening in Russia—express trains, free food for children, theaters, the International. They listen with delight and disbelief. I think—you'll have your diamond-studded sky, everything and everyone will be turned upside down and inside out for the umpteenth time, and [I] feel sorry for them."

"My usual system": perhaps it is kind to scatter false consolations among the doomed. Or else it is not kindness at all, merely a writer's mischief or a rider's diversion—the tormented mice of Galicia entertained by a cat in Cossack dress. Sometimes he is recognized as a Jew (once by a child), and then he half-lies and explains that he has a Jewish mother. But mainly he is steadfast in the pretense of being Lyutov. And nervy: the *Diary* begins on June 3, in Zhitomir, and on July 12, one day before Babel's twenty-sixth birthday, he notes: "My first ride on horseback." In no time at all he is, at least on horseback, like all the others: a skilled and dauntless trooper. "The horse galloped well," he says on that first day. Enchanted, proud, he looks around at his companions: "red flags, a powerful, well-knit body of men, confident commanders, calm and experienced eyes of topknotted Cossack fighting men, dust, silence, order, brass band." But moments later the calm and experienced eyes are searching out plunder in the neat cottage of an immigrant Czech family, "all good people." "I took nothing, although I could have," the new horseman comments. "I'll never be a real Budyonny man."

The real Budyonny men are comely, striking, stalwart. Turning off a highway, Babel catches sight of "the brigades suddenly appear[ing], inexplicable beauty, an awesome force advancing." Another glimpse: "Night . . . horses are quietly snorting, they're all Kuban Cossacks here, they eat together, sleep together, a splendid silent comradeship . . . they sing songs that sound like church music in lusty voices, their devotion to horses, beside each man a little heap—saddle, bridle, ornamental saber, greatcoat, I sleep in the midst of them."

Babel is small, his glasses are small and round, he sets down secret sentences. And meanwhile his dispatches, propaganda screeches regularly published in *Red Cavalryman*, have a different tone: "Soldiers of the Red Army, finish them off! Beat down harder on the opening covers of their stinking graves!" And: "That is what they are like, our heroic nurses! Caps off to the nurses! Soldiers and commanders, show respect to the nurses!" (In the *Diary* the dubious propagandist writes satirically, "Opening of the Second Congress of the Third International, unification of the peoples finally realized, now all is clear . . . We shall advance into Europe and conquer the world.")

And always there is cruelty, and always there are the Jews. "Most of the rabbis have been exterminated." "The Jewish cemetery . . . hundreds of years old, gravestones have toppled over . . . overgrown with grass, it has seen Khmelnitsky, now Budyonny . . . everything repeats itself, now that whole story—Poles, Cossacks, Jews—is repeating itself with stunning exactitude, the only new element is Communism." "They all say they're fighting for justice and they all loot." "Life is loathsome, murderers, it's unbearable, baseness and crime." "I ride along with them, begging the men not to massacre prisoners . . . I couldn't look at their faces, they bayoneted some, shot others, bodies covered by corpses, they strip one man while they're shooting another, groans, screams, death rattles." "We are destroyers . . . we move like a whirlwind, like a stream of lava, hated by everyone, life shatters, I am at a huge, never-ending service for the dead . . . the sad senselessness of my life."

The Jews: "The Poles ransacked the place, then the Cossacks." "Hatred for the Poles is unanimous. They have looted, tortured, branded the pharmacist with a red-hot iron, put needles under his nails, pulled out his hair, all because somebody shot at a Polish officer." "The Jews ask me to use my influence to save them from ruin, they are being robbed of food and goods . . . The cobbler had looked forward to Soviet rule—and what he sees are Jew-baiters and looters . . . Organized looting of a stationer's shop, the proprietor in tears, they tear up everything . . . When night comes the whole town will be looted—everybody knows it."

The Jews at the hands of the Poles: "A pogrom . . . a naked, barely breathing prophet of an old man, an old woman butchered, a child with fingers chopped off, many people still breathing, stench of blood, everything turned upside down, chaos, a mother sitting over her sabered son, an old woman lying twisted up like a pretzel, four people in one hovel, filth, blood under a black beard, just lying there in the blood."

The Jews at the hands of the Bolsheviks: "Our men nonchalantly walking around looting whenever possible, stripping mangled corpses. The hatred is the same, the Cossacks just the same, it's nonsense to think one army is different from another. The life of these little towns. There's no salvation. Everyone destroys them." "Our men were looting last night, tossed out the Torah scrolls in the synagogue and took the velvet covers for saddlecloths. The military commissar's dispatch rider examines phylacteries, wants to take the straps." The *Diary* mourns, "What a mighty and marvelous life of a nation existed here. The fate of Jewry."

And then: "I am an outsider." And again: "I don't belong, I'm all alone, we ride on . . . five minutes after our arrival the looting starts, women struggling, weeping and wailing, it's unbearable, I can't stand these never-ending horrors . . . [I] snatch a flatcake out of the hands of a peasant woman's little boy." He does this mechanically, and without compunction.

"How we eat," he explains. "Red troops arrive in a village, ransack the place, cook, stoves crackling all night, the householders' daughters have a hard time" (a comment we will know how to interpret). Babel grabs the child's flatcake—a snack on the fly, as it were—on August 3. On July 25, nine days earlier, he and a riding companion, Prishchepa, a loutish syphilitic illiterate, have burst into a pious Jewish house in a town called Demidovka. It is the Sabbath, when lighting a fire is forbidden; it is also the eve of the Ninth of Av, a somber fast day commemorating the destruction of the Temple in Jerusalem. Prishchepa demands fried potatoes. The dignified mother, a flock of daughters in white stockings, a scholarly son, are all petrified; on the Sabbath, they protest, they cannot dig potatoes, and besides, the fast begins at sundown. "Fucking Yids," Prishchepa yells; so the potatoes are dug, the fire to cook them is lit.

Babel, a witness to this anguish, says nothing. "I keep quiet, because I'm a Russian"—will Prishchepa discover that Lyutov is only another Yid? "We eat like oxen, fried potatoes and five tumblersful of coffee each. We sweat, they keep serving us, all this is terrible, I tell them fairy tales about Bolshevism." Night comes, the mother sits on the floor and sobs, the son chants the liturgy for the Ninth of Av—Jeremiah's Lamentations: "they eat dung, their maidens are ravished, their menfolk killed, Israel subjugated." Babel hears and understands every Hebrew word. "Demidovka, night, Cossacks," he sums it up, "all just as it was when the Temple was destroyed. I go out to sleep in the yard, stinking and damp."

And there he is, New Soviet Man: stinking, a sewer of fairy tales, an unbeliever—and all the same complicit. Nathalie Babel said of her father that nothing "could shatter his feeling that he belonged to Russia and that he had to share the fate of his countrymen. What in so many people would have produced only fear and terror, awakened in him a sense of duty and a kind of blind heroism." In the brutal light of the *Diary*—violation upon violation—it is hard not to resist this point of view. Despair and an abyss of cynicism do not readily accord with a sense of duty; and whether or not Babel's travels with the Cossacks—and with Bolshevism altogether—deserve to be termed heroic, he was anything but blind. He saw, he saw, and he saw.

It may be that the habit of impersonation, the habit of deception, the habit of the mask, will in the end lead a man to become what he impersonates. Or it may be that the force of "I am an outsider" overwhelms the secret gratification of having got rid of a fixed identity. In any case, the *Diary* tells no lies. These scenes in a journal, linked by commas quicker than human breath, run like rapids through a gorge—on one side the unrestraint of violent men, on the other the bleaker freedom of unbelonging. Each side is subversive of the other; and still they embrace the selfsame river.

To venture yet another image, Babel's *Diary* stands as a tragic masterwork of breakneck cinematic "dailies"—those raw, unedited rushes that expose the director to himself. If Trilling, who admitted to envy of the milder wilderness that was Hemingway, had read Babel's *Diary*—what then? And who, in our generation, should read the *Diary*? Novelists and poets, of course; specialists in Russian literature, obviously; American innocents who define the world of the Twenties by jazz, flappers, and Fitzgerald. And also: all those who protested Claude Lanzmann's film *Shoah* as unfair to the psyche of the Polish countryside; but, most of all, the cruelly ignorant children of the Left who still believe that the Marxist Utopia requires for its realization only a more favorable venue, and another go.

No one knows when or exactly how Babel perished. Some suppose he was shot immediately after the NKVD picked him up and brought him to Moscow's Lyubanka prison, on May 16, 1939. Others place the date of his murder in 1941, following months of torture.* More than fifty years later, as if the writer were sending forth phantoms of his first and last furies, Babel's youthful *Diary* emerges. What it attests to above all is not simply that fairy tales can kill—who doesn't understand this?—but that Bolshevism was lethal in its very cradle.

Which is just what S., my ironical Muscovite cousin, found so pathetically funny when, laughing at our American stupidity, she went home to Communism's graveyard.

---

*But a letter from Robert Conquest, dated May 15, 1995, offers the following: "Babel's fate is in fact known. Arrested on 16 May 1939, he was subjected to three days and nights of intensive interrogation on 29–31 May, at the end of which he confessed. At various interrogations over the year he withdrew that part of his confession that incriminated other writers. At his secret trial on 26 January 1940, he pled not guilty on all counts. The main charges were of Trotskyism; espionage for Austria and France (the latter on behalf of André Malraux); and involvement in a terrorist plot against Stalin and Voroshilov by former NKVD chief Nikolai Yezhov, whose wife Babel knew. He was shot at 1:40 A.M. the next day."

GEORGE STEINER AND THE ERRATA OF HISTORY

I GNAZIO SILONE, the renowned Italian novelist who was early attracted to revolutionary politics, once testified that it was an act of greed during an earthquake in the Abruzzi village of his boyhood that turned him to Communism. While Silone's mother lay buried under rubble, with only one arm exposed, his uncle—until that moment in every way a good man—looted her housekeeping cache. "I think that night my attitude to money became tinged with a profound horror."

Communism's centrally defining seductiveness has never been politics in the Roman sense of *civitas*, the mundane social mechanisms of civil order, so much as it has been a metaphysical denial of greed. In "Proofs," George Steiner's arresting novella of Communism's 1989 collapse—the opening fiction of his *Proofs and Three Parables*—the Marxist purists are all messianic spiritualists swept away by seizures of justice and radical love. Like Silone, they are Italians who remember Il Duce with revulsion, and they are similarly in search of the transcendent insight that catapulted them into a belief as indissoluble and sacramental as any other species of immovable faith. Silone famously left the Party and disavowed it: "the forgetting of the end in the means, the acceptance of a new servitude masked by the theory of historical necessity, seemed to me to be disastrous. My 'way out' had led me into a concentration camp."

The few quixotic members of Steiner's last-ditch Circle for Marxist Revolutionary Theory and Praxis have not recanted, though they too are no longer of the Party: they were expelled for protesting the brutalities of Soviet tanks in Hungary. Yet they cannot expel the primordial ideal from their own bosoms—they watch with shocked bemusement as the Berlin Wall crumbles, as the tyrannies of Prague, Warsaw, Budapest, Sofia all dissolve. The visionaries of the CMRTP do not obscure Stalin's atrocities—"The perversion is monstrous"—but they cannot snuff the redemptive dream that has animated their meager lives. All the same, in the annus mirabilis of 1989, it is not the state that is withering away, as Marx predicted, but the dream itself. The CMRTP, with no recruits and a lost agenda, is compelled to disband. The rhapsody jangles, the maggots have eaten Utopia.

In the Circle's chief visionary, whom the others call *"Professore"* because of his erudite intensity, Steiner has contrived a seamless and apposite metaphor: the *Professore* is a proofreader of such flawless purity that he "had not rival in the arts of scruple." His perfectionism is such that even paper litter in the streets cannot escape his fastidious eye: "if the winds blew a piece toward his feet, he would pick it up, smooth it, read closely, and make any correction needed. Then he would deposit it in the garbage receptacle." And finally, after debating the genesis of Marxist hope until dawn, the proofreader cries out: "Utopia simply means *getting it right*! Communism means taking the errata out of history. Out of man. Reading proofs."

The errata of history and of humankind comprise the obsessive counterminings of Steiner's narrative. His models are Dostoyevsky's Grand Inquisitor, the dialectical segments of *The Magic Mountain*, Chekhov's more argumentative and theorizing characters—in short, the fiction of ideas, wherein ideas are indistinguishable from passions, and culture is defined by its loftiest urgencies. Steiner's Marxists, contending on behalf of the ordinary human article, are nevertheless consummate elitists. They look to Olympus or Sinai, or to the holy men of the West: Plato, Schubert, Shakespeare, Einstein, Mozart, Cézanne, Marx above all. They are the gravest of theologians, with a weak sense of irony and hardly a glimmer of the comedy struck off by human unpredictability. They will find origins, they believe, in outcome.

So Father Carlo, the renegade priest, has learned to see that "at the heart of Communism is the lie. . . . The systematic bribing and betrayal of human hope. . . . Your earthly messiahs turned out to be nothing but hypocritical hoodlums. Lords of lice." But he dismisses Christianity as "aspirin" and ends by praising American consumerism. "A country," the *Professore* retorts, "which no poem can shake. Where no philosophic argument matters." And of Bolshevism even in the hour of its rot he declares, "Yes, we got it wrong. Hideously wrong. . . . But the big error, the overestimate of man from which the mistake came, is the single most noble motion of the human spirit in our awful history."

Yet here Steiner's tragic satire springs its terrible trap. The perfectionist erratum-catcher, having proclaimed that the "hopes of a Communist are a way of seeing with absolute clarity," is gradually losing his eyesight to glaucoma; his vision is compromised. If Utopia is "reading proofs," then Communism's landscape has been turned into an uncorrectable jungle of typos and ignoramus blunders.

George Steiner may be a philosophical essayist who writes fiction—his last, "The Portage to San Cristobal of A.H.," notorious for giving Hitler the last word, was also a narrative of history's outcome—but it is contentious fiction with the blood of life in it. The blood of life, that is, if it is understood that our lives hang on what we think and believe (or what others lead us to think and believe) as much as on what we feel and do. Even the sexual occasions in "Proofs" are stimulated by a union of belief: idea is as elemental as pulse.

The three "parables" that follow are, it seems to me, unnecessarily drawn under this portentous head, which can suggest Khalil Gibran as readily as Kafka. What is meant to have, in "A Conversation Piece," the resonance of rabbinic disputation (notable for its succinctness), is rather more redolent of a grandiloquent translation from the Persian: "blessed be the hem of His unsayable Name and the fire-garment of His glory." The subject is what Hebrew scripture calls the *akedah*, Abraham's "binding" of his son Isaac, who is saved from sacrifice by divine intent. Though the dialogue is mazy with speculations concerning the purport of God's way with Abraham, the speakers are finally gathered under the spigot of gas. "There is no ram now and the bush is burning." Having pierced us with this twentieth-century denouement, does Steiner mean us to infer that the Holocaust was God's will?

"Noël, Noël" is a short story told from the viewpoint of a family pet, for whom the pleasures of Christmas are violated by what appears to be an act of incest. "Desert Island Discs" proposes a sound-archive that includes Fortinbras's belch, the "sibilant swerve (in G minor) of the steel nib on Rudolf Julius Emmanuel Clausius's pen in the instant in which this pen wrote the n in the exponential n minus x to the nth power in the equation of entropy," and other captured acuities. A witty piece, its format moving between poetry and a conceit.

But in this little book of fables for the intellect, it is the canny agility and breadth of "Proofs" that leave the most enduring traces. With all their weary pathos, Steiner's incurable visionaries will likely find their way into the accumulating archive of Communism's spiritual doom.

MARK
TWAIN'S
VIENNA

SOME INTRODUCTORY
MUSINGS ON THE NATURE
OF THE FACSIMILE

I N CONTEMPLATING the difference between a Victorian museum and one of our own era, what is the instantly recognizable contemporary element? Never mind that display cases have evolved from what used to be called "vitrines" (glass boxes on wooden legs); or that pictures are no longer strung from rococo cornices; or that museum visitors, too, have evolved—from isolated passionate starers to dogged mobs in motion, with headsets plugged into their ears. The absolute difference is in the growth of the lobby shop: here nearly every treasure of the galleries overhead appears in facsimile. The past is exactly duplicated in the present: for a few dollars you can own a Canaanite clay oil lamp or a carved Egyptian cat.

Jorge Borges in one of his ingenious *ficciones* imagines the paradox of a man who has written a "modern" *Don Quixote*, identical in every syllable to Cervantes' *Don Quixote*. Yet the difference is extreme: whereas the original work manifested a robust contemporary style of speech appropriate to the seventeenth century, the modern duplicate turns out to be hopelessly archaic. Or consider the plaster casts of those pitifully fleeing figures of Pompeii, whose shapes have already been preserved, two thousand years ago, in cooled volcanic ash: sculpted twice, they are twice removed from the ancient catastrophe they copy.

The idea of the facsimile is, in our time, itself a kind of volcanic eruption: this or that newfangled device can spew out an instantaneous copy of practically anything. All the same, there is a divide between the original and its imitator. The divide is history. When you purchase one of those clay oil lamps from a museum shop, and take it home and put it on a shelf, you may dream over it all you like, summoning up the past with your marveling caress—but the past of what? Its history is a molding machine in Newark, New Jersey. The original of anything carries the force of its own contemporaneity. Polishing my grandmother's brass candlesticks, I feel how *her* hand once did the same, and her spirit accompanies the act. Rare-book collectors know all this: the living touch of an aging binding is instinct with its period, and with the breath of its first owner.

A facsimile edition is something else altogether. Though it suggests a Zeitgeist long evaporated, still it can only *suggest*; so it places on its readers a burden of history-imagining that a genuine first edition will not. A first edition of an old book is an heirloom, a relic, an authentic survival of the past; in its own presence and essence, it *is* the past, a palpable instance of time-travel. But a facsimile edition, because it is the product of machined reproduction, stirs up a quandary: even if we are seduced into pretending so, ancestral eyes and hands did *not* encounter this very volume.

The quandary is this. Mark Twain in any available edition—and there are scores of these—augurs a reader's private exchange with an American classic. But Mark Twain in a facsimile edition is designed to be a wholly dissimilar experience; and yet it is not, and cannot be. Touch a facsimile volume, and what you touch is the refined technology of photocopying—no time-travel in *that*. I am looking now at a facsimile of a Harper & Brothers publication of *The Man That Corrupted Hadleyburg and Other Stories and Essays*, dated 1900. The print is large and clear, the margins generous. There is a frontispiece photograph of Mark Twain, captioned "S. L. Clemens." The copyright, curiously, is not in the name of S. L. Clemens (or of his pseudonym), but in that of Olivia L. Clemens, his wife. (She died in 1904, predeceasing him by six years). The fifteen items in the Table of Contents disclose their sources; of periodicals once renowned (*Harper's Magazine, The Century, The Cosmopolitan, The New York World, The Youth's Companion, The Forum, McClure's,* and *The North American Review*), only *Harper's* recognizably survives. The several illustrations (artist unidentified), with their captions excerpted from the text, are redolent of nineteenth-century charm—the charm of skilled and evocative drawings—and may make us nostalgic for a practice long in disuse: every tale equipped with its visual interpretation. (But it was a practice serious authors grew tired of and finally could no longer endure. Henry James, for instance, banished internal illustrations from his New York Edition and turned to photography for the frontispiece.)

A facsimile volume, then, can offer only this much of "history": a list of forgotten magazines, a handful of old-fashioned drawings, an imitative binding. The rest of it is the job of reading; and a facsimile volume, despite its hope of differentiating itself from an ordinary sort of book, reads, after all, like any other reprint. With this caution. A run-of-the-mill reprint will supply you with a text—fiction or essay—and leave you on your own, so to speak. A facsimile edition, on the other hand, because it deals in reproductive illusion—like that clay oil lamp bought in a museum gift shop—demands what illusion always demands: confirmation (or completion) in solid data. In brief: context or setting.

If I read "The Man That Corrupted Hadleyburg" in an indifferent or insipid edition, I read it as a celebrated story by Mark Twain, with all that signifies intrinsically. But if I read that same story in an ambitious and even beautiful facsimile format, the extrinsic urges itself on the text with the inexorability of a compensating force. The facsimile volume advertises a false authenticity—but it can lay no claim to being a historical object, any more than the museum-shop lamp can. Without the testimony of the archaeologists to give it context, the duplicate clay is merely last Tuesday's factory item; and without the surround of 1900, what is the *raison d'être* of an imitation 1900 edition? The facsimile cries out for an adumbration of the world into which the original was introduced; that is its unique and pressing power, and the secret of its admittedly physical shock on our senses. Reproduction exacts history.

"THE MAN That Corrupted Hadleyburg" was written in 1898, in Europe: specifically, Vienna. Mark Twain was still under the shadow of an indelible bereavement; only two years earlier, in 1896, Susy, the oldest and probably the most literarily gifted of the three Clemens daughters, had suddenly been carried off by cerebral meningitis. Restlessness and grief drove Mark Twain and his family—his wife Livy and their two remaining daughters, Clara and Jean—from England to Switzerland to Vienna, where they settled for nearly two years. Clara had come to study piano and voice with distinguished Viennese teachers; Jean was being treated, intermittently and inconclusively, for epilepsy. But Mark Twain was there, willy-nilly, as Mark Twain abroad—which could only mean Mark Twain celebrated and lionized. Vienna was a brilliant magnet for composers and concert artists, for playwrights and satirists, for vivid promoters of liberal and avant-garde ideas. Mark Twain was courted by Hapsburg aristocrats—countesses and duchesses—and by diplomats and journalists and dramatists. He spoke at pacifist rallies and collaborated in the writing of a pair of plays urging women's suffrage (they never reached the stage and the manuscripts have not survived). He obliged this or that charity by giving public readings; one of them, in February 1898, was attended by Dr. Sigmund Freud. Set within resplendent architecture and statuary, the intellectual life of the city dazzled.

But there was another side to fin-de-siècle Vienna: its underside. Vienna was (then and later) notoriously, stingingly, passionately antisemitic. The familiar impulses that jubilantly welcomed Hitler's *Anschluss* in 1938, and defiantly elected Kurt Waldheim, a former Nazi, as president of Austria in 1986, were acted upon with equal vigor (and venom) in 1898, when the demagogue Karl

Lueger held office as Vienna's popular mayor; and Lueger was a preparatory template for the Nazi politics that burgeoned in Vienna only two and a half decades on. In Mark Twain's Vienna, the cultural elite included prominent Jewish musicians and writers, among whom he flourished companionably; his daughter Clara married Ossip Gabrilowitsch, a Russian Jewish composer-pianist and fellow music student. These warm Viennese associations did not escape the noisome antisemitic press, which vulgarly denounced Mark Twain either as Jew-lover or as himself a secret Jew.

In 1898, the European press in general—whether in Paris or Brussels or Berlin or Vienna or even Moscow—was inflamed by an international controversy: the fever of the Dreyfus Affair was erupting well beyond France itself, where Captain Alfred Dreyfus, a Jewish army officer, had been falsely incriminated on a charge of treason. Polity after polity was split between Dreyfusards and anti-Dreyfusards; and in Vienna, Mark Twain boldly stood for Dreyfus's innocence. In 1898, Zola published his great *J'Accuse*, and escaped arrest by fleeing to England. It was the year of a vast European poisoning, by insidious sloganeering and hideous posters and caricatures; no single country went unsullied.

And it was in this atmosphere that Mark Twain sat down to write "The Man That Corrupted Hadleyburg"—a story about a town in which moral poisoning widens and widens, until no single person remains unsullied. No one can claim that the Dreyfus Affair, a conspiracy to entrap the innocent, impinged explicitly on Mark Twain's tale of a citizenry brought down by revenge and spreading greed. But the notion of a society—even one in microcosm, like Hadleyburg—sliding deeper and deeper (and individual by individual) into ethical perversion and contamination was not far from a portrait of a Europe undergoing the contagion of its great communal lie. The commanding theme of "The Man That Corrupted Hadleyburg" *is* contagion; and also the smugness that arises out of self-righteousness, however rooted in lie it may be.

Hadleyburg's lie is its belief in its own honesty; it has, in fact, sheltered itself against the possibility of corruption, teaching "the principles of honest dealing to its babies in the cradle," and insulating its young people from temptation, "so that their honesty could have every chance to harden and solidify, and become a part of their very bone." Yet the absence of temptation is commonly no more than the absence of a testing occasion, and when temptation finally does come to Hadleyburg, no citizen, despite stringent prior training, can withstand it. Dishonest money-lust creeps over the town, first infiltrating a respectable old couple, then moving from household to household of nineteen of the town's most esteemed worthies. An archetypal narrative, it goes without saying: the devil tempting the seemingly pure, who turn out to be as flawed as the ordinary human article usually is. The Faustian bargain trades innocence for gold.

A first reading of "The Man That Corrupted Hadleyburg"—i.e., a first reading *now*, nearly a century after its composition—is apt to disappoint through overfamiliarity. It is not that familiarity lessens art; not in the least; more often it intensifies art. The experience of one *Hamlet* augments a second and a third, and this is as true of *Iolanthe* as it is of Shakespeare; but surely we don't go to *Hamlet* or *Iolanthe* for the *plot*. In the last several decades Hadleyburg, as the avatar of a corrupted town, has reappeared in short stories by Shirley Jackson ("The Lottery") and I. B. Singer ("The Gentleman from Cracow"), and in *The Visit*, a chilling drama by Friedrich Dürrenmatt. And not only through such literary means: in the hundred years since Mark Twain invented Hadleyburg, a proliferation of story-appliances (radio, film, television, and video-recorders), spilling out scores of Hadleyburgs, has acquainted us with (and doubtless hardened us against) the stealthy despoliation of an idyllic town by a cunning stranger. Hadleyburg, for us, is largely a cinematic cliché worn down, by now, to a parody of itself; nor do we have any defense against our belatedness (to use a critical term made famous by Harold Bloom).

But all that applies only to a first reading, when what will stand out is, mainly, the lineaments of the narrative itself. Behind the recognizable Faustian frame are two unlikely categories of ingenuity. The first touches on the identity of the tempter. Hadleyburg, we are told, "had the ill luck to offend a passing stranger . . . a bitter man and vengeful."

All through his wanderings during a whole year he kept his injury in mind, and gave all his leisure moments to trying to invent a compensating satisfaction for it. He contrived many plans, and all of them were good, but none of them was quite sweeping enough; the poorest of them would hurt a great many individuals, but what he wanted was a plan which would comprehend the entire town, and not let so much as one person escape unhurt. At last he had a fortunate idea, and when it fell into his brain it lit up his whole head with an evil joy.

We know no more than this about the injured stranger and never will know more. (Here the illustrator has supplied a gloating figure in overcoat, top hat, and cravat, rubbing his hands together and hooking his feet around the legs of a chair. Ears, nose, and chin are each pointedly pointed, and you almost expect to catch the point of a tail lashing behind.) There is no shred of a hint concerning the nature of the offense, or exactly who committed it. This forcefully suggests the Demiurge, who hates the human race simply for its independent existence, especially when that existence is embroidered by moral striving; the devil requires no motive. And as the powerful sovereign of a great and greatly populated kingdom, he has no need of revenge. The Demiurge's first and last urge is gluttony—the lust to fatten his kingdom with more and more souls. Vengeance is clearly a human trait, not the devil's; so we may conclude that the "passing stranger" is, in truth, no different in kind from any indigenous citizen of Hadleyburg, and that the vengeful outlander and the honest native are, in potential and surely in outcome, identical.

And, indeed, at the end of the day, when Hadleyburg has been fully corrupted, there is nothing to choose between the "evil joy" of the schemer and the greedy dreams of the townsfolk who scheme to enrich themselves through lies. The contest is not between the devil and man, but between man and man.* And it is not so much a contest as a confluence. In other words, we may be induced to imagine that *all* the citizens of Hadleyburg are "passing strangers": strangers to themselves. They have believed that they

*Mark Twain and an avalanche of literature before him employ "man" to represent humankind; and so will I, without a trace of feminist shame, when the grace of a sentence depends on it.

are one thing—pure hearts burnished and enameled by honesty—and they learn that they are another thing: corruptible, degraded, profoundly exposed.

Then is the corrupter of Hadleyburg *not* the devil? And if he is not, is there, after all, *no* Faustian frame? Is what we have, instead, the textual equivalent of the sort of optical illusion that permits you to perceive, with unqualified clarity, two different pictures, but never at the same instant? Nearly everyone has experienced the elusive vase that suddenly shows itself as a pair of silhouettes, and the maddening human profiles that unaccountably flash out of sight to reveal a vase: is *this* the conceptual design of Mark Twain's narrative? That the outline of the corrupter is inseparable from the outline of the corrupted—that they are one and the same, ineluctably and horribly fused—but that our gaze is barred from absorbing this metaphorical simultaneity? A far more subtle invention than the Faustian scaffold on which this tale has always been said to depend.

On the other hand, Hadleyburg's tempter (whether or not he is intended to be a Mephistophelean emblem) *does* have a palpable identity of another kind—one we can easily grasp; and this is Mark Twain's second category of ingenuity. The stranger is a man who relishes the manipulation of words: certain phrases must be reproduced, and they must be precisely the *right* phrases, every syllable perfected. When a sack is deposited at the house of Mr. and Mrs. Richards, an explanatory note is attached. The note is far from brief; it has a plot, a trajectory, a climactic purpose; it promises as much as the opening of a fairy tale. The sack, it claims, "contains gold coin weighing a hundred and sixty pounds four ounces," and should be given as a reward of gratitude to the unknown Hadleyburg citizen who long ago unwittingly earned it. The sack's donor was once a gambler who was spurred to reform because a man of the town gave him twenty dollars and spoke a sentence that "saved the remnant of my morals." That man, the schemer's note continues—and we have understood from the beginning that all this is a spurious concoction—that man "can be identified by the remark he made to me; I feel persuaded that he will remember it."

This is a story, then, that hangs on a set of words—fictitious, invented words—and as the narrative flies on with increasing complexity, devising painful joke after painful joke, it soon becomes clear that "The Man That Corrupted Hadleyburg" is less about gold than it is about language. A sentence that is *almost* "correct" but contains a vagrant "very," is deemed fraudulent; eventually all versions of the elusive remark fall under a cloud of fraudulence, and threaten the town, and expose its infamous heart. And ultimately even hard gold coin is converted into language, in the form of written checks. It is language itself, even language subjected to comedy, that is revealed as the danger, as a conduit to greed, as an entangler in shame and sin and derision.

Which probably *does* return us to the devil. And why not? Mark Twain, early and late, is always preoccupied with the devil and his precincts: the devil is certainly the hero of *The Mysterious Stranger* (a work that is also a product of Vienna), where he is a grand imaginer who appears under the name of Dream, though his dreams are human nightmares, and his poetry destroys. In this view (and who will separate it from Mark Twain's metaphysical laughter?), the devil is a writer, and the corrupter of Hadleyburg a soulless figure who comprehends that words can carry more horror, and spread more evil joy, than any number of coveted treasures in a sack: even in the saving light of ridicule.

AND IF WE are returned to the devil and his precincts, we are also returned to Vienna. Under the purposefully ambiguous title "Stirring Times in Vienna," Mark Twain published in *Harper's*, in the latter part of 1897, four pieces of journalism reporting on sessions of the parliament of the Hapsburg empire, then known as Austria-Hungary—a political amalgam of nineteen national enclaves that endured for fifty-one years until its dissolution after the First World War. The Austrian parliament, situated in Vienna, and conducted in German (the empire's official language), is, in Mark Twain's rendering, a non-homogeneous Hadleyburg corrupted well past mere greed into the contagion of chaos and contumely. The Hadleyburg townsfolk are uniformly named Richards and Burgess and Goodson and Wilson and Billson; and yet their interests conflict as if they held nothing in common. In the Austrian parliament it is certain that nothing is held in common: the native languages of the members are Polish, Czech, Romanian, Hungarian, Italian, German, etc., and the motley names correspond to their speakers' origins. What is at issue, in December of 1897, is a language dispute. The Bohemians are demanding that Czech replace German as Bohemia's official language; the government (i.e., the majority party) has acceded. But the German-speaking Austrians, who comprise only one-fourth of the empire's entire population, are enraged, and are determined to prevent the government from pursuing all other business—including the ratification of the indispensable *Ausgleich*, the renewable treaty of confederation linking Austria and Hungary—unless and until German is restored in Bohemia.

The analogy with Hadleyburg is not gratuitous. Here again the crux is language. In Hadleyburg there are nineteen worthies complicit in the turmoil of communal shame; in the Austrian parliament there are nineteen states. And just as the nineteen leading citizens of Hadleyburg furiously compete, so do the Austrian parliamentarians: "Broadly speaking, all the nations in the empire hate the government—but they all hate each other too, and with devoted and enthusiastic bitterness; no two of them can combine; the nation that rises must rise alone." And if we can recognize in Hadleyburg the dissolving Austria-Hungary of the 1890's, we can surely recognize the disintegrated components of the former Yugoslavia in the 1990's. Hadleyburg may be emblematic of the imperial parliament in Vienna seventeen years before the outbreak of war in Sarajevo in 1914; even more inescapably, it presages the fin-de-siècle Sarajevo of our own moment.

Yet there is a difference—of reportage—between Mark Twain's Vienna and contemporary Bosnia that turns out to be not quite what we would expect. The facsimile volume presents us with a pair of century-old photographs, one showing the exterior of the parliament, the other a violent interior scene. The parliament buildings appear to stretch over three or four city blocks, with all the majesty of a row of imperial palaces. The interior—"its panelled sweep relieved by fluted columns of distinguished grace and dignity, which glow softly and frostily in the electric light"—offers a mob of unruly screamers, a good number of them clubbing their desks with wooden planks. The photographs are necessarily static and silent, and we might be induced to feel technologically superior in a news-gathering way to a generation that perforce had to do without CNN or Court TV (not omitting the impact of the Army-McCarthy hearings of the 1950's); whereas *we* have television (and the prose of Peter Arnett). Vienna in 1897 had only Mark Twain; and imagination confirms which medium overpowers (or, as we are wont to put it, "outperforms") which. What TV anchor, accompanied by what "brilliant camerawork," can match this introspective portrait of the parliament's Polish president?

> He is a gray-haired, long, slender man, with a colorless long face, which, in repose, suggests a death-mask; but when not in repose is tossed and rippled by a turbulent smile which washes this way and that, and is not easy to keep up with—a pious smile, a beseeching and supplicating smile; and when it is at work the large mouth opens, and the flexible lips crumple, and unfold, and crumple again, and move around in a genial and persuasive and angelic way, and expose large glimpses of teeth; and that interrupts the sacredness of the smile and gives it momentarily a mixed worldly and political and satanic cast.

As for the rest of the assembly, they are "religious men, they are earnest, sincere, devoted, and they hate the Jews."

Mark Twain's dispatches reached New York without tampering. The imperial press was subject to a heavy and capricious censorship; so it is possible that the readers of *Harper's* were more intimately informed of the degradation of an allegedly democratic parliament than the citizens of Austria or of its eighteen coequal provinces. The tactics of the Opposition—i.e., of the Germans who refuse to allow the Czechs their own tongue—begin reasonably enough, in parliamentary fashion, with a heroic one-man filibuster lasting twelve hours. At the speaker's first words, however, decorum instantly and repeatedly gives way to yells, the beating of desks with long boards, and the clamor of threats and name-calling astonishingly gutter-bred. (The members of the assembly include princes, counts, barons, priests, lawyers, judges, physicians, professors, merchants, bankers—and also "that distinguished religious expert, Dr. Lueger, Bürgermeister of Vienna.") A number of these shouted declarations vibrate with a dread familiarity, as if a recording of the sounds of the Vienna of 1938 are somehow being hurled back into that earlier time, forty years before: "The Germans of Austria will neither surrender nor die!" "It's a pity that such a man [one willing to grant language rights to the Czechs] should be a leader of the Germans; he disgraces the German name!" "And *these* shameless creatures are the leaders of the German People's Party!" "You Jew, you!" "I would rather take my hat off to a Jew!" "Jew flunky! Here we have been fighting the Jews for ten years and now you are helping them to power again. How much do you get for it?" "You Judas!" "Schmeel Leeb Kohn! Schmeel Leeb Kohn!"

But let us not misrepresent by overselection. Tainting their opponents with "Jew" may be the most scurrilous offense these princes, counts, barons, priests, judges, etc., can settle on, but it is not the most imaginative. There are also the following: "Brothelknight!" "East German offal-tub!" "Infamous louse-brat!" "Cowardly blatherskite!"—along with such lesser epithets as "Polish dog," "miserable cur," and *"Die Grossmutter auf dem Misthaufen erzeugt worden"* (which Mark Twain declines to translate from the original).

In short: a parliamentary riot that is soon to turn into street riots. The fourth and last dispatch records the arrival of the militia:

> And now we see what history will be talking of five centuries hence: a uniformed and helmeted battalion of bronzed and stalwart men marching in double file down the floor of the House—a free parliament profaned by an invasion of brute force! . . . They ascended the steps of the tribune, laid their hands upon the inviolable persons of the representatives of a nation, and dragged and tugged and hauled them down the steps and out at the door.

"The memory of it," Mark Twain concludes—and by now all satire is drained away—"will outlast all the thrones that exist today. In the whole history of free parliaments the like of it had been seen but three times before. It takes its imposing place among the world's unforgettable things."

He is both wrong and right. Wrong, because the December 1897 parliamentary upheaval in Vienna is of course entirely forgotten, except by historian-specialists and readers of Mark Twain's least-known prose. And right, because it is an indelible precursor that not merely portends the profoundly unforgettable Viennese mob-events of 1938, but thrusts them into our teeth with all their bitter twentieth-century flavor. Here is no déjà vu, but its prophesying opposite. Or, to say it otherwise: a twenty-year-old rioter enjoying Mark Twain's Vienna easily becomes a sixty-year-old Nazi enjoying *Anschluss* Vienna.

In the immediate wake of the introduction of the militia, the government

> came down with a crash; there was a popular outbreak or two in Vienna; there were three or four days of furious rioting in Prague, followed by the establishing there of martial law; the Jews [who were by and large German-speaking] and Germans were harried and plundered, and their houses destroyed; in other Bohemian towns there was rioting—in some cases the Germans being the rioters, in others the Czechs—and in all cases the Jew had to roast, no matter which side he was on.

ALL THIS was in progress while Europe continued to boil over Dreyfus. Living on top of the fire, so to speak, Mark Twain could hardly overlook the roasting Jews. Consequently, a few months after his parliamentary reports, he published in *Harper's*, in March of 1898, a kind of sequel to "Stirring Times in Vienna"—a meditation entitled "Concerning the Jews." Part polemic, part reprimand, part self-contradictory panegyric, the essay was honorably motivated but ultimately obtuse and harmful. The London *Jewish Chronicle*, for example, commented at the time: "Of all such advocates, we can but say 'Heaven save us from our friends.' " (In the United States in the 1930's, pro-Nazi groups and other antisemites seized on portions of the essay to suggest an all-American signature for the promulgation of hate.)

Mark Twain was not unaware that Sholem Aleichem, the classic Yiddish writer, was affectionately called "the Jewish Mark
Twain." This was because Sholem Aleichem, like his American
counterpart, was a bittersweet humorist and a transcendent hu-
manist; and also because he reflected his village Jews, sunk in
deepest poverty, as intimately and faithfully as Mark Twain recorded the homespun villages of his American South. Both men
were better known by their pen names than by their actual names;
both stood for liberty of the oppressed; both were eagerly read by
the plain people—the "folk"; and both were nearly unprecedented
as popular literary heroes. Sholem Aleichem certainly read Mark
Twain (possibly in German translation), but it is hardly likely that
Mark Twain read Sholem Aleichem. Even the smallest inkling of
Sholem Aleichem's social content would have stood in the way of
the central canard of "Concerning the Jews." And to contradict
that canard, and to determine the real and typical condition of the
shtetl-bound mass of European Jews, Mark Twain had only to
look over his shoulder at those Jewish populations nearest to hand
in Austro-Hungarian Galicia. Instead he looked to the old hostile
myths.

To be sure, "Concerning the Jews" is remembered (perhaps
mainly by those who have never read it) as charmingly philosemitic. A single witty—and famous—sentence supports that
view: "All that I care to know is that a man is a human being—that
is enough for me; he can't be any worse." And we can believe
Mark Twain—we *do* believe him—when he avers that he makes
"no uncourteous reference" to Jews in his books "because the disposition is lacking." Up to a point the disposition *is* lacking; there
is plenty of evidence for it. A curious science-fiction sketch called
"From the 'London Times' of 1904"—written about the same time
as "Concerning the Jews," and striking for its "invention" of the
"telectrophonoscope," or television—turns out to be a lampoon
of "French Justice" as exemplified in the punishment of the innocent Dreyfus; and if a savage satire can be felt to be delectable, this
one is.

The disposition is lacking in other, less political, directions. Jewish charitableness, Jewish generosity, Jewish responsibility are all acknowledged—for the moment. The facts, Mark Twain declares,

> are all on the credit side of the proposition that the Jew is a good and orderly citizen. Summed up, they certify that he is quiet, peaceable, industrious, unaddicted to high crime and brutal dispositions; that his family life is commendable; that he is not a burden upon public charities; that he is not a beggar; that in benevolence he is above the reach of competition. These are the very quintessentials of good citizenship.

And all this is followed by another accolade: the Jew is honest. The proof of it is that the "basis of successful business is honesty; a business cannot thrive where the parties to it cannot trust each other." Who will not affirm this generality? Now add to the assertion of Jewish honesty this quip about the "Jewish brain," from a letter to an American friend, written from Vienna in 1897: "The difference between the brain of the average Christian and that of the average Jew . . . is about the difference between a tadpole's and an Archbishop's." We may laugh at this, but let liberal laughter be on its guard: the Jew, the essay continues, "has a reputation for various small forms of cheating . . . and for arranging cunning contracts which leave him an exit but lock the other man in, and for smart evasions which find him safe and comfortable just within the strict letter of the law, when court and jury know very well that he has violated the spirit of it." From none of this does Mark Twain dissent. So much for his honest Jewish businessman. And so much for praise of the "Jewish brain," which takes us straightway to "cunning contracts" and "smart evasions" and the old, old supersessionist proposition that Judaism attends to the "letter," and not to the "spirit."

Still, the overriding engine of this essay is situated in a much larger proposition. "In all countries," Mark Twain tells us, "from the dawn of history, the Jew has been persistently and implacably hated, and with frequency persecuted." From the dawn of history? And if so, why? Not because the Jew has been millennially blamed for the Crucifixion; "the reasons for it are older than that event," and reside entirely in the Jew's putative economic prowess; theology doesn't apply; at least the Gospels and Pauline and Augustinian traditions don't apply. Skip the Crucifixion, then; penetrate even more deeply behind the veil, into those still earlier mists of pre-history, and let the fault land on Joseph in Egypt—Joseph the provider, "who took a nation's money all away, to the last penny." *There* is your model for "the Jew"! "I am convinced," Mark Twain insists, "that the persecution of the Jew is not due in any large degree to religious prejudice." And here is his judgment of the root of the matter:

> No, the Jew is a money-getter; and in getting his money he is a very serious obstruction to less capable neighbors who are on the same quest. . . . In estimating worldly values the Jew is not shallow, but deep. With precocious wisdom he found out in the morning of time that some men worship rank, some worship heroes, some worship power, some worship God, and that over these ideals they dispute and cannot unite—but that they all worship money; so he made it the end and aim of his life to get it. He was at it in Egypt thirty-six centuries ago; he was at it in Rome . . .; he has been at it ever since. The cost to him has been heavy; his success has made the whole human race his enemy—but it has paid, for it has brought him envy, and that is the only thing which men will sell both soul and body for.

Reading this, who can help thinking that all of it could go down quite nicely in the Austrian parliament of late 1897, not to mention the Viennese street? There is enough irony here to make even the devil weep. The truth is that Mark Twain was writing of Jews as "money-getters" at a time when the mass emigration of poor Jews by the hundreds of thousands had already begun to cram the steerage compartments of transoceanic ships—Jews in flight from economic hopelessness; and when the meanest penury was the lot of most Jews; and when Jewish letters and Jewish lore and Jewish wit took "poor" to be synonymous with "Jew." And here comes Mark Twain, announcing that the Jew's "commercial importance is extravagantly out of proportion to the smallness of his bulk." He might have taken in the anguished testimony of Sholem Aleichem's Jews; or the deprivations of Galician Jews down the road, so to speak, from Vienna; or the travail of Russian Jews penned into the Pale of Settlement. Or, in his native land, he might have taken in the real status of all those small storekeepers whose names he notes on their shop-signs (Edelstein, Blumenthal, Rosenzweig), while observing that "commercial importance" means railroads, banks, mining, insurance, steel, shipping, real estate, etc., etc.—industries where he would have been hard put to find a single Jew.

As it happens, he took in almost none of it; and, though eschewing theology, let himself be taken in by an ancient theological canard: the legacy, via the Judas legend, of the Jew's affinity for money—the myth of the Rich Jew, the Jew Usurer. The very use of the generic phrase "the Jew" suggests stigma. Mythology, it develops, is the heart and muscle of Mark Twain's reputedly "philosemitic" essay—the old myths trotted out for an airing in the American idiom. He said he lacked the disposition for slander. It would be wrong to dismiss this statement; but perhaps it would be fairer to suppose that he lacked the disposition for disciplined caution. He knew nothing of Jewish literary or jurisprudential civilization, or of the oceanic intellectual traditions of Jewish biblical commentary; he approached the Joseph tale with the crudity of a belligerent village atheist, and employed it to defame on economic grounds exactly as the charge of deicide defamed on theological grounds.

Yet he was surely capable of renouncing a canard when someone helped him to prise out the truth. The Jew, he had written, "is charged with an unpatriotic disinclination to stand by the flag as a soldier." "You feed on a country," he accused, "but you don't like to fight for it." Nevertheless there is appended, at the end of this essay, a remarkable Postscript: "The Jew as Soldier," wherein instance after historical instance of Jewish "fidelity" and "gallant soldiership" is cited—in the American Revolution, the War of 1812, the Mexican War, and especially the Civil War. It is not the admission of canard that is remarkable, but rather the principle drawn from it: "It is not allowable to endorse wandering maxims upon supposition." That, overall, and despite its contrary motivation, is a precise characterization of "Concerning the Jews"—the endorsement of wandering maxims upon supposition. Only compare

George Eliot's "The Modern Hep Hep"—a chapter in her *Impressions of Theophrastus Such*, published just twenty years before Mark Twain's wandering maxims—to see what a generalized essay concerning the Jews, engaging Mark Twain's own questions, might attain to.

MARK TWAIN'S twenty months of residence in Vienna were among his most prolific. The fifteen short works collected in the 1900 edition of *The Man That Corrupted Hadleyburg and Other Stories and Essays* are a fraction of his output during this period; but they reflect the entire arsenal of his art: the occasionally reckless polemic, the derisive irony, the intelligent laughter, the verbal stilettoes, the blunt country humor, the fervent despair, the hidden jeer, the relishing of palaver and tall tale, the impatient worldliness, the brilliant forays of language—sometimes for purposes of search-and-destroy, sometimes for a show of pure amazement, sometimes for plain delight in the glory of human oddness; most often for story-telling's fragile might. Nothing is too trivial, nothing too weighty. And frequently the trivial and the weighty are enmeshed, as in Hadleyburg, when the recitation of a handful of words touches on depths of deceit. Or as in a lightly turned sketch—"My Boyhood Dreams"—that teases such eminences as William Dean Howells and John Hay (U.S. Secretary of State in 1898) with their failure to fulfill their respective childhood ambitions—steamboat mate and auctioneer; never mind that these "ambitions" are wholly of Mark Twain's antic invention. But even so playful an oddment as this begins with a bitter reference to the humiliated Dreyfus.

In fact, aboard Mark Twain's prose you cannot very long rely on the "lightly turned"—whatever sets out with an elfin twitch of the nostrils or a Mona Lisa half-smile is likely to end in prophetic thunder. "My First Lie, and How I Got Out of It" starts off with a diaper pin and a twinkle, but its real theme is indifference to injustice—"the silent assertion that there wasn't anything going on in which humane and intelligent people were interested." From slaveholding to Dreyfus is but a paragraph's leap: "From the beginning of the Dreyfus case to the end of it all France . . . lay under the smother of the silent-assertion lie that no wrong was being done to a persecuted and unoffending man." And from Dreyfus how far is it to the "silent National Lie," "whole races and peoples conspir[ing] to propagate gigantic mute lies in the interest of tyrannies and sham"? Beware Mark Twain when his subject looks most severely simple or mild-manneredly innocent: you may speedily find yourself aflame in a fiery furnace of moral indignation.

Sketches, fables, diatribes. Eight months before his death in 1910 he wrote, "I am full of malice, saturated with malignity." More than two decades earlier he had exclaimed to Howells that his was "a pen warmed up in hell." Yet—with relative benignity—the remainder of this volume treats of artists who are ignored while alive and valued only posthumously ("Is He Living or Is He Dead?"); of a train companion determined to set right every minor annoyance ("Travelling with a Reformer"); and of a celebrated inventor ordered by the Austrian government to teach grade school ("The Austrian Edison Keeping School Again"). But that is scarcely the finish of it—there are other exuberances. "The Private History of the 'Jumping Frog' Story" not only supplies an ancient Greek version of the joke, but bursts into a spoof of word-for-word translation from the French. "How to Tell a Story" will remind readers of nighttime ghost-scares at summer camp, while "The Esquimau Maiden's Romance"—an unrestrained comic lecture on the relative nature of wealth—would hardly pass muster in a contemporary multiculturalist classroom. "About Play-Acting" compares a serious drama in Vienna with the frivolous offerings cut from the New York theater advertisements of Saturday, May 7, 1898; Broadway at this hour (despite spectacular technical advances) is not a whit more substantive or sophisticated. "At the Appetite Cure," with its praise of starvation as the key to health, reflects Mark Twain's own belief in the curative virtues of abstinence from food—a crank piece; but here the jokes are crude and cruel, with a Teutonic edge of near-sadism. All the same, the most stirring—the most startling—real-life narrative in this volume, "My Debut as a Literary Person," concerns starvation: in extremis, at sea, in a small boat, after a shipwreck. Mark Twain defines it in a minor way as a journalistic scoop, but for power, passion, character, and suspense, it belongs among his masterworks.

All these romances—some as slight as skits, and one as rich and urgent as a novel—were set down in Mark Twain's Vienna: a cosmopolis driven by early modernism, saturated in music and theater, populated by gargantuan cultural figures whose influence still shakes the world (Sigmund Freud and Theodor Herzl, to mention only these), ruled by rogues (two of Hitler's idols among them), on occasion ruled by mobs; a society gaudily brilliant, acutely civilized, triumphantly flourishing, and also shameless, brutal. Part heaven, part the devil's precinct. An odd backdrop for a writer reared in Hannibal, Missouri. But in Vienna Mark Twain was close to the peak of what he called his "malignity," and Vienna served him.

Along with Dreyfus in Paris, it gave him a pen warmed up in the local hell.

SAUL
BELLOW'S
BROADWAY

On Broadway it was still bright afternoon and the gassy air was motionless under the leaden spokes of sunlight, and sawdust footprints lay about the doorways of butcher shops and fruit stores. And the great, great crowd, the inexhaustible current of millions of every race and kind pouring out, pressing round, of every age, of every genius, possessors of every human secret, antique and future, in every face the refinement of one particular motive or essence—*I labor, I spend, I strive, I design, I love, I cling, I uphold, I give way, I envy, I long, I scorn, I die, I hide, I want.* Faster, much faster than any man could make the tally. The sidewalks were wider than any causeway; the street itself was immense, and it quaked and gleamed . . .

THIS IS Saul Bellow's "Broadway uptown" in the middle of the twentieth century. "The carnival of the street," he called it, "the dust going round like a woman on stilts." Four and a half decades on, the Upper West Side (roughly from the Seventies all the way up to Columbia University on 116th Street) still clings to Broadway's pouring, pressing, teeming wadi, and the dizzying dust, though descended from its stilts, still goes round and round, crawling into your nostrils and stippling its egalitarian stucco over every race and kind. The fruit stores are still there, run by Koreans. The inexhaustible current of voices is still there, though you are less likely to hear remnants of Yiddish and more likely to hear torrents of Spanish, in dialects up from the Caribbean, from Colombia, Peru, the Dominican Republic, even Mexico. The elderly ladies are still there in the coffee shops, "rouged and mascaraed and hennaed and [they] used blue hair rinse and eye shadow and wore costume jewelry, and many of them were proud and stared at you with expressions that did not belong to their age," and though they still take you in with their youth-ravenous painted stares, the blue hair is as out-of-date as the butcher shop sawdust, and their old New York faces compete now with the Inca faces from the side-street tenements and the lost faces of the homeless on their shreds of blankets. The butcher shops, meanwhile, have mostly been swallowed up by the supermarket chains. And the "cafeteria with the gilded front" is gone.

All the same, Bellow's Broadway uptown—*Seize the Day* was first published in 1956—is nearly intact: the hurrying anonymous lives, the choked and throbbing urban air, the heavy sunlight that makes you "feel like a drunkard." Re-entering the theater of this short novel after more than forty years, you will find the scenery hardly altered.

What *has* altered is the cultural scenery, so to speak, outside the novel.

In 1953, Bellow's *The Adventures of Augie March* struck out on a course so independent from the tide of American fiction that no literary lessons could flow from it: it left no wake, and cut a channel so entirely idiosyncratic as to be uncopyable. Much earlier, Ernest Hemingway had engineered another radical divergence in the prose of the novel: having inherited the stylistic burden of the nineteenth century, with its elaborate "painting" of interiors and landscapes, its obligatory omniscience, and its essaylike moralizing, he mopped up the excess moisture ("clotting the curds," he called it) and lopped subordinate clauses and chopped dialogue and left little of the old forest of letters standing. An army of succinctness-seekers followed in a movement that accommodated two or three generations of imitators, until finally the distinctive Hemingway dryness flaked off into lifeless desiccation. The Hemingway sentence became a kind of ancestral portrait on the wall, and died of too many descendants. *Augie March*, by contrast (though it had its own ancestors, not so much in style as in character), was in itself too fecund to produce epigones or copyists or offspring—as if every source and resource of procreation were already contained in, or used up by, its own internal energies.

Though a generation apart, both prose revolutions, one much-imitated, the other mimic-proof, were surrounded by an alert and welcoming system. The system was, simply, the idea of the novel as urgent and necessary, as a ubiquitous expectation of life, and it is only in retrospect that we are led to call it a system; once it was as manifest as the kitchen table, on which a novel often lay. Yet it was a system even then, though as little noted as the circulation of the blood: it was the air, it was being itself—an organization of those elements intended, as Bellow said in his 1976 Nobel speech, "to represent mankind adequately." Under that system the novel was looked to; it was awaited. Hemingway's *The Old Man and the Sea* (itself charged with being imitation Hemingway) took up a whole issue of *Life* magazine, which was to the early Fifties what television later became.

In a 1991 interview, Bellow described those old habits and sensations as the outer system penetrating the inner: "Literature in my early days was still something you lived by; you absorbed it, you took it into your system. Not as a connoisseur, aesthete, lover of literature. No, it was something on which you formed your life, which you ingested so that it became part of your substance, your path to liberation and full freedom." He went on, "I think the mood of enthusiasm and love for literature, widespread in the twenties, began to evaporate in the thirties."

One could take issue with the designated decade; probably every fevered reader will choose the hour of her own youth as that Golden Age when literature was woven into the sinews of the world. What we can be certain of is that the old system (and "The Old System" is the title of one of Bellow's crankiest short stories) is gone—gone *as* a system, meaning as a collective perception, or as the lining, as it were, of a corpus of time. Individuals, of course, go on being born into the life-shock of print, into the recognition (as Bellow set it out in his introduction to Allan Bloom's *The Closing of the American Mind*) that poets and novelists "give new eyes to human beings, inducing them to view the world differently, converting them from fixed modes of experience."

But in the absence of the old system this wizardlike conversion no longer tosses rapturous signals from reader to reader—so that hearing the phrase "the haying scene," said just like that, will instantly sweep one into the fields with Levin, joyful among the reapers. For that to happen, *Anna Karenina* must be common property. There is plenty of common property nowadays—so many globally-fixed modes of experience, pictures clicked into place by that household appliance all families, the richest and the poorest, live with and through. But the images of television, and of film, are immutable and uniform; everything arrives ready-made, already "processed," already envisioned, and, in effect, already *seen*. If literature can give new eyes to human beings, it is because the thing held in common is separately imagined. Utter "I would prefer not," and out of these few words Bartleby materializes, your Bartleby and my Bartleby, a mutual Bartleby: yet the seeing differs from mind to mind. And at the same time a tunnel has been dug from mind to mind, and an unsuspected new current runs between them.

"In the greatest confusion," Bellow comments, "there is still an open channel to the soul. It may be difficult to find because by midlife it is overgrown, and some of the wildest thickets that surround it grow out of what we describe as our education. But the channel is always there, and it is our business to keep it open, to have access to the deepest part of ourselves—to that part of us which is conscious of a higher consciousness, by means of which we make final judgments and put everything together." (Be assured that the channel Bellow speaks of is not NBC's Channel

Four.) And it is literature that assists in driving a chink into that higher consciousness.

Inklings of the deepest part of ourselves; flashes of the indelible, or call it lightnings from an inner storm—Levin mowing with the peasants, Bartleby's "I would prefer not" in Melville's industrious Wall Street.

And truly Levin had never drunk any liquor so good as this warm water with green bits floating in it, and a taste of rust from the tin dipper. And immediately after this came the delicious slow saunter, with his hand on the scythe, during which he could wipe away the streaming sweat, take deep breaths of air, and look about at the long string of mowers . . .

The longer Levin mowed, the oftener he felt the moments of unconsciousness in which it seemed not his hands that swung the scythe, but the scythe moving of itself, a body full of life and consciousness of its own, and as though by magic, without thinking of it, the work turned out regular and well-finished of itself. These were the most blissful moments.

"I would prefer not to," said he.

I looked at him steadfastly. His face was leanly composed; his grey eye dimly calm. Not a wrinkle of agitation rippled him. Had there been the least uneasiness, anger, impatience or impertinence in his manner; in other words, had there been anything ordinarily human about him; doubtless I should have violently dismissed him from the premises. But as it was, I should have as soon thought of turning my pale plaster-of-paris bust of Cicero out of doors . . .

"I would prefer not to," he replied in a flute-like tone. It seemed to me that while I had been addressing him, he carefully revolved every statement that I made; fully comprehended the meaning; could not gainsay the irresistible conclusion; but, at the same time, some paramount consideration prevailed with him to reply as he did.

To these some will want to add certain culminating lines from *The Death of Ivan Ilyich*:

It occurred to him that what had appeared perfectly impossible to him before, namely that he had not spent his life as he should have done, might after all be true. It occurred to him that his scarcely perceptible attempts to struggle against what was considered good by the most highly placed people, those scarcely noticeable impulses which he had immediately suppressed, might have been the real thing, and all the rest false. And his professional duties and the whole arrangement of his life and of his family, and all his social and official interests, might all have been false. He tried to defend all those things to himself and suddenly felt the weakness of what he was defending. There was nothing to defend.

Tommy Wilhelm of *Seize the Day* is present in this company of the higher consciousness, and his convulsion of grief at a stranger's funeral—a great and turbulent wave of introspective terror—belongs with literature's most masterly scenes of transfiguring self-disclosure:

> Standing a little apart, Wilhelm began to cry. He cried at first softly and from sentiment, but soon from deeper feeling. He sobbed loudly and his face grew distorted and hot, and the tears stung his skin . . .
> Soon he was past words, past reason, coherence. He could not stop. The source of all tears had suddenly sprung open within him, black, deep, and hot, and they were pouring out and convulsed his body, crippling the very hands with which he held the handkerchief. His efforts to collect himself were useless. The great knot of ill and grief in his throat swelled upward and he gave in utterly and held his face and wept. He cried with all his heart . . .
> "The man's brother, maybe?"
> "Oh, I doubt that very much," said another bystander. "They're not alike at all. Night and day."

WHEN *Seize the Day* first appeared, the old system was fully at work. Ah! How to describe it? Hunger, public hunger; and then excitement, argument, and, among writers, the wildly admiring disturbances of envy. A new book by Bellow! You lived by it, you absorbed it, you took it into your system. *Augie March* had been published three years earlier, in 1953; Bellow was thirty-eight. It was his third novel, following *Dangling Man* (1944) and *The Victim*

(1947). These were received, as Diana Trilling put it in the *Nation* in 1948, as "solidly built of fine, important ideas"; Bellow was recognized as a philosophical novelist. But *Augie March* was an eruption, a tumult, a marvel; a critical deluge pursued it. Original even in the scope of its ambition in a mostly narrow decade, it was a work that turned over American fiction, breaking through all restraints of language (mixing the lavish with the raffish) and of range: the barriers of inhibition kicked down, the freed writer claiming authority over human and planetary organisms.

There was, besides, another element in Bellow's prose—in the coloration of his mind—that could not be immediately detected, because it contradicted a taken-for-granted sentiment about human character: that the physical body is simply a shell for the nature hidden within, that what I look like is not what I truly am, that my disposition is masked by the configuration of my features. The American infatuation with youth tends to support this supposition: a very young face *is* a sort of mask, and will generally tell you nothing much, and may, in fact, mislead you. Bellow in a way has invented a refreshed phrenology, or theory of the humors; in any case, by the time *Seize the Day* arrived, it was clear he was on to something few moderns would wish to believe in: the human head as characterological map. But such a premise is not a retreat or a regression to an archaic psychology. It is an insight that asks us to trust the condition of art, wherein the higher consciousness can infiltrate portraiture. Disclosure is all. Human flesh has no secrets: Levin's hand on the scythe is the teacher of Levin's soul, Ivan Ilyich in his body's decay reads the decay of his soul, Bartleby's frozen serenity incarnates a consummate innerness. Bellow, like every artist, is no dualist—his bodies are not bodies, they are souls. And the soul, too, is disparaged by moderns as an obscurantist archaism.

But Bellow's art escapes the judgment of the merely enlightened. The nursery-rhyme proverb may be more to his liking: my face is my fortune. If manners are small morals, as Hobbes said, then bodies and faces may be morals writ large; or what is meant by soul. Here is Dr. Tamkin, a central character of *Seize the Day*— who may not be a doctor at all:

What a creature Tamkin was when he took off his hat! The indirect light showed the many complexities of his bald skull, his gull's nose, his rather handsome eyebrows, his vain mustache, his deceiver's brown eyes. His figure was stocky, rigid, short in the neck, so that the large ball of the occiput touched his collar. His bones were peculiarly formed, as though twisted twice where the ordinary human bone was turned only once, and his shoulders rose in two pagodalike points. At mid-body he was thick. He stood pigeon-toed, a sign perhaps that he was devious or had much to hide. The skin of his hands was aging, and his nails were moonless, concave, clawlike, and they appeared loose. His eyes were as brown as beaver fur and full of strange lines. The two large brown naked balls looked thoughtful—but were they? And honest—but was Dr. Tamkin honest?

And here is a minor character, the manager of a brokerage office, no more than a walk-on:

Silvery, cool, level, long-profiled, experienced, indifferent, observant, with unshaven refinement, he scarcely looked at Wilhelm. . . . The manager's face, low-colored, long-nostriled, acted as a unit of perception; his eyes merely did their reduced share. Here was a man . . . who knew and knew and knew.

And about whom there is nothing further to know. What more would the man's biography provide, how would it illuminate? Bellow's attraction to the idea of soul may or may not be derived from an old interest in Rudolf Steiner; but no one will doubt that these surpassingly shrewd, arrestingly juxtaposed particulars of physiognomy are inspired grains of what can only be called human essence.

Dr. Tamkin, curiously, is both essence and absence: which is to say he is a con man, crucially available to begin with, and then painfully evaporated. Wilhelm, strangled by his estranged wife's inflated expenses, father of two boys, runaway husband who has lost his job—salesman for a corporation that promised him advancement and then fired him in an act of nepotism—is drawn to Tamkin as to a savior. Tamkin takes Wilhelm's last seven hundred dollars, introduces him (bewilderingly) to the commodities market, pledges a killing in lard, and meanwhile spills out advice on how to live: Tamkin is a philosopher and amateur poet. Wilhelm's vain and indifferent father, Dr. Adler, an elderly widower, also supplies advice, but brutally, coldly.

Much of this futile counsel takes place in the Gloriana, a residence hotel within view of the Ansonia, an ornate Stanford White-era edifice which "looks like a baroque palace from Prague or Munich enlarged a hundred times, with towers, domes," a leftover from the socially ambitious Broadway of a former age. Despite its name, the Gloriana's glory days are well behind it; its denizens are chiefly retired old Jews like Wilhelm's fastidious father and the ailing Mr. Perls, who drags "a large built-up shoe." Wilhelm at forty-four may be the youngest tenant, and surely the healthiest—"big and fair-haired," "mountainous," with "a big round face, a wide, flourishing red mouth, stump teeth." But he is also the humblest: failed husband, failed actor still carrying a phony Hollywood name, broke, appealing to his father for the rent money, pleading with his wife not to squeeze him so hard.

Though maimed and humiliated, Wilhelm is no cynic; he is a not-so-naive believer in search of a rescuer. And because he is hopeful and almost gullible, and definitely reckless, a burnt-out sad sack, he is aware of himself as a hapless comic figure. "Fair-haired hippopotamus!" he addresses his lumbering reflection in the lobby glass. And later, heartlessly: "Ass! Idiot! Wild boar! Dumb mule! Slave!"

Wilhelm may seem even to himself to be a fool, but there are no outright fools in Bellow's varied worlds: all his clowns are idiosyncratic seers. Wilhelm sees that his father is mesmerized by old age as death's vestibule, incapable of compassion beyond these margins: a confined soul, disappointed in his son, Dr. Adler, though affluent enough, refuses him help. "He doesn't forget death for one single second, and that's what makes him like this," Wilhelm thinks. "And not only is death on his mind but through money he forces me to think about it, too. It gives him power over me." Wilhelm may be a hollow flounderer in all other respects—work, wife, sons, father, lover, past, future, all lost—but he can *see.* And he sees a glimmering in Tamkin, a market gambler with

Wilhelm's money, a fly-by-night speculator, a trickster, a kind of phantom appearing and disappearing at will, an opportunist and exploiter, plainly shady if not an out-and-out crook—he sees that Tamkin is somehow and despite everything a man in whom to put his trust. Pragmatically, this will turn out to be a whopper of a mistake; yet Wilhelm, in a passion of nihilist self-seeing, embracing his blunders, defines himself through misjudgment and miscalculation:

> . . . since there were depths in Wilhelm not unsuspected by himself, he received a suggestion from some remote element in his thoughts that the business of life, the real business—to carry his peculiar burden, to feel shame and impotence, to taste these quelled tears—the only important business, the highest business was being done. Maybe the making of mistakes expressed the very purpose of his life and the essence of his being here. Maybe he was supposed to make them and suffer from them here on this earth. And though he had raised himself above Mr. Perls and his father because they adored money, still they were called to act energetically and this was better than to yell and cry, pray and beg, poke and blunder and go by fits and starts and fall upon the thorns of life. And finally sink beneath that watery floor—would that be tough luck, or would it be good riddance?

And still there is hope's dim pulse:

> "Oh, God," Wilhelm prayed, "Let me out of my trouble. Let me out of my thoughts, and let me do something better with myself. For all the time I have wasted I am very sorry. Let me out of this clutch and into a different life. For I am all balled up. Have mercy."

Mercy is what Tamkin brings, even if only briefly, fitfully, almost unrecognizably; he sports "a narrow smile, friendly, calming, shrewd, and wizardlike, patronizing, secret, potent." He spins out sensational stories, difficult to credit, speaks of "love," "spiritual compensation," "the here-and-now," brags of reading Aristotle in Greek ("A friend of mine taught me when I was in Cairo"); he declares himself to be "a psychological poet." His topic is the nature of souls:

"In here, the human bosom—mine, yours, everybody's—there isn't just one soul. There's a lot of souls. But there are two main ones, the real soul and a pretender soul. Now! Every man realizes that he has to love something or somebody. He feels that he must go outward. 'If thou canst not love, what art thou?' Are you with me?"

"Yes, Doc, I think so," said Wilhelm, listening—a little skeptically, but nonetheless hard.

". . . The interest of the pretender soul is the same as the interest of the social life, the society mechanism. This is the main tragedy of human life. Oh, it is terrible! Terrible! You are not free. Your own betrayer is inside of you and sells you out. You have to obey him like a slave. He makes you work like a horse. And for what? For who?"

"Yes, for what?" The doctor's words caught Wilhelm's heart. "I couldn't agree more," he said. "When do we get free?"

Tamkin carries on, catching and catching Wilhelm's heart: "The true soul is the one that pays the price. It suffers and gets sick, and it realizes that the pretender can't be loved. Because the pretender is a lie. The true soul loves the truth." Garble and gobbledygook, but with a magnetism that can seduce: love, truth, tragedy, the importance of one's own depths. "As a matter of fact," Tamkin winds up, "you're a profound personality, with very profound creative capacities but also disturbances." Wilhelm falls for all this and at the same time doubts. Tamkin soothes, procrastinates, plunges into tangential narratives, distracts, eats, philosophizes, and finally hands Wilhelm four stanzas of semiliterate self-help verse studded with greatness, joy, beauty, ecstasy, glory, power, serenity, eternity. "What kind of mishmash, claptrap is this!" Wilhelm shouts in his thoughts. Yet Tamkin continues to lure him; at the brokerage office, where the doctor, an operator, hurries from stocks to commodities and back again, Wilhelm's breast swarms with speculations about the speculator: "Was he giving advice, gathering information, or giving it, or practicing—whatever mysterious profession he practiced? Hypnotism? Perhaps he could put people in a trance while he talked to them."

In the large and clumsy Wilhelm there is a large and clumsy

shard of good will, a privately spoken, half-broken unwillingness
to be driven solely by suspicion: Tamkin is right to count two dis-
parate souls—only, for Wilhelm, which is the pretender, which the
true? Is hopeful trust the true soul, and suspicious doubt the pretender? Or the other way around? For a time it hardly matters:
Tamkin is a doctor to Wilhelm's sorrow, a teacher of limitlessness,
a snake-oil charlatan whose questionable bottles turn out to contain an ancient and legitimate cure for mortality's anxieties: seize
the day. And he is the elfish light that dances over the blackened
field, the ignis fatuus of wish and illusion, the healer of self-
castigation. The effectively fatherless Wilhelm finds in Tamkin a
fairy godfather—but, as might be expected in the land of wishes,
one whose chariot melts to pumpkin at the end of the day. Yet
again and again, swept away by one fantastic proposition or another, Wilhelm, moved, is led to respond, "This time the faker
knows what he's talking about." Or: "How does he know these
things? How can he be such a jerk, and even perhaps an operator,
a swindler, and understand so well what gives?"

Wilhelm is absurd; sometimes he is childish, and even then,
longing for pity and condemning himself for it, he muses: "It is my
childish mind that thinks people are ready to give it just because
you need it." In spite of a depth of self-recognition, he will burst
out in infantile yells and preposterous gestures. Complaining to
his father how his wife's conduct and her attitudes suffocate him,
he grabs his own throat and begins to choke himself. A metaphor
turns into a boy's antics. And after an argument with his wife on
a public telephone—during which she accuses him of thinking
"like a youngster"—he attempts to rip the telephone box off its
wall. There is something of the Marx Brothers in these shenani-
gans, and also of low domestic farce. "I won't stand to be howled
at," cries his wife, hanging up on him. But a man's howl, of anguish or rage, belongs to the Furies, and is not a joke.

Nor is the timing of these incidents. It is the day before Yom
Kippur, the Day of Atonement, comprising the most solemn
hours of the Jewish liturgical calendar. Old Mr. Rappoport, half-
blind, whom Wilhelm encounters at the broker's, reminds him of
his synagogue obligations. Wilhelm replies that he never goes; but

he reflects on his mother's death, and remembers the ruined bench next to her grave. Dr. Adler, preoccupied with dying as his near destination, has no interest in religion. Wilhelm, though, is fixed on his own destiny, with or without God; and Tamkin is a fixer—a repairer—of destiny and of despair. Yet who is more farcical than Tamkin? Bellow once noted—commenting on the tone of traditional Jewish story-telling—how "laughter and trembling are so curiously intermingled that it is not easy to determine the relations of the two. At times the laughter seems simply to restore the equilibrium of sanity; at times the figures of the story, or parable, appear to invite or encourage trembling with the secret aim of overcoming it by means of laughter."

Seize the Day is such a parable; or, on second thought, perhaps not. The interplay of the comic and the melancholic is certainly there—but a parable, after all, is that manner of fable which means to point a moral, or, at the least, to invoke an instructive purpose. The "secret aim," as Bellow has it, is generally more significant than the telling or the dramatis personae. Bellow's fiction hardly counts as "moral" or instructive (though there are plenty of zealous instructors wandering through). His stories look for something else altogether: call it wisdom, call it ontology, or choose it from what Tamkin in free and streaming flight lets loose: "Creative is nature. Rapid. Lavish. Inspirational. It shapes leaves. It rolls the waters of the earth. Man is the chief of this." A tornado of made-up maxims and twisted tales, Tamkin is among the great comic characters (comedy being a corridor to wisdom, though not the only one): that he flaunts his multiple astonishments in the modest compass of a short novel is a Bellovian marvel. And he is, besides, Bellow's sentry in reverse, standing watch over an idea of fiction that refuses borders.

Bellow is sometimes said to be the most "European" of American writers—perhaps because of his familiarity with the century's intellectual currents, his regard for history, the dense and forceful knit of his prose, the sense that nothing has been left out: that what is there is *complete*. That may be why one is compelled to think of the grand Russians when contemplating Bellow (hence Levin, hence Ivan Ilyich); even when his characters attend to the trivial, metaphysics enters—as when old Mr. Perls observes that in New York if "you wanted to talk about a glass of water, you had to start back with God creating the heavens and the earth." Wilhelm himself, in the subway tunnel under Times Square, invents a "larger body"—all the unsavory and strange-looking underground people united with him in "a blaze of love."

The larger body, so to speak, of *Seize the Day* is the union of Wilhelm with Bartleby: one can imagine that if Melville had allowed Bartleby a voice beyond those ineluctable, forlorn, perplexingly spare syllables, Wilhelm's own torrent of yearning, his thwarted expression of the higher consciousness, are what would have emerged. The linking of Bellow with Europeanness, on the other hand, equates depth and scope with those castled and worn and battered lands, overlooking Melville of New York—Melville who is not nearly an ancestor or relative of Bellow's, but not a stranger either. Bellow's famous sentence is irrefragably American, a wise-guy (or wisdom-guy) contrivance soaked in learning and pathos and irony and inquisitiveness and knowhow—and exactly balanced, in *Seize the Day*, between the con artist's lingo and God's machinery of existence.

In the last one hundred and forty years Bartleby's Wall Street has altered past recognition. After the flash-by of only forty years Wilhelm's Broadway is scarcely different. You are not likely to catch sight of Bartleby sidling by the Exchange in the deserted dusk of the business district, but up there on roiling Broadway, not far from the Gloriana and the Ansonia, you might possibly hear Tamkin still working his clientele, promising a killing in rye. So they live on, these two New York stories—as queerly close, in the long view, as the Twin Towers; two heartstruck urban tales made to outlast much else.

RUSHDIE
IN THE
LOUVRE

A WHILE AGO—it was in Paris, in the Louvre—I saw
Salman Rushdie plain. He was sitting in a high-backed chair at the
foot of an incalculably long banquet table fitted out with two rows
of skinny microphones, each poking upward like a knuckly finger.
His hands lay docile, contained, disciplined, on a dark-red leather
portfolio stamped with his name in gilt. A gargantuan crystal
chandelier, intricately designed, with multiple glinting pendants,
hung from a ceiling painted all over with rosy royal nymphs—a
ceiling so remote that the climate up there seemed veiled in haze.
Who could measure that princely chamber, whether in meters or
in history? And all around, gold, gold gold.

The day before, in a flood of other visitors, I had penetrated
an even more resplendent hall of the Louvre, the Galerie
d'Apollon—a long, spooky corridor encrusted with kingly treasures: ewers and reliquaries of jasper and crystal, porphyry vases,
scepters of coronations anciently repudiated, and, forlorn in their
powerlessness, the Crown Jewels. All these hide in the gloom of
their glass cases, repelling whatever gray granules of light drizzle

down from above, throwing a perpetual dusk over the march of regal portraits that once commanded awe, and now, in the half-dark, give out a bitter look of faint inner rot. Here, among its glorious leavings, one can feel the death of absolutism. "I can stand a great deal of gold," Henry James once said; and so could the kings of France, and the Napoleons who succeeded them, all devoted to the caressings and lustings of gold—Midaslike objects of gold, soup bowls and spoons, fretwork and garnishings and pilasters of gold, gold as a kind of contagion or irresistible eruption.

James was enchanted; for him that rash of gold hinted at no disease, whether of self-assertion or force of terror. He equated the artist's sovereign power with what he had "inhaled little by little" in the Gallery of Apollo—"an endless golden riot and relief, figured and flourished in perpetual revolution, breaking into great high-hung circles and symmetries of squandered picture, opening into deep outward embrasures," a glory that signified for him "not only beauty and art and supreme design but history and fame and power." On his deathbed, confused by a stroke, he imagined himself to be Napoleon in the midst of a project of renovating the Louvre: "I call your attention," he dictated to his secretary, "to the precious enclosed transcripts of plans and designs for the decoration of certain apartments of the palaces here, of the Louvre and the Tuileries, which you will find addressed in detail to artists and workmen who are to take them in hand."

James's Napoleonic hallucination of 1916 has been realized seven decades later. Artists and workmen *have* taken the Louvre and the Tuileries in hand. There are cranes and sandy excavations—a broad tract of these at the end of the gardens of the Tuileries abutting the Louvre—and then, suddenly, there is the great living anti-Ozymandian I. M. Pei Pyramid, swarming with visitors, a peaked postmodernist outcropping of glass and steel in the wide square courtyard of this brilliant old palace: a purposeful visual outrage conceived in amazing wit and admirable utility, flanked by a triplet of smaller pyramids like three echoing laughters. The apartments of the Louvre's Richelieu wing, where Rushdie sat—balding, bearded, in sober coat and tie—was undergoing reconstruction: visitors' shoes left plaster-powder footprints on the red-carpeted grand stair. But visitors were few, anyhow, during the renovation, when the Richelieu was closed to the public. On the day Rushdie came, the entire Louvre was closed, and the Richelieu wing was effectively sealed off by a formidable phalanx of security men in black outfits, with black guns at their hips. Rushdie's arrival was muted, unnoticed; out of the blue he was there, unobtrusive yet somehow enthroned—ennobled—by the ongoing crisis of terror that is his visible nimbus.

He was attending a seminar of the Académie Universelle des Cultures, the brainchild of then President François Mitterrand. The Academy's president, appointed by Mitterrand, is Elie Wiesel, recipient of the Nobel Peace Prize, and there are nine other Nobel-winning members, among them Wole Soyinka of Nigeria (in Literature), and the Americans Joshua Lederberg (in Medicine and Physiology) and Toni Morrison (the 1993 laureate in Literature). The official meeting place of this newborn organization—it is still in the process of formulating its by-laws and refining its overall aims—is in the Richelieu apartments. Unlike the twilight majesties of the Gallery of Apollo, the Academy's space is brightly warmed in sun from immense windows. Peering out, one sees a bit of courtyard, but mainly the long line of an encircling balcony, ranged with mammoth stone figures in plumed Monte Cristo headgear and buckled eighteenth-century pumps, the very soles of which seem mountainously tall. It is as if hallucinations can inhabit even daylight. A low door—low in relation to the ceiling—opens into what might pass for a giantess's pantry, a series of closets white with plaster dust and smelling of an unfinished moistness, and then a sort of gangway leading to just-installed toilets. On the day Rushdie came, it was up to an armed guard to decide whether or not to let one through to the plumbing.

The other end of this vast sanctum is the threshold to salon after palatial salon, magnificence serving as vestibule to still more magnificence, everything freshly gilded everywhere: the Napoleonic dream re-imagined for the close of a century that has given new and sinister vitality to the meaning of absolutism. The gas chambers and the ovens; the gulag; and finally the terror that invents car bombs, airplane hijackings, ideological stabbings of civilians at bus stops, the murder of ambassadors and Olympic athletes and babies in their cribs, the blowing up of an embassy in Buenos Aires, the World Trade Center in New York, the financial district of London, a restaurant in Paris, a synagogue in Istanbul. Under the shadow of this decades-long record, the setting of a price on a novelist's head is hardly a culmination, though it is surely, in an era of imaginative atrocity, a new wrinkle, a kind of hallucination in itself. Hallucination, after all, is make-believe taken literally; dream assessed as fact.

Long before he dreamt himself the imperial Napoleon ordering the rehabilitation of the Louvre, Henry James had a dream of limitless terror. The dream was of the Gallery of Apollo—but now those inhalations of absolutism were wholly altered: what had been seen as the potency of fame and the absolute rule of beauty and art turned away its sublime face to reveal absolutism's underside, a thing uncompromisingly deadly, brutal, irrational. Artist and dreamer, James in his nightmare is being pursued down the length of the Galerie d'Apollon by an "appalling" shape intent on murdering him. (Note the dreamer's pun: Apollo, appalling. Supremacy transmogrified into horror.) A door is shut against the powerful assassin; the assassin—"the awful agent, creature, or presence, whatever he was"—presses back. And then, all at once, in a burst of opposing power, the dreamer defends himself: "Routed, dismayed, the tables turned upon him by my so surpassing him for straight aggression and dire intention, my visitant was already but a diminished spot in the long perspective, the tremendous, glorious hall, . . . over the far-gleaming floor of which, cleared for the occasion of its great line of priceless *vitrines* down the middle, he sped for *his* life, while a great storm of thunder and lightning played through the deep embrasures of high windows on the right."

Not far from the Gallery of Apollo, the Richelieu apartments of the Louvre do not quake with the storm of nightmare, but the members of the Academy (men and women from the four corners of our slightly ovoid planet), discreet, courtly, inhale the appalling breath of the pursuer. The image of routing is dim: what weapon is there against a hidden assassin who may strike a moment from now, or tomorrow, or the day after? The arsenal of intellect—what we mean by the principles or intuitions of culture—is helpless before such willed, wild atrocity: anybody here might overnight become Rushdie. The Academy's President, a survivor of Auschwitz, has already *been* Rushdie: a human being pitilessly hunted as prey. No one cranes down the endless table, with its line of microphones, to gape at this newest human prey; yet Rushdie's quiet reality is electrifying, a prodigy in itself. It is his first appearance at a meeting since his unanimous election to the Academy. His arrival was hinted at—discreetly, elusively—by President Wiesel the evening before, but would the man who is hunted and stalked actually show up? His plain humanity is a marvel—a fellow sitting in a chair, loosening his tie, taking off his jacket as the afternoon warms. He is no metaphor, no legend, no symbol. His fame, once merely novelist's fame, is now the fame of terror. A writer has been transmuted into a pharaoh, wrapped in hiddenness, mummified in life. It happens that Rushdie nowadays looks more scribbler than pharaoh: a certain scruffiness of falling-out hair and indecisive beard, the telltale fleshiness of the sedentary penman; the redundant mien of someone who hates wearing a tie. How different from that slender princeling who, at the Forty-eighth International PEN Conference in New York in 1986, stood up to speechify in the aisle! What we saw then was a singularly beautiful young man got up in a bright Indian (or perhaps pseudo-Indian) tunic, black-haired, black-eyed, as ravishing in outline as some gilt Persian miniature. I no longer recollect what he said on that occasion, though I retain something of his point of view: rigidly "Third World," loyally "progressive." A document protesting Middle Eastern terrorism was circulating through that body for some days; Rushdie did not append his name to it.

The bristling protection that surrounds him now is an offense, an enormity: professional, determined, watchful, admitting no breach; above all, conducted on a kingly scale. There is a twist of corruption—civilization undone—in Rushdie's necessary retinue, a retinue that shocks: all these sentries, these waiting police cars in the courtyard, dedicated to the preservation of a single human life. Or one could easily, and more justly, claim the opposite: that it is civilization's high humane standard, a society's concrete and routine glory, that so much sheltering force should be dedicated to the protection of one man under threat. But the first response is the sharper one: the sensation of recoil from the stealthily meandering armed men in black, the armed men lurking on the way to the toilet, the squad of armed men churning in this or that passageway or bunched oddly against a wall. When, at the beginning of the year, President Mitterrand came for the official inauguration of the Académie Universelle des Cultures, the crush of television cameras, reporters, ambassadors, distinguished oglers, assorted intellectuals, and the charmed hoopla of fervent French *gloire* brought in the wake of the President's footsteps a troop of security men drumming over the Louvre's burnished floors—but there was nothing grim in that train. It signified honor and festivity. Monarchs and presidents may have to live like targets in danger of being detonated; for their guests at a celebration, though, that busy retinue, however fearsomely occupied, registers as innocently as a march of bridesmaids. Rushdie, by contrast, is tailed by a reminder of death. Whoever is in a room with him, no matter how secured against intruders, remembers that the would-be assassin is on the alert for opportunity, whether for greed or for God.

Rushdie's so-called blasphemy is the fabrication of literalists whose piety can be respected but whose literalism assumes what may not be assumed: that the Creator of the Universe can be diminished by any human agency, that the sacred is susceptible of human soiling. How can a novel blaspheme? How can a work of art (which can also mean a work of dream, play, and irony) blaspheme? Islam, like Judaism, is not an iconic creed (both are famously the opposite), but the philosophers of even iconic religious expressions like medieval Christianity and classical Hinduism do not locate the divine literally in paint or carving, and know that art, while it may, for some, kindle reverence, cannot be a medium for the soiling of the sacred. Art cannot blaspheme because it is not in the power of humankind to demean or besmirch the divine. Can a man's book tarnish God? "Where wast thou when I laid the foundations of the earth?" the Lord rebukes Job.

"Knowest thou the ordinances of heaven? canst thou set the do-
minion thereof in the earth? . . . Who hath put wisdom in the
inward parts? or who hath given understanding to the heart?" After which, Job is chastened enough to "lay mine hand upon my
mouth."

Men who were not there when the foundations of the earth
were laid nevertheless lay their hands on a novelist's mouth. One
of Rushdie's translators, the Japanese Hitoshi Igarashi, has been
murdered; another, the Italian Ettore Capriolo, was seriously
wounded. The American publishers of the paperback *Satanic
Verses* hide behind an anonymous "consortium." And meanwhile
Rushdie walks or rides nowhere without his train of guards. After
lunching in a dining room of the Pyramid, the other members of
the Academy stroll the few yards across the Louvre's inner court
to return to the Richelieu for the afternoon plenary; but Rushdie,
emerging alone from the Pyramid like the pharaonic figure he has
been made into, is invisibly placed, alone, in a limousine that
moves with glacial languor from one part of the courtyard to the
other, accompanied by security men slowly pacing beside it and all
around it. Rushdie is the prisoner both of his protectors and of his
accusers.

In the eyes of his accusers, his very existence is a blasphemy to
be undone and a blemish to be annihilated. Barricaded day and
night against fanatic absolutists who look for a chance to kill, who
despise reason and discourse, repudiate compromise, and reject
amelioration, he has become, in his own person, a little Israel—or,
rather, Israel as it felt its circumstances until just recently, before
the Rabin-Arafat peace accord (and as it continues to feel them
vis-à-vis Hamas and other rejectionists). This is something that, in
all logic, has cried out to be said aloud ever since the *fatwa* was
first promulgated; but Rushdie's defenders, by and large, have not
said it—some because they feared to exacerbate his situation (but
how could it have been worsened?), some because they have
themselves been among Israel's fiercest ideological opponents.
But one fact is incontrovertible: for the mullahs of Iran, who op-
pose both recognition and peace, Rushdie and the Jews of Israel
are to be granted the same doom. What can be deduced from this

ugly confluence is, it seems to me, also incontrovertible: morally and practically, there is no way to distinguish between the terrorist whose "cause" is pronounced "just" (and whose assaults on civilians are euphemized as political or religious resistance) and the terrorist who seeks to carry out the mullahs' *fatwa* against Rushdie (a call to assassination euphemized as religious duty). One cannot have exculpated Arafat's Fatah for its long-standing program of bloodshed—not yet wholly suppressed—directed against both Jews and Arabs (the latter for what is termed "collaboration"), while at the same time defending Rushdie and deploring his plight. And in one way, after all, Rushdie is better off than women knifed on street corners or bus passengers blown up: he is at every moment under the surveillance of his security team. On the other hand, individual civilians on their errands, exposed to the brutal lottery of ambush, have their lucky and unlucky days; Rushdie, no longer a civilian, drafted into the unwilling army of victimhood, has drawn the targeted ticket. All his days are unlucky.

But like James in the Gallery of Apollo, today in the Louvre he means to turn the tables.

Why link Henry James and Salman Rushdie? They are separated by a century. They were born continents apart. One is a vast and completed library; the other, unfathomable as to his ultimate stature, is in the middle of the way. Moreover (as for the issue of terror), what threatens Rushdie has a name, *fatwa*, and a habitation—Iran, and all those other places and men and women driven by the mullahs' imaginings of God's imperatives. Whereas what threatened James was no more than his own imagination, an extrusion of the psyche's secrets, nothing enacted in the world of real and ferocious event. What threatened James was a fable of his own making. But a dream, gossamer and ephemeral though it may be, is like a *genius loci*, the spirit of a site, which can send out exhalations with the force of ciphers or glyphs. Ciphers can be decoded; glyphs can be read across centuries. (Is it the Louvre itself that will speak up for Rushdie? Wait and see.) There is, besides, an arresting nexus of situation and temperament. Like James, Rushdie left the country of his birth for England: each sought, and won, a literary London life. Each kept a backward-glancing eye on his native society. As James never abandoned interest, inquisitiveness, sympathy, and the sometimes adversarial passions of kinship with regard to America, so Rushdie retains a familial, historical and scholarly connection to Islam, warmed by kinship, interest, sympathy. Both men were charged with apostasy—James because near the end of his life, out of gratitude to Britain, he gave up his American citizenship; Rushdie more savagely, on account of having written a fable. Both are in thrall to fable; both have an instinct for the intercultural tale of migration, what James called "the international theme." Both are beguiled by notions of assimilation and strangeness, of native and newcomer.

There is more. Rushdie, like James, is secular, history-minded, skeptical, impatient with zealotry. James's father, though harmless enough, was a man metaphysically besotted, a true believer, dogmatically sunk in Swedenborgian fogs. Having been reared in an atmosphere of private fanaticism, James repudiated its public expression wherever he encountered it. He had nothing but contempt for the accusers of Dreyfus, the French Jewish army officer condemned for treason. He followed the case day by day. "I sit . . . and read L'Affaire Dreyfus. What a bottomless and sinister *affaire* and in what a strange mill it is grinding. . . . I eat and drink, I sleep and dream Dreyfus." He did better than that. He wrote to Zola to congratulate him on the publication of *J'Accuse*, a defense of Dreyfus—"one of the most courageous things ever done"—for which Zola was brought to trial and convicted. In James's view, if Zola had not fled from his sentencing, "he would have been torn *limb from limb* by the howling mob in the street."

Bottomless and sinister; apostasy and treason; the howling mob in the street. It is all familiar and instantly contemporary. The determination of the anti-Dreyfusards in France, and their fellow travelers all over Europe, to destroy an innocent and consummately patriotic Frenchman by conspiracy and forgery, and especially by the incitement of mobs, reminds one that the concept of *fatwa* is not held exclusively by mullahs. And Rushdie too has been conspired against by a kind of forgery: having written a fable, he is represented as having issued a curse; he is charged with betraying Islam. Dreyfus was charged with betraying France. Millions were avid to believe it, until his champion Zola turned the tables on the persecutors.

It is now clearer than ever that Rushdie is resolved to become, however obliquely, his own champion. Though ringed always by his ferocious security apparatus, he ventures more and more into the hot zone of political suasion. His meeting with President Clinton at the White House in November of 1993 may have constituted, for Rushdie, the hottest—the most influential—zone of all. The mullahs, whose denunciations followed immediately, hardly disagreed, and the White House visit triggered instant State Department warnings to Americans overseas about possible retaliation. No one forgets the murder of that translator; as the anonymity of Rushdie's paperback publishers shows, it is not easy for others to speak up for him. Even among writers' organizations, Rushdie's cause is sometimes reduced to a half-yawning obligatory gesture; after a while even a celebrated crisis grows humdrum and loses the glamor that writers notoriously enjoy. Wole Soyinka (himself in difficulties with an undemocratic regime in Nigeria) points out that standing up for Rushdie is currently out of fashion and looked down on among certain "multicultural" academics: it is considered an intellectual offense to the mores and sensibilities of another culture—very much in the spirit of the Congress on Human Rights in Vienna not long ago, where the idea of the universalism of human rights was initially resisted either as prejudicial to national sovereignty, or else as an objectionable parochial contrivance being foisted on societies that are satisfied with their own standards and values. The danger in defending Rushdie's right to exist is no longer the simple business of turning oneself into one more lightning rod to attract the assassins. Nowadays, standing up for Rushdie brings another sort of risk: it places one among the stereotypers and the "Orientalists," as they are often called, who are accused of denigrating whole peoples. To stand up for Rushdie is to display a colonialist mentality. A man's right to exist is mired in the politics of anti-colonialism—and never mind the irony of this, given Rushdie's origins as a Muslim born in India.

Though Iran responded to Rushdie's White House appearance by labeling the President "the most hated man before all the Muslims of the world," and though the majority of other Muslim governments have shown official indifference to Rushdie's situation, not all Muslims have been silent, even in the face of personal endangerment. One hundred Muslim and Arab writers and intellectuals have contributed to *For Rushdie*, a volume of poems and essays protesting the *fatwa*—among them the Egyptian Nobel winner Naguib Mahfouz, later attacked and seriously injured by a Muslim extremist in Cairo, and for the same reasons cited by the mullahs of Iran. "Without freedom," one of the essayists in *For Rushdie* wrote, "there is no creation, no life, no beauty."

In the Academy's afternoon plenary session, André Miquel, the president of the Collège de France and a distinguished specialist in Arabic literature, proposes a resolution condemning the systematic assassination of Algerian intellectuals by fundamentalist extremists. The language of the resolution is plain: "A terrible thing is happening in Algeria—people are being killed simply because they think." This action comes under the heading of Intervention, the Academy's chosen topic for its first year of life—a philosophic theme, but spurred on by the urgencies of Bosnia and Somalia. (Marc Kravetz, editor-in-chief of the French newspaper *Libération*, a visiting lecturer at this session, counts forty separate conflicts ongoing in the world. How many are cause for intervention, and by whom, and for whom?) Rushdie, who had earlier quietly remarked that he "hoped to speak of something besides myself," keeps to his word. Without directly offering himself in illustration, he argues against "the specific thrust of the motion," and suggests that the particular case of Algeria is "typical, part of a larger phenomenon, not just an isolated thing"—that "there is a concentrated program to oppress intellectuals in many countries." Yashar Kemal, of Turkey (currently in trouble with his own government), mentions the killings in southern Turkey by Hezbollah, the Party of God, and the murder of Turkish intellectuals "fighting for lay principles." The resolution is altered. "In many countries, and recently in Algeria," it now begins, "a terrible thing is happening." Someone raises a question of credibility: is it appropriate for an Academy as newly formed as this one to be sending out resolutions? Don't we first have to settle down a little, and acquire a recognizable character? To which Rushdie replies: "We should issue motions even if the Academy is newborn. *We* are not newborn."

Luc Ferry, a professor of philosophy at the University of Caen, and another visitor to the plenary, had described Muslim societies, insofar as they fail to separate religion from matters like human rights, as "premodern." Rushdie, scribbling away as Ferry develops this idea, disputes the term. Moral fundamentalism, Rushdie argues, is not premodern but postmodern—in short, decidedly contemporary. Secular ideals, though they may be taken for granted in Europe, are very seriously under threat elsewhere. In Saudi Arabia, for instance, modernity has been declared to be against religion, and its practitioners denounced as heretical. The concept of human rights is regarded by fundamentalists as an expression of modernity, and is rejected and despised. Moreover, not only are there conflicts between opposing cultures—between, say, fundamentalism and the secularizing West—but the same kind of conflict can occur *within* a culture, and on its own ground. Finally, if intervention means that you set out from home to supply assistance to another people, then what of terror, which leaves its place of origin to seek you out and destroy you in your own country? "Terror," Rushdie finishes, "is a reverse form of intervention."

He had, as he had promised, not spoken of himself or of his condition. Though composed and eloquent, he had not spoken much at all. When he was neither speaking nor writing, he sat very still, as immobile as a Buddha statue. One got the impression (but impressions can violate) that he had learned to be still; that he had taught himself to be *that* still. He was, in fact, a magnet of stillness—it was as if that great splendid room were shrinking to a single point of awareness: Rushdie sitting there in his shirtsleeves.

Come back now to Henry James, and the glyphs he has left behind. In another part of the Louvre on this day, past turnings of corridors, is the darkened Gallery of Apollo, empty but for its portraits and carvings and accretions of gold—as deserted as it was in

James's hot imagining, when the appalling pursuer scrabbled after him over those polished floors. The ghosts of the Louvre are many—kings, cardinals, emperors. Add to these the generations of museum-goers; remember also that Emerson walked here when America itself was almost new—Emerson, whose mind James once described as a "ripe unconsciousness of evil." In this fanciful place it is today not possible to escape the fullest, ripest consciousness of evil; Rushdie's hunted presence draws it out. He is poet, fabulist, ironist; he is the one they want to kill because his intelligence is at play. But these ancient galleries, these tremendous, glorious halls, reverberate with a memory of the tables being turned, the pursuer diminished and in flight. Dream? Hallucination? Rushdie in Paris calls up that old nightmare of panic in the Louvre, and how the stalker was driven to retreat. And Paris itself calls up Dreyfus, who was no dream, and the heroic Zola, who routed evil with reason. Still, there is a difference. The terror of our time is stone deaf to reason, and it is not enough for the Dreyfus of our time to suffer being Dreyfus. Against all the odds, he must take on being Zola too.

OF CHRISTIAN
HEROISM

*There is a story about Clare Boothe Luce complaining that she
was bored with hearing about the Holocaust. A Jewish friend of
hers said he perfectly understood her sensitivity in the matter;
in fact, he had the same sense of repetitiousness and fatigue,
hearing so often about the Crucifixion.*
—Herbert Gold, "Selfish Like Me"

I.

O F THE GREAT European murder of six million Jews, and
the murderers themselves, there is little to say. The barbaric years
when Jews were hunted down for sport in the middle of the twentieth century have their hellish immortality, their ineradicable in-
famy, and will inflame the nightmares—and (perhaps) harrow the
conscience—of the human race until the sun burns out and takes
our poor earth-speck with it. Of the murder and the murderers everything is known that needs to be known: how it was done, who
did it, who helped, where it was done, and when, and why. Especially why: the hatred of a civilization that teaches us to say No to
hatred.

Three "participant" categories of the Holocaust are commonly
named: murderers, victims, bystanders.* Imagination demands a
choosing. Which, of this entangled trio, are we? Which are we
most likely to have become? Probably it is hardest of all to imagine
ourselves victims. After all, we were here and not there. Or we

---

*We owe the perception of these categories to Raul Hilberg's *Perpetrators, Victims,
Bystanders.*

were Gentiles and not Jews or Gypsies. Or we were not yet born. But if we had already been born, if we were there and not here, if we were Jews and not Gentiles . . .

"If" is the travail of historians and philosophers, not of the ordinary human article. What we can be sure of without contradiction—we can be sure of it because we *are* the ordinary human article—is that, difficult as it might be to imagine ourselves among the victims, it is not in us even to begin to think of ourselves as likely murderers. The "banality of evil" is a catchword of our generation; but no, it is an unusual, an exceptional, thing to volunteer for the S.S.; to force aged Jews to their knees to scrub the gutter with their beards; to empty Zyklon B canisters into the hole in the roof of the gas chamber; to enact those thousand atrocities that lead to the obliteration of a people and a culture.

The victims take our pity and our horror, and whatever else we can, in our shame, cede to their memory. But they do not puzzle us. It does not puzzle us that the blood of the innocent cries up from the ground—how could it be otherwise? Even if humanity refuses to go on remembering, the voices crushed in the woods and under the fresh pavements of Europe press upward. The new plants that cover the places where corpses were buried in mass pits carry blood in their dew. Basement-whispers trouble the new blocks of flats that cover the streets where the flaming Warsaw Ghetto fell. The heavy old sideboards of the Thirties that once stood in Jewish dining rooms in certain neighborhoods of Berlin and Vienna are in Catholic and Protestant dining rooms now, in neighborhoods where there are no longer any Jews; the great carved legs of these increasingly valued antiques groan and remember the looting. The books that were thrown onto bonfires in the central squares of every German city still send up their flocks of quivering phantom letters.

All that—the looting, the shooting, the herding, the forced marches, the gassing, the torching of synagogues, the cynicism, the mendacity, the shamelessness, the truncheons, the bloodthirstiness, the fanaticism, the opportunism, the Jews of Europe as prey, their dehumanization, the death factories, the obliteration of a civilization, the annihilation of a people—all that it is possible to study, if not to assimilate. Pious Jews, poor Jews, secular Jews, universalist Jews, baptized Jews, Jews who were storekeepers, or doctors, or carpenters, or professors, or teamsters, Jewish infants and children—all annihilated. Thousands upon thousands of Jewish libraries and schools looted and destroyed. Atrocity spawns an aftermath—perhaps an afterlife. In the last four decades the documents and the testimonies have been heaped higher and higher—yet a gash has been cut in the world's brain that cannot be healed by memorial conferences or monuments. Lamentation for the martyred belongs now to the history of cruelty and to the earth. There is no paucity of the means to remember; there may be a paucity of the will to remember. Still, we know what we think of the murders and the murderers. We are not at a loss to know how to regard them.

But what of the bystanders? They were not the criminals, after all. For the bystanders we should feel at least the pale warmth of recognition—call it self-recognition. And nowadays it is the bystanders whom we most notice, though at the time, while the crimes were in progress, they seemed the least noticeable. We notice them now because they are the ones we can most readily identify with. They are the ones imagination can most readily accommodate. A bystander is like you and me, the ordinary human article—what normal man or woman or adolescent runs to commit public atrocities? The luck of the draw (the odds of finding oneself in the majority) saves the bystander from direct victimhood: the Nuremberg "racial" laws, let us say, are what exempt the bystander from deportation. The bystander is, by definition, not a Jew or a Gypsy. The bystander stays home, safe enough if compliant enough. The bystander cannot be charged with taking part in any evil act; the bystander only watches as the evil proceeds. One by one, and suddenly all at once, the Jewish families disappear from their apartments in building after building, in city after city. The neighbors watch them go. One by one, and suddenly all at once, the Jewish children disappear from school. Their classmates resume doing their sums.

The neighbors are decent people—decent enough for ordinary purposes. They cannot be blamed for not being heroes. A hero—

like a murderer—is an exception and (to be coarsely direct) an abnormality, a kind of social freak. No one ought to be expected to
become a hero. Not that the bystanders are, taken collectively, altogether blameless. In the Germany of the Thirties it was they—
because there were so many of them—who created the norm.
The conduct of the bystanders—again because there were so
many of them—defined what was common and what was uncom-
mon, what was exceptional and what was unexceptional, what
was heroic and what was quotidian. If the bystanders in all their
numbers had not been so docile, if they had not been so conciliatory, or, contrariwise, if they had not been so "inspired" (by slo-
gans and rabble-rousers and uniforms and promises of national
glory), if they had not acquiesced both through the ballot box and
alongside the parades—if, in short, they had not been *so many*—
the subject of heroism would never have had to arise.

When a whole population takes on the status of bystander, the
victims are without allies; the criminals, unchecked, are strength-
ened; and only then do we need to speak of heroes. When a field
is filled from end to end with sheep, a stag stands out. When a
continent is filled from end to end with the compliant, we learn
what heroism is. And alas for the society that requires heroes.

Most of us, looking back, and identifying as we mainly do with
the bystanders—because it is the most numerous category, into
which simple demographic likelihood thrusts us; or because
surely it is the easiest category, the most recognizably human, if
not the most humane—will admit to some perplexity, a perplexity
brought on by hindsight. Taken collectively, as I dared to do a moment ago, the bystanders are culpable. But taking human beings
collectively is precisely what we are obliged not to do. Then consider the bystanders not as a group, not as a stereotype, but one
by one. If the bystander is the ordinary human article, as we have
agreed, what can there be to puzzle us? This one, let us say, is a
good and zealous hater (no one can deny that hating belongs to
the ordinary human article), encouraged by epaulets, posters,
flashy rhetoric, and pervasive demagoguery. And this one is an envious malcontent, lustful for a change of leadership. And this one
is a simple patriot. And this one, unemployed, is a dupe of the

speechmakers. Such portraits, both credible and problematical, are common enough. But let us concede that most of the bystanders were quiet citizens who wanted nothing more than to get on with their private lives: a portrait entirely palatable to you and me. The ordinary human article seeks nothing more complex than the comforts of indifference to public clamor of any kind. Indifference is a way of sheltering oneself from evil; who would interpret such unaggressive sheltering as a contribution to evil? The ordinary human article hardly looks to get mixed up in active and wholesale butchery of populations; what rational person would want to accuse the bystander—who has done no more than avert her eyes—of a hardness-of-heart in any way approaching that of the criminals? That would be a serious lie—a distortion both of fact and of psychological understanding.

Yet it is the nature of indifference itself that bewilders. How is it that indifference, which on its own does no apparent or immediate positive harm, ends by washing itself in the very horrors it means to have nothing to do with? Hoping to confer no hurt, indifference finally grows lethal; why is that? Can it be that indifference, ostensibly passive, harbors an unsuspected robustness? The act of turning toward—while carrying a club—is an act of brutality; but the act of turning away, however empty-handed and harmlessly, remains nevertheless an *act*. The whole truth may be that the idea of human passivity is nothing but the illusion of wistful mortals; and that waking into the exigencies of our own time—whichever way we turn, toward or away—implies action. To be born is to be compelled to act.

One of the most curious (and mephitic) powers of indifference is its retroactive capacity: it is possible to be indifferent *nunc pro tunc*. I am thinking of a few sentences I happened to be shown the other day: they were from the pen of a celebrated author who was commenting on a piece of so-called "Holocaust writing." "These old events," he complained, "can rake you over only so much, and then you long for a bit of satire on it all. Like so many others of my generation"—he was a young adult during the Forties—"who had nothing to do with any of it, I've swallowed all the guilt I can bear, and if I'm going to be lashed, I intend to save my skin for more recent troubles in the world."

Never mind the odd protestation of innocence where nothing has been charged—what secret unquiet lies within this fraying conscience? What is odder still is that a statement of retroactive indifference is represented as a commitment to present compassion. As for present compassion, does anyone doubt that there is enough contemporary suffering to merit one's full notice? Besides, a current indifference to "these old events" seems harmless enough now; the chimneys of Dachau and Birkenau and Belsen have been cold for fifty years. But does this distinguished figure—a voice of liberalism as well as noteworthy eloquence—suppose that indifference to "old events" frees one for attention to new ones? In fact, indifference to past suffering is a sure sign that there will be indifference to present suffering. Jaded feelings have little to do with the staleness of any event. To be "jaded" is to decline to feel at all.

And that is perhaps the central point about indifference, whether retroactive or current. Indifference is not so much a gesture of looking away—of choosing to be passive—as it is an active disinclination to feel. Indifference shuts down the humane, and does it deliberately, with all the strength deliberateness demands. Indifference is as determined—and as forcefully muscular—as any blow. For the victims on their way to the chimneys, there is scarcely anything to choose between a thug with an uplifted truncheon and the decent citizen who will not lift up his eyes.

II.

WE HAVE spoken of three categories: criminal, victim, bystander. There is a fourth category—so minuscule that statistically it vanishes. Fortunately it is not a category that can be measured by number—its measure is metaphysical and belongs to the sublime. "Whoever saves a single life," says the Talmud, "is as one who has saved an entire world." This is the category of those astounding souls who refused to stand by as their neighbors were being hauled away to the killing sites. They were willing to see, to judge, to decide. Not only did they not avert their eyes—they set out to rescue. They are the heroes of Nazified Europe. They are Polish, Italian, Romanian, Russian, Hungarian, French, Yugoslavian, Swiss, Swedish, Dutch, Spanish, German. They are Catholic and Protestant. They are urban and rural; educated and uneducated; sophisticated and simple; they include nuns and socialists. And whatever they did, they did at the risk of their lives.

It is typical of all of them to deny any heroism. "It was only decent," they say. But no: most people are decent; the bystanders were decent. The rescuers are somehow raised above the merely decent. When the rescuers declare that heroism is beside the point, it is hard to agree with them.

There is, however, another view, one that takes the side of the rescuers. Under the steady Jerusalem sun stands a low and somber building known as Yad Vashem: a memorial to the Six Million, a place of mourning, a substitute for the missing headstones of the victims; there are no graveyards for human beings ground into bone meal and flown into evanescent smoke. But Yad Vashem is also a grove of celebration and honor: a grand row of trees, one for each savior, marks the valor of the Christian rescuers of Europe, called the Righteous Among the Nations. Mordechai Paldiel, the director of the Department for the Righteous at Yad Vashem, writing in *The Jerusalem Post* not long ago, offered some arresting reflections on the "normality" of goodness:

> We are somehow determined to view these benefactors as heroes: hence the search for underlying motives. The Righteous persons, however, consider themselves as anything but heroes, and regard their behavior during the Holocaust as quite normal. How to resolve this enigma?
>
> For centuries we have undergone a brain-washing process by philosophers who emphasized man's despicable character, highlighting his egotistic and evil disposition at the expense of other attributes. Wittingly or not, together with Hobbes and Freud, we accept the proposition that man is essentially an aggressive being, bent on destruction, involved principally with himself, and only marginally interested in the needs of others. . . .

Goodness leaves us gasping, for we refuse to recognize it as a natural human attribute. So off we go on a long search for some hidden motivation, some extraordinary explanation, for such peculiar behavior.

Evil is, by contrast, less painfully assimilated. There is no comparable search for the reasons for its constant manifestation (although in earlier centuries theologians pondered this issue).

We have come to terms with evil. Television, movies and the printed word have made evil, aggression and egotism household terms and unconsciously acceptable to the extent of making us immune to displays of evil. There is a danger that the evil of the Holocaust will be absorbed in a similar manner; that is, explained away as further confirmation of man's inherent disposition to wrongdoing. It confirms our visceral feeling that man is an irredeemable beast, who needs to be constrained for his own good.

In searching for an explanation of the motivations of the Righteous Among the Nations, are we not really saying: what was wrong with them? Are we not, in a deeper sense, implying that their behavior was something other than normal? . . . Is acting benevolently and altruistically such an outlandish and unusual type of behavior, supposedly at odds with man's inherent character, as to justify a meticulous search for explanations? Or is it conceivable that such behavior is as natural to our psychological constitution as the egoistic one we accept so matter-of-factly?

It is Mr. Paldiel's own goodness that leaves me gasping. How I want to assent to his thesis! How alluring it is! His thesis asserts that it is the rescuers who are in possession of the reality of human nature, not the bystanders; it is the rescuers who are the ordinary human article. "In a place where there are no human beings, *be* one"—it is apparent that the rescuers were born to embody this rabbinic text. It is not, they say, that they are exceptions; it is that they are human. They are not to be considered "extraordinary," "above the merely decent."

Yet their conduct emphasizes—exemplifies—the exceptional.

For instance:

Giorgio Perlasca, an Italian from Padua, had a job in the Spanish Embassy in Budapest. When the Spanish envoy fled before the invading Russians, Perlasca substituted the Spanish "Jorge" for the Italian "Giorgio" and passed himself off as the Spanish chargé d'affaires. He carried food and powdered milk to safe houses under the Spanish flag, where several hundred Jews at a time found a haven. He issued protective documents that facilitated the escape of Jews with Spanish passes. "I began to feel like a fish in water," he said of his life as an impostor: the sole purpose of his masquerade was to save Jews. And he saved thousands.

Bert Berchove was a Dutch upholsterer who lived with his wife and two children in a large apartment over his shop, in a town not far from Amsterdam. At first he intended to help only his wife's best friend, who was Jewish; her parents had already been deported. Berchove constructed a hiding place in the attic, behind a false wall. Eventually thirty-seven Jews were hidden there.

In a Dominican convent near Vilna, seven nuns and their mother superior sheltered a number of Jews who had escaped from the ghetto, including some poets and writers. The fugitives were disguised in nuns' habits. The sisters did not stop at hiding Jews: they scoured the countryside for weapons to smuggle into the ghetto.

Who will say that the nuns, the upholsterer, and the impostor are not extraordinary in their altruism, their courage, the electrifying boldness of their imaginations? How many nuns have we met who would think of dressing Jewish poets in wimples? How many upholsterers do we know who would actually design and build a false wall? Who among us would dream of fabricating a fake diplomatic identity in order to save Jewish lives? Compassion, it is clear, sharpens intuition and augments imagination.

For me, the rescuers are *not* the ordinary human article. Nothing would have been easier than for each and every one of them to have remained a bystander, like all those millions of their countrymen in the nations of Europe. It goes without saying that the bystanders, especially in the occupied lands, had troubles enough of their own, and hardly needed to go out of their way to acquire new burdens and frights. I do not—cannot—believe that human beings are, without explicit teaching, naturally or intrinsically altruistic. I do not believe, either, that they are naturally vicious, though they can be trained to be. The truth (as with most truths) seems to be somewhere in the middle: most people are born bystanders. The ordinary human article does not want to be disturbed by extremes of any kind—not by risks, or adventures, or unusual responsibility.

And those who undertook the risks, those whose bravery steeped them in perilous contingencies, those whose moral strength urged them into heart-stopping responsibility—what (despite their demurrals) are they really, if not the heroes of our battered world? What other name can they possibly merit? In the Europe of the most savage decade of the twentieth century, not to be a bystander was the choice of an infinitesimal few. These few are more substantial than the multitudes from whom they distinguished themselves; and it is from these undeniably heroic and principled few that we can learn the full resonance of civilization.

EXISTING
THINGS

F IRST INKLING. If I were to go back and back—*really* back, to earliest consciousness—I think it would be mica. Not the prophet Micah, who tells us that our human task is to do justly, and to love mercy, and to walk humbly with our God; but that other still more humble mica—those tiny glints of isinglass that catch the sun and prickle upward from the pavement like shards of star-stuff. Sidewalks nowadays seem inert, as if cement has rid itself forever of bright sprinklings and stippled spangles. But the pavement I am thinking of belongs to long ago, and runs narrowly between the tall weeds of empty lots, lots that shelter shiny green snakes.

The lots are empty because no one builds on them; it is the middle of the summer in the middle of the Depression, childhood's longest hour. I am alone under a slow molasses sun, staring at the little chips of light flashing at my feet. Up and down the whole length of the street there is no one, not a single grownup, and certainly, in that sparse time, no other child. There is only myself and these hypnotic semaphores signaling eeriness out of the ground. But no, up the block a little way, a baby carriage is entrusted to the idle afternoon, with a baby left to sleep, all by itself, under white netting.

If you are five years old, loitering in a syrup of sunheat, gazing at the silver-white mica-eyes in the pavement, you will all at once be besieged by a strangeness: the strangeness of understanding, for the very first time, that you are really alive, and that the world is really true; and the strangeness will divide into a river of wonderings.

Here is what I wondered then, among the mica-eyes:

I wondered what it would be like to become, for just one moment, every kind of animal there is in the world. Even, I thought, a snake.

I wondered what it would be like to know all the languages in the world.

I wondered what it would be like to be that baby under the white netting.

I wondered why, when I looked straight into the sun, I saw a pure circle.

I wondered why my shadow had a shape that was me, but nothing else; why my shadow, which was almost like a mirror, was not a mirror.

I wondered why I was thinking these things; I wondered what wondering was, and why it was spooky, and also secretly sweet, and amazingly *interesting*. Wondering felt akin to love—an uncanny sort of love, not like loving your mother or father or grandmother, but something curiously and thrillingly other. Something that shone up out of the mica-eyes.

Decades later, I discovered in Wordsworth's *Prelude* what it was:

> . . . *those hallowed and pure motions of the sense*
> *Which seem, in their simplicity, to own*
> *An intellectual charm;*
> . . . *those first-born affinities that fit*
> *Our new existence to existing things.*

And those existing things are *all* things, everything the mammal senses know, everything the human mind constructs (temples or equations), the unheard poetry on the hidden side of the round earth, the great thirsts everywhere, the wonderings past wonderings.

First inkling, bridging our new existence to existing things. Can one begin with mica in the pavement and learn the prophet Micah's meaning?

THE BREAK

I WRITE THESE WORDS at least a decade after the terrifying operation that separated us. Unfortunately, no then current anaesthesia, and no then accessible surgical technique, was potent enough to suppress consciousness of the knife as it made its critical blood-slice through the area of our two warring psyches. It is the usual case in medicine that twins joined at birth are severed within the first months of life. Given the intransigence of my partner (who until this moment remains recalcitrant and continues to wish to convert me to her loathsome outlook), I had to wait many years until I could obtain her graceless and notoriously rancorous consent to our divergence.

The truth is I have not spoken to her since the day we were wheeled, side by side as usual, on the same gurney, into the operating room. Afterward it was at once observed (especially by me) that the surgery had not altered her character in any respect, and I felt triumphantly justified in having dragged her into it. I had done her no injury—she was as intractable as ever. As for myself, I was freed from her proximity and her influence. The physical break was of course the end, not the beginning, of our rupture; psychologically, I had broken with her a long time ago. I disliked her then, and though shut of her daily presence and unavoidable attachment, I dislike her even now.

Any hint or symptom of her discourages me; I have always avoided reading her. Her style is clotted, parenthetical, self-indulgent, long-winded, periphrastic, in every way excessive— hard going altogether. One day it came to me: why bother to keep up this fruitless connection? We have nothing in common, she and I.

To begin with, I am honest; she is not. Or, to spare her a moral lecture (but why should I? what has she ever spared *me*?), let me put it that she is a fantasist and I am not. Never mind that her own term for her condition is, not surprisingly, realism. It is precisely her "realism" that I hate. It is precisely her "facts" that I despise.

Her facts are not my facts. For instance, you will never catch me lying about my age, which is somewhere between seventeen and twenty-two. She, on the other hand, claims to be over sixty. A preposterous declaration, to be sure—but see how she gets herself up to look the part! She is all dye, putty, greasepaint. She resembles nothing so much as Gravel Gertie in the old Dick Tracy strip. There she is, done up as a white-haired, dewlapped, thick-waisted, thick-lensed hag, seriously myopic. A phenomenal fake. (Except for the nearsightedness, which, to be charitable, I don't hold against her, being seriously myopic myself.)

Aging is certainly not her only pretense. She imagines herself to be predictable; fixed; irrecoverable. She reflects frequently— tediously—on the trajectory of her life, and supposes that its arc and direction are immutable. What she has done she has done. She believes she no longer has decades to squander. I know better than to subscribe to such fatalism. Here the radical difference in our ages (which began to prove itself out at the moment of surgery) is probably crucial. It is her understanding that she is right to accept her status. She is little known or not known at all, relegated to marginality, absent from the authoritative anthologies that dictate which writers matter.

She knows she does not matter. She argues that she has been in rooms with the famous, and felt the humiliation of her lesserness, her invisibility, her lack of writerly weight or topical cachet. In gilded chambers she has seen journalists and cultural consuls cluster around and trail after the stars; at conferences she has been shunted away by the bureaucratic valets of the stars. She is aware that she has not written enough. She is certainly not read. She sees with a perilous clarity that she will not survive even as "minor."

I will have none of this. There was a time—a tenuous membrane still hung between us, a remnant of sentiment or nostalgia on my part—when she was fanatically driven to coerce me into a similar view of myself. The blessèd surgery, thank God, put an end to all that. My own ambition is fresh and intact. I can gaze at her fearfulness, her bloodless perfectionism and the secret crisis of confidence that dogs it, without a drop of concern. You may ask: why am I so pitiless? Don't I know (I know to the lees) her indiscipline, her long periods of catatonic paralysis, her idleness, her sleepiness?

Again you ask: do you never pity her? Never. Hasn't she enough self-pity for the two of us? It is not that I am any more confident or less fearful; here I am, standing at the threshold still, untried, a thousand times more diffident, tremulous, shy. My heart is vulnerable to the world's distaste and dismissiveness. But oh, the difference between us! I have the power to scheme and to construct—a power that time has eroded in her, a power that she regards as superseded, useless. Null and void. Whatever shreds remain of her own ambitiousness embarrass her now. She is resigned to her failures. She is shamed by them. To be old and unachieved: ah.

Yes, ah! Ah! This diminution of hunger in her disgusts me; I detest it. She is a scandal of sorts, a superannuated mourner: her Promethean wounds (but perhaps they are only Procrustean?) leak on her bed when she wakes, on the pavement when she walks. She considers herself no more than an ant in an anthill. I have heard her say of the round earth, viewed on films sent back from this or that space shuttle, that Isaiah and Shakespeare are droplets molten into that tiny ball, and as given to evaporation as the pointlessly rotating ball itself. Good God, what have I to do with any of that? I would not trade places with her for all the china in Teaneck.

Look, there is so much ahead! Forms of undiminished luminescence: specifically, novels. A whole row of novels. All right, let her protest if it pleases her—when *she* set out, the written word was revered; reputations were rooted in literariness—poets, novelists. Stories are electronic nowadays, and turn up in pictures: the victory, technologically upgraded, of the comic book. The writer is at last delectably alone, dependent on no acclaim. It is all for the sake of the making, the finding, the doing: the Ding-an-Sich. The wild *interestingness* of it! I will be a novelist yet! I feel myself becoming a voluptuary of human nature, a devourer, a spewer, a seer, an ironist. A hermit-toiler. I dream of nights without sleep.

She, like so many of her generation, once sought work and recognition. Perhaps she labored for the sake of fame, who knows? Five or six of her contemporaries, no more, accomplished that ubiquitous desire. But here in the gyre of my eighteenth year, my goatish and unbridled twentieth, my muscular and intemperate and gluttonous prime, it is fruitfulness I am after: despite the unwantedness of it—and especially despite *her*—I mean to begin a life of novel-writing. What do I care? I have decades to squander.

As for her: coward, whining wizened hoary fake—I deny her, I denounce her, I let her go!

OLD HAND
AS NOVICE

I REMEMBER precisely the moment I knew I wanted to write a play: it was in an out-of-the-way theater, the Promenade, on Broadway in the Seventies, somewhere in the middle of the second act of *The Common Pursuit*, a melancholic comedy by the British playwright Simon Gray. The play was a send-up of the passionate Cambridge cenacle attached to *Scrutiny*, that fabled literary periodical presided over by F. R. Leavis, an eminent critic of forty years ago; it followed the rise and fall and erotic history of its madly literary protagonists from cocky youth to sour middle age. Madly literary myself, I sat electrified in the seductive dark of the Promenade, flooded by an overpowering wish: Some day!

And I remember precisely the moment I discovered the first sinister fumes brewed up by those liars and obfuscators who dare to term themselves "revisionists," but are more accurately named Holocaust deniers. It was the late summer of 1961. My husband and I had just rented an apartment in a building so new that the fresh plaster, not yet fully dried, was found to be congenial to a repulsive army of moisture-seeking insects rather prettily called silverfish. How to rid ourselves of this plague? Off we went to the town library, to look for a book on household infestation. The helpful volume we hit on happened to be translated, and very nicely so, from the German. It recommended a certain gas with a record of remarkable success in the extermination of vermin. An asterisk led to a slyly impassive footnote at the bottom of the page, utterly deadpan and meanly corrupt: "Zyklon B, used during the Second World War."

How the delectable theatrical dark came to be entangled with the dark of Zyklon B, the death-camp gas, I can hardly fathom; but when, after years of feeling unready, I did finally undertake to write a play, it turned out to be tempestuously and bitterly political—nothing in the least like that dream of literary laughter the Promenade had inspired long before. Its salient theme was Holocaust denial: a trap contrived out of cunning, deceit, and wicked surprise. Yet a not inconsequential literary issue stuck from the start to the outer flanks of my play, and continued to dog it: the ill-humored question of the playwright's credentials.

Of course there is nothing new in a writer's crossing from one form into another; no one is startled, or aggrieved, by a novelist turned essayist, or by a poet who ventures into fiction. The radical divide is not in the writer, but in the mode, and mood, of reception. Reading is the expression of a profound social isolation. As in getting born or dying, you are obliged to do it alone; there is no other way. Theater—like religion, its earliest incarnation—is a communal rite. Study a row of faces transfixed in unison by a scene on a stage, and you will fall into a meditation on anatomical variety irradiated by a kind of dramaturgical monotheism: the infusion of a single godly force into so many pairs of luminously staring eyes.

Theater *is* different from fiction, yes; an untried genre for the novice playwright, a dive into strangeness: that mysterious hiatus in the dark, that secret promissory drawing of breath just before the stage lights brighten. Nevertheless a novice is not the same as an amateur. An amateur worships—is glamorized by—the trappings of an industry, including the excitements of being "inside." Theater industry (or call it, as anthropologists nowadays like to do, theater culture), with all its expertise, protocol, hierarchy, jargon, tradition, its existential hard knocks and heartbreak, its endemic optimism and calloused cynicism, its experience with audiences, its penchant for spectacle, still cannot teach a writer the writer's art—which is not on the stage, but in the ear and in the brain. Though a novice playwright will certainly be attentive to "technique," to "knowhow," real apprenticeship is ultimately always to the self; a writer's lessons are ineluctably internal. As a beginning novelist long ago, I learned to write dialogue not in a fiction workshop ruled by a sophisticated "mentor," but by reading Graham Greene's *The Heart of the Matter* over and over again. There were uncanny reverberations in those short, plain sentences, and a peculiarly suspenseful arrest of a character's intent. The perfected work was the mentor.

Let me not arrogantly misrepresent. There is plenty for an uninitiated playwright to learn from the living air of a reading, a rehearsal, a developing performance in the theater itself; and from an actor's cadence or lift of the eyelid; and from an impassioned talk with a seasoned playwright (and no one is more openly generous than lifelong playwrights, who are a band of mutually sympathizing cousins); and above all from a trusted and trusting director who recognizes the writer *as writer*. Besides, a novelist's perspective is hardly akin to a playwright's. Novels are free to diverge, to digress, to reflect, to accrete. Proust is a gargantuan soliloquizer. Tolstoy encompasses whole histories. George Eliot pauses for psychological essays. A novel is like the physicist's premise of an expanding universe—horizon after horizon, firmament sailing past firmament. But a play is just the reverse: the fullness of the universe drawn down into a single succinct atom—the all-consuming compactness and density of the theorist's black hole. Everything converges in the dot that is the stage. A novelist seeking to become a playwright will uncover new beauty—structure and concision; the lovely line of the spine and the artfully integrated turn of each vertebra.

Yet always a gauntlet is thrown down before the newcomer playwright (especially one who has arrived from the famously sequestered craft of fiction), and that is the many-fingered image of "collaboration." I want to say quickly—against all the power and authority of theatrical magnates and magi, against the practice and conviction of all those who know more and better than an uninformed interloper like myself—that the term "collaboration," as I have heard it used again and again, is a fake, a fib, and a sham. The truth stands clarified: no matter what the genre, a writer is necessarily an autonomous, possessed, and solitary figure generating furies. Imagination is a self-contained burning, a fire that cannot be fed from without. The idea of a "collaborative art" is an idea out of Oz—i.e., it supplies you with a phony wizard haranguing into a megaphone. No one can claim ascendancy over a writer's language or imagination, and anyone who tries—and succeeds—is an invader, an editor, or just a run-of-the-mill boss. Writers cloutless and consequently docile will likely acquiesce—but what will come out of it is what editors and bosses always get: something edited, something obliging. An artificial voice. A dry wadi where the heart of a river might have roiled. In the name of a putative collaborative art, a novice playwright (even if an old hand as a writer) will be manipulated by the clever, patronized by the callow, humiliated by the talentless. Generations of clichés will pour down. To become master over a writer is not, as it happens, to become a master of writing.

But if the notion of a collaborative art is simply authoritarian make-believe, the experience of *skills* in collaboration is the rapt and gorgeous satisfaction of theater—the confluence of individual artists, each conceptually and temperamentally singular. The brainy director's orchestral sensibility; the actors' transformative magickings (a gesture over nothingness will build you the solidest phantom table conceivable); dramatic sculptures hewn of purest light; inklings sewn into a scene by the stitch of a tiny sound; a dress that is less a costume than a wise corroboration; a set that lands you unerringly in the very place you need to be; and the sine qua non of the producers' endlessly patient acts of faith—all these carry their visionary plenitude. Novice playwrights—and veterans, too, I believe—will fall on their knees in gratitude.

To return to the matter of credentials. A bird can fly over any continent you choose; it's the having wings that counts. A writer can be at home in novel, story, essay, or play; it's the breathing inside a blaze of words that counts. However new to theater culture, a writer remains exactly that—the only genuine authority over the words and the worlds they embody.

And if the play should vanish away without being realized in a theater before an audience (nine times out of ten, plays are snowflakes in July), the disappointed scribbler will peacefully turn back to the blessèd privacy of a secluded desk—where the writer not only acts all the roles, wears all the costumes, and dreams all the scenery, but is both determined producer and tireless director, unwaveringly committed to fruition; and where there is no mistaking who is sovereign.

SEYMOUR:
HOMAGE
TO A
BIBLIOPHILE

NYONE WHO sets out to tell her own peculiar Seymour story takes no risks of parochialism: nothing can be more certain than that *my* Seymour will be *your* Seymour; and vice versa. There are two reasons for this confidence. The first is that I came to Seymour late, and found him in all the ripened wholeness of his absolute Self—Seymour to the full, Seymour to the dazzling brim. By the time I got to know him—less than two years, it turned out, before he left us to join Keats in Heaven—it was plain he had been *this* Seymour, and no other, for a long while: a man of such spirited sweetness, airiness, and diffident wit, a man of such ungrudging jauntiness and sprightly gentleness, an affectionate idealist so luminously elevated by humane imagination, that I understood at once I had fallen into an amazement.

Figuring out the substantial character and content of that amazement took a little longer. No one had told me, when we were introduced—a handshake at the Rosenbach Museum in Philadelphia—that Mr. Seymour Adelman was (as a Rosenbach publication itself puts it) "a famous Philadelphia bookman." What

I saw was a tall gentleman, conventionally distinguished, but with one shoulder just a shade tipped down, as if this business of looking distinguished had happened in spite of himself, without his meaning it to; as if he worried that looking important would make him seem self-important. At that moment he had no smile; he wasn't exactly at ease; it appeared he didn't like being "introduced." He was probably afraid that his credentials were about to be reeled off, and he would stand exposed for what he was: one of the most passionate bibliophiles on the American scene, a collector in whom the near evidence of a poet's mind and hand inspired rapt and tremulous awe. There was no reasonable way, really, for Seymour to be introduced. He would have had to be defined, and that would have made him bashful.

Now if, at that early encounter, Seymour *had* been defined, this is what I would most likely have heard: "Please meet Mr. Adelman, in whom the acquisitive faculty is a lesser, though essential, aspect of the delectably inquisitive. Curiosity and rapture, infatuation and fascination—these are what motivate Mr. Adelman. If he has contrived to live in the presence of a marvelous thing—a letter, a document, a manuscript, a drawing, a broadside, a painting—it isn't simply to *own* it, like some possessive tycoon, but to enter its intelligence, to dream himself into it. Please note that Mr. Adelman has dreamed himself into American and British history and painting and literature, and beyond—even into the boxing ring! Collecting is the domestication of beloved apparitions, so it's no wonder that Mr. Adelman has chosen to set up housekeeping in the most sumptuous of all the palaces of the imagination. He doesn't mean to stay there alone, though—the windows and doors are wide open, with Mr. Adelman waving like mad at the front gate, calling out 'Come and see!' to every fellow dreamer."

But since no one said any of this, I had no idea of what lay ahead. I had never known a private collector, and thought of "bookmen," when I thought of them at all, as pinched experts on the condition of old leather bindings. I had the low notion that bibliophilism belonged to the extrinsic, the superficial, the merely valuable—the farthest pole from true poets and their true lives.

Seymour contradicted all that. I followed him down into the

hold of the Canaday Library of Bryn Mawr College, into his captain's cabin—Room A-10. These were high seas! "Do you like A. E.
Housman?" he asked: testing a potential member of the crew. I
confessed to having been smitten at the age of sixteen. "Well,
then," said Seymour, and put into my hands an autographed tran-
script of "Loveliest of trees, the cherry now / Is hung with bloom
along the bough." Housman at his purest, most lyrical, most crystal. And set down by the poet's own pen. Seymour's pride in this
fabled cargo rocked the little room like a fresh wave—not the
pride of ownership, but something else: a cheerful reverence, one
might call it, a kind of patriotism for beauty and grace. Elation,
perhaps, over the seamless continuity of art.

The next moment I was gazing down at still another Housman
manuscript, also in Housman's own hand:

> *Marinade of 4 Anchovy*
> *2 Soy*
> *3 Ketchup*
> *A little treacle with vinegar*
> *Draw out the gut, but do not split the fish*
> *Bake in a closed vessel for 3 hours in a slow oven*

It was a recipe for pickled herring. "I am happy indeed,"
Seymour wrote me afterward, "that you recovered quickly from
the encounter with Pickled Herring à la Housman. I might add
that yours was a very mild case; most visitors to A-10, after even
the merest glimpse of the recipe, collapse in a heap, gasping, and
are routinely taken to Bryn Mawr Hospital."

In return, I sent him a rhyme.

> *Loveliest of fish, the herring now*
> *Is hung with vinegar above its brow,*

it brazenly began. The "future home" of my letter, Seymour responded grandly, "is A-10, where I know it will be welcomed by its
peers—my Keats and Shelley and Wordsworth and Coleridge and
Tennyson letters." And he emblazoned his signature with a flour-
ish: "Now, hence, and forever."

Now, hence, and forever. The loyal little "my" that preceded those noble names of English literature—for Seymour, it was "my" Keats, "my" Shelley, "my" Wordsworth, and all the rest, not because he had won these consummately precious world-treasures at hard auction, not because he had been victorious over other collectors (though the triumph of the chase ought not to be discounted), but because he had made a pact with genius. He offered his own life, a life of veneration and concentration and care—a dedicated curatorship; and genius, on its side, was simply to give him leave to warm his hands at its fires. A covenant both modest and glorious.

Seymour liked to say that it was "the malignant influence of mathematics" that exiled him from the University of Pennsylvania after his sophomore year. More likely it was the beneficent promptings of immortality. It seems clear that Seymour had to be himself—a visionary seeker—no matter what: he went in a straight line from earliest youth. In 1924, still in his teens, he bought, for thirteen dollars, a letter by Charles Dickens, written in Philadelphia. He was attracted from the first by the halo of stubbornness that surrounds imaginative literature, the deep radiances only poets have the obstinacy to see all the way down into; and it was these flashes from the fiery hoop of eternity Seymour was secretly after. (Now, hence, and forever!)

He could sometimes cloak the sight of this blazing wheel behind the charming sleight-of-hand of the jokes and stories that teased his own ambition, but it was there all the same, and probably all the time. Here it is hidden in the catalogue note to Item 184 in the Adelman Collection:

> WINSTON CHURCHILL
> Typed letter signed, to
> Seymour Adelman.
> Roquebrune, France, 14 March 1959

In regard to this letter, mentioning Dunkirk, it can be stated, on the highest authority, that its recipient has not yet fully recovered from the joyous shock of receiving it. He had expected, at most, a note of acknowledgment signed by one of Churchill's five secretaries.

This appears in the heart of much other Churchilliana, but what rushes up out of the surprise in Seymour's voice—*his* voice unquestionably, as plain as a fingerprint—is the terrible heat of history: history as furnace and forge. Seymour was out to touch, even if only with the tip of his thumbnail, the heaving flames of that part of eternity which was his own time.

Yet he rarely left Philadelphia. "During the last eleven years," he said in 1962, and again in 1974, "I have not been away from Philadelphia for twenty-four consecutive hours. And if my luck holds out, I look forward to another uninterrupted decade or two within the city limits." The London he knew inside out was a map drawn in its gossamer particularity on the underside of his eyelids. (A map preserved, by the way, in Seymour's most delightful essay, the celebrated "Changing Patterns in the Function of Travel Agencies.") He could voyage to this handy London at will—"we're going to see Shelley plain!"—and always find his favorite poets at home when he knocked. (He never actually admitted to it, but there is a hint or two in some of his paragraphs that he may have gone on these phantom journeys to London in the family car, with "my mother and sister on the lookout for scrimshaw and samplers, and my father on the lookout for reckless drivers," right there over the Atlantic.)

Though there is no mistaking the inimitable apparatus of Seymour's magnetism for anyone else's, there is, anyhow, a second reason for a limitlessly recognizable and universal Seymour. It can be witnessed in an arresting painting by Seymour's friend, Susan Macdowell Eakins, the widow of Thomas Eakins. An elegant young man in spectacles is reading in a beautifully carved chair. One long leg is crossed over the other. The head, too, is long, the hair richly thick. A nearby table holds books, a periodical, a splendid vase, an intricate little sculpture; also the young man's stylish fedora and fringed scarf. On a wall behind, nearly lost in dimness, is a work by Thomas Eakins. A bright sheet has fallen beside the young man's chair—a poster by Lovat Fraser, for a performance of *The Beggar's Opera* at London's Lyric Theatre. The young man has so far never been to London—it is 1932. The fingers of his right hand press dreamily into the pages of his book. If you stare long enough (not at the angelic mouth, but at the serious eyes), you can see the immortal Seymour just beginning a characteristic smile. The portrait is called, unsurprisingly, "The Bibliophile." It is a singular representation of an American Muse: Seymour as the embodiment—the ingathering—of imagination, of heritage, of civilization and its arts.

SEYMOUR, A FAMOUS Philadelphia bookman, has finally left the city limits. He is in London at last—the true London, the London of the English poets. A hundred geniuses of the English tongue are streaming toward him. Dickens, Yeats, Hardy, Matthew Arnold, Max Beerbohm, Stevenson, Wilde, Hazlitt, Chatterton, Ralph Hodgson, Rupert Brooke, Isaac Rosenberg—they are all hugely curious about the Adelman Collection. They want to look themselves up in the catalogue. Seymour, meanwhile, is taking tea with Keats. Tomorrow he will nibble herring with Housman. He is planning to treat FitzGerald—the FitzGerald of the *Rubáiyát*—to some vanilla ice cream, Seymour's own favorite. Churchill has asked for an appointment. Wordsworth is waiting eagerly on the doormat. The incandescent ring of eternity fires the horizon, and Seymour is reaching out to collect it.

> *And, south or north, 'tis only*
> *A choice of friends one knows,*
> *And I shall ne'er be lonely*
> *Asleep with these or those.*

—A. E. Housman, "Hughley Steeple"

HELPING
T. S. ELIOT
WRITE BETTER
(NOTES TOWARD
A DEFINITIVE
BIBLIOGRAPHY)

I̤T IS NOT yet generally known to the world of literary scholarship that an early version of T. S. Eliot's celebrated poem, "The Love Song of J. Alfred Prufrock," first appeared in *The New Shoelace*, an impoverished publication of uncertain circulation located on East Fifteenth Street. Eliot, then just out of Harvard, took the train down from Boston carrying a mottled manila envelope. He wore slip-on shoes with glossy toes. His long melancholy cheeks had the pallor associated in those days with experimental poets.

The New Shoelace was situated on the topmost floor of an antique factory building. Eliot ascended in the elevator with suppressed elation; his secret thought was that, for all he knew, the young Henry James, fastidiously fingering a book review for submission, might once have entered this very structure. The brick walls smelled of old sewing machine oil. The ropes of the elevator, visible through a hole in its ceiling, were frayed and slipped occasionally; the car moved languidly, groaning. On the seventh floor Eliot emerged. The deserted corridor, with its series of shut doors, was an intimidating perplexity. He passed three with frosted glass panels marked by signs: BIALY'S WORLDWIDE NEEDLES; WARSHOWER WOOL TRADING CORP.; and MEN. Then came the exit to the fire escape. *The New Shoelace*, Eliot reasoned, must be in the opposite direction. MONARCH BOX CO.; DIAMOND'S LIGHTING FIXTURES—ALL NEW DESIGNS; MAX'S THIS-PLANET-ONLY TRAVEL SERVICE; YANKELOWITZ'S ALL-COLOR BRAID AND TRIM; LADIES. And there, at the very end of the passage, tucked into a cul-de-sac, was the office of *The New Shoelace*. The manila envelope had begun to tremble in the young poet's grip. Behind that printed title reigned Firkin Barmuenster, editor.

In those far-off days, *The New Shoelace*, though very poor, as its shabby furnishings readily attested, was nevertheless in possession of a significant reputation. Or, rather, it was Firkin Barmuenster who had the reputation. Eliot was understandably cowed. A typist in a fringed scarf sat huddled over a tall black machine, looking rather like a recently oppressed immigrant out of steerage, swatting the keys as if they were flies. Five feet from the typist's cramped table loomed Firkin Barmuenster's formidable desk, its surface hidden under heaps of butter-spotted manuscript, odoriferous paper bags, and porcelain-coated tin coffee mugs chipped at their rims. Firkin Barmuenster himself was nowhere to be seen.

The typist paused in her labors. "Help you?"

"I am here," Eliot self-consciously announced, "to offer something for publication."

"F.B. stepped out a minute."

"May I wait?"

"Suit yourself. Take a chair."

The only chair on the horizon, however, was Firkin Barmuenster's own, stationed forbiddingly on the other side of the awe-inspiring desk. Eliot stood erect as a sentry, anticipating the footsteps that at last resounded from the distant terminus of the corridor. Firkin Barmuenster, Eliot thought, must be returning from the door marked MEN. Inside the manila envelope in Eliot's fevered grasp, "The Love Song of J. Alfred Prufrock" glowed with its incontrovertible promise. One day, Eliot felt sure, it would be one of the most famous poems on earth, studied by college freshmen and corporate executives on their way up. Only now there were these seemingly insurmountable obstacles: he, Tom Eliot, was painfully young, and even more painfully obscure; and Firkin Barmuenster was known to be ruthless in his impatience with bad writing. Eliot believed in his bones that "Prufrock" was not bad writing. He hoped that Firkin Barmuenster would be true to his distinction as a great editor, and would be willing to bring out Eliot's proud effort in the pages of *The New Shoelace*. The very ink-fumes that rose up out of the magazine excited Eliot and made his heart fan more quickly than ever. Print!

"Well, well, what have we here?" Firkin Barmuenster inquired, settling himself behind the mounds that towered upward from the plateau of his desk, and reaching into one of the paper bags to extract a banana.

"I've written a poem," Eliot said.

"We don't mess with any of those," Firkin Barmuenster growled. "We are a magazine of opinion."

"I realize that," Eliot said, "but I've noticed those spaces you sometimes leave at the bottom of your articles of opinion, and I thought that might be a good place to stick in a poem, since you're not using that space for anything else anyhow. Besides," Eliot argued in conciliatory fashion, "my poem also expresses an opinion."

"Really? What on?"

"If you wouldn't mind taking half a second to look at it—"

"Young man," Firkin Barmuenster barked rapidly, "let me tell you the kind of operation we run here. In the first place, these are modern times. We're talking 1911, not 1896. What we care about here are up-to-date issues. Politics. Human behavior. Who rules the world, and how. No wan and sickly verses, you follow?"

"I believe, sir," Eliot responded with grave courtesy, "that I own an entirely new Voice."

"Voice?"

"Experimental, you might call it. Nobody else has yet written this way. My work represents a revolt from the optimism and cheerfulness of the last century. Dub it wan and sickly if you will—it is, if you don't mind my blowing my own horn"—but here he lowered his eyes, to prove to Firkin Barmuenster that he was aware of how painfully young, and painfully obscure, he was—"an implicit declaration that poetry must not only be found *through* suffering, but can find its own material only *in* suffering. I insist," he added even more shyly, "that the poem should be able to see beneath both beauty and ugliness. To see the boredom, and the horror, and the glory."

"I like what you say about the waste of all that white space," Firkin Barmuenster replied, growing all at once thoughtful. "All right, let's have a look. What do you call your jingle?"

" 'The Love Song of J. Alfred Prufrock.' "

"Well, that won't do. Sit down, will you? I can't stand people standing, didn't my girl tell you that?"

Eliot looked about once again for a chair. To his relief, he spied a high stool just under the single grimy window, which gave out onto a bleak airshaft. A stack of back issues of *The New Shoelace* was piled on it. As he gingerly removed them, placing them with distaste on the sooty sill, the cover of the topmost magazine greeted Eliot's eye with its tedious headline: MONARCHY VS. ANARCHY—EUROPE'S POLITICAL DILEMMA. This gave poor Tom Eliot a pang. Perhaps, he reflected fleetingly, he had brought his beloved "Prufrock" to the wrong crossroads of human aspiration? How painfully young and obscure he felt! Still, a novice must begin somewhere. Print! He was certain that a great man like Firkin Barmuenster (who had by then finished his banana) would sense unusual new talent.

"Now, Prudecock, show me your emanation," Firkin Barmuenster demanded, when Eliot had dragged the stool over to the appropriate spot in front of the editor's redoubtable desk.

"Prufrock, sir. But I'm Eliot." Eliot's hands continued to shake as he drew the sheets of "Prufrock" from the mottled manila envelope.

"Any relation to that female George?" Firkin Barmuenster free-associated companionably, so loudly that the fringed typist turned from her clatter to stare at her employer for a single guarded moment.

"It's *Tom*," Eliot said; inwardly he burned with the ignominy of being so painfully obscure.

"I like that. I appreciate a plain name. We're in favor of clarity here. We're straightforward. Our credo is that every sentence is either right or wrong, exactly the same as a sum. You follow me on this, George?"

"Well," Eliot began, not daring to correct this last slip of the tongue (Freud was not yet in his heyday, and it was too soon for the dark significance of such an error to have become public knowledge), "actually it is my belief that a sentence is, if I may take the liberty of repeating myself, a kind of Voice, with its own suspense, its secret inner queries, its chancy idiosyncrasies and soliloquies. Without such a necessary view, one might eunuchize, one might render neuter—"

But Firkin Barmuenster was already buried in the sheets of "Prufrock." Eliot watched the steady rise and fall of his smirk as he read on and on. For the first time, young Tom Eliot noticed Barmuenster's style of dress. A small trim man lacking a mustache but favored with oversized buff teeth and grizzled hair the color of ash, Barmuenster wore a checkered suit of beige and brown, its thin red pinstripe running horizontally across the beige boxes only; his socks were a romantic shade of robin's egg blue, and his shoes, newly and flawlessly heeled, were maroon with white wing-tips. He looked more like a professional golfer down on his luck than a literary man of acknowledged stature. Which, Eliot mused, was more representative of Barmuenster's intellectual configuration—his sartorial preferences or the greasy paper bags under his elbows? It was impossible to decide.

Firkin Barmuenster kept reading. The typist went on smacking imaginary flies. Eliot waited.

"I confess," Firkin Barmuenster said slowly, raising his lids to confront the pallid face of the poet, "that I didn't expect anything this good. I like it, my boy, I like it!" He hesitated, gurgling slightly, like a man who has given up pipe-smoking once and for all. And indeed, Eliot spied two or three well-chewed abandoned pipes in the tumbler that served as pencil-holder; the pencils, too, were much-bitten. "You know our policy on fee, of course. After we get finished paying Clara and the rent and the sweeping up and the price of an occasional banana, there's not much left for the writer,

George—only the glory. I know that's all right with you, I know you'll understand that what we're chiefly interested in is preserving the sanctity of the writer's text. The text is holy, it's holy writ, that's what it is. We'll set aside the title for a while, and put our minds to it later. What's the matter, George? You look speechless with gratitude."

"I never hoped, sir—I mean, I *did* hope, but I didn't think—"

"Let's get down to business, then. The idea is excellent, first-rate, but there's just a drop too much repetition. You owned up to that yourself a minute ago. For instance, I notice that you say, over here,

> *In the room the women come and go*
> *Talking of Michelangelo,*

and then, over *here*, on the next page, you say it again."

"That's meant to be a kind of *refrain*," Eliot offered modestly.

"Yes, *I* see that, but our subscribers don't have *time* to read things twice. We've got a new breed of reader nowadays. Maybe back, say, in 1896 they had the leisure to read the same thing twice, but our modern folks are on the run. I see you're quite a bit addicted to the sin of redundancy. Look over here, where you've got

> *'I am Lazarus, come back from the dead,*
> *Come back to tell you all, I shall tell you all'—*
> *If one, settling a pillow by her head,*
> *Should say: 'That is not what I meant at all;*
> *That is not it, at all.'*

Very nice, but that reference to the dead coming back is just too iffy. I'd drop that whole part. The pillow, too. You don't need that pillow; it doesn't do a thing *for* you. And anyhow you've said 'all' four times in a single place. That won't do. It's sloppy. And who uses the same word to make a rhyme? Sloppy!" Barmuenster iterated harshly, bringing his fist down heavily on the next banana, peeled and naked, ready for the eating. "Now this line down here, where you put in

> *No! I am not Prince Hamlet, nor was meant to be,*

well, the thing to do about that is let it go. It's no use dragging in
the Bard every time you turn around. You can't get away with that
sort of free ride."

"I thought," Eliot murmured, wondering (ahead of his time)
whether banana-craving could somehow be linked to pipe-
deprivation, "it would help show how Prufrock feels about
himself—"

"Since you're saying he *doesn't* feel like Hamlet, why put Hamlet *in*? We can't waste words, not in 1911 anyhow. Now up here, top
of the page, you speak of

> *a pair of ragged claws*
> *scuttling across the floor of silent seas.*

Exactly what kind of claws are they? Lobster claws? Crab? Precision, my boy, precision!"

"I just meant to keep it kind of general, for the atmosphere—"

"If you *mean* a crustacean, *say* a crustacean. At *The New Shoelace*
we don't deal in mere metonymy."

"Feeling is a kind of meaning, too. Metaphor, image, allusion,
lyric form, melody, rhythm, tension, irony, above all the objective
correlative—" But poor Tom Eliot broke off lamely as he saw the
older man begin to redden.

"Tricks! Wool-pullers! Don't try to tell Firkin Barmuenster
about the English language. I've been editing *The New Shoelace*
since before you were born, and I think by now I can be trusted
to know how to clean up a page of words. I like a clean page, I've
explained that. I notice you have a whole lot of question marks all
over, and they go up and down the same ground again and again.
You've got *So how should I presume?* and then you've got *And how
should I presume?* and after that you've got *And should I presume?*
You'll just have to decide on how you want that and then keep to
it. People aren't going to make allowances for you forever, you
know, just because you're painfully young. And you shouldn't put
in so many question marks anyhow. You should use nice clean de-
clarative sentences. Look at this, for instance, just look at what a
mess you've got here—

Helping T. S. Eliot Write Better

I grow old . . . I grow old . . .
I shall wear the bottoms of my trousers rolled.

Shall I part my hair behind? Do I dare to eat a peach?
I shall wear white flannel trousers and walk upon the beach.
I have heard the mermaids singing, each to each.

That won't *do* in a discussion of the aging process. There you go repeating yourself again, and then that question business cropping up, and 'beach' and 'each' stuck in just for the rhyme. Anybody can see it's just for the rhyme. All that jingling gets the reader impatient. Too much baggage. Too many *words*. Our new breed of reader wants something else. Clarity. Straightforwardness. Getting to the point without a whole lot of nervous distraction. Tell me, George, are you serious about writing? You really want to become a writer some day?"

The poet swallowed hard, the blood beginning to pound in his head. "It's my life," Eliot answered simply.

"And you're serious about getting into print?"

"I'd give my eyeteeth," admitted Tom.

"All right. Then you leave it to me. What you need is a good clean job of editing. Clara!" he called.

The fringed typist glanced up, as sharply as before.

"Do we have some white space under any of next issue's articles?"

"Plenty, F.B. There's a whole slew of white at the bottom of that piece on Alice Roosevelt's new blue gown."

"Good. George," the editor pronounced, holding out his viscid hand in kindness to the obscure young poet, "leave your name and address with Clara and in a couple of weeks we'll send you a copy of yourself in print. If you weren't an out-of-towner I'd ask you to come pick it up, to save on the postage. But I know what a thrill real publication in a bona fide magazine is for an aspiring novice like yourself. I recollect the days of my own youth, if you'll excuse the cliché. Careful on the elevator—sometimes the rope gets stuck on that big nail down near the fifth floor, and you get a bounce right up those eyeteeth of yours. Oh, by the way—any suggestions for the title?"

The blood continued to course poundingly in young Tom Eliot's temples. He was overwhelmed by a bliss such as he had never before known. Print! "I really think I still like 'The Love Song of J. Alfred Prufrock,'" his joy gave him the courage to declare.

"Too long. Too oblique. Not apropos. Succinctness! You've heard of that old maxim, 'So that he who runs may read?' Well, my personal credo is: *So that he who shuns may heed.* That's what *The New Shoelace* is about. George, I'm about to put you on the map with all those busy folks who shun versifying. Leave the title to me. And don't you worry about that precious Voice of yours, George—the text is holy writ, I promise you."

Gratefully, Tom Eliot returned to Boston in high glee. And within two weeks he had fished out of his mailbox the apotheosis of his tender years: the earliest known publication of "The Love Song of J. Alfred Prufrock."

It is a melancholy truth that nowadays every company president can recite the slovenly unedited opening of this justly famous item—

> *Let us go then, you and I,*
> *When the evening is spread out against the sky*
> *Like a patient etherized upon a table;*
> *Let us go, through certain half-deserted streets,*
> *The muttering retreats*
> *Of restless nights in one-night cheap hotels, etc.*

—but these loose and wordy lines were not always so familiar, or so easily accessible. Time and fate have not been kind to Tom Eliot (who did, by the way, one day cease being painfully young): for some reason the slovenly unedited version has made its way in the world more successfully during the last eighty years than Barmuenster's conscientious efforts at perfection. Yet the great Firkin Barmuenster, that post-fin-de-siècle editor renowned for meticulous concision and passionate precision, for launching many a new literary career, and for the improvement of many a flaccid and redundant writing style, was—though the fact has so far not yet reached the larger reading public—T. S. Eliot's earliest supporter and discoverer.

For the use of bibliographers and, above all, for the delectation of poetry lovers, the complete text of "The Love Song of J. Alfred Prufrock" as it appeared in *The New Shoelace* of April 17, 1911, follows:

THE MIND OF MODERN MAN
by
George Eliot

(Editor's Note: A new contributor, Eliot is sure to be heard from in the future. Out of respect for the author's fine ideas, however, certain purifications have been made in the original submission on the principle that, in the Editor's words, GOOD WRITING KNOWS NO TRICKS, SO THAT HE WHO SHUNS MAY HEED.)

On a high-humidity evening in October, shortly after a rainfall, a certain nervous gentleman undertakes a visit, passing through a bad section of town. Arriving at his destination, the unhappy man overhears ladies discussing an artist well-known in history (Michelangelo Buonarroti, 1475–1564, Italian sculptor, painter, architect, and poet). Our friend contemplates his personal diffidence, his baldness, his suit and tie, and the fact that he is rather underweight. He notes with some dissatisfaction that he is usually addressed in conventional phrases. He cannot make a decision. He believes his life has not been well-spent; indeed, he feels himself to be no better than a mere arthropod (of the shelled aquatic class, which includes lobsters, shrimps, crabs, barnacles, and wood lice). He has been subjected to many social hours timidly drinking tea, for, though he secretly wishes to impress others, he does not know how to do so. He realizes he is an insignificant individual, with a small part to play in the world. He is distressed that he will soon be eligible for an old age home, and considers the advisability of a fruit diet and of permitting himself a greater relaxation in dress, as well as perhaps covering his bald spot. Thus, in low spirits, in a markedly irrational frame of mind, he imagines he is encountering certain mythological females, and in his own words he makes it clear that he is doubtless in need of the aid of a reliable friend or kindly minister. (As are, it goes without saying, all of us.)

AGAINST
MODERNITY

Annals of the Temple
1918–1927

A CENTURY, like any entrenched institution, runs on inertia and is inherently laggard. Even when commanded by the calendar, it will not easily give up the ghost. The turn of the century, as the wistful phrase has it, hardly signifies the brisk swing of a gate on its hinge: a century turns, rather, like a rivulet—a silky, lazy, unwitting flow around a silent bend. Whatever the twenty-first century (seemingly only minutes away) may bring, we, entering it, will go on being what we are: creatures born into, and molded and muddied by, the twentieth.

And the twentieth, too, did not properly begin with the demise of the nineteenth. When the fabled Armory Show introduced modern art to New York in 1913, the American cultural establishment (to use a term typically ours, not theirs) was in the governing hands of men born before the Civil War—men who were marked by what Santayana, as early as 1911, had already condemned as "the genteel tradition." Apart from the unjust condescensions of hindsight, and viewed in the not-so-easily-scorned light of its own standards, what *was* the genteel tradition? Its adherents, after all, did not know themselves to be pre-modernist; they did not know that a volcanic alteration of taste and expression was about to consume the century; they did not know that irony and pastiche and parody and a conscious fever of innovation-through-rupture would overcome notions of nobility, spirituality, continuity, harmony, uncomplicated patriotism, romanticized classicism. It did not occur to them that the old patterns were threadbare, or could be repudiated on grounds of exhaustion.

To be able to say what the men of the genteel tradition (its constituents were nearly all men) did know, and what they saw themselves as, and what they in fact were, would lead us directly to the sublimely conceived fellowship they established to embody their ideals—a kind of latterday temple to the Muses. And the word "temple" is apt: it calls up an alabaster palace on a hill; an elite priesthood; ceremonial devotions pursued in a serious though lyrical frame of mind—a resolute thoughtfulness saturated in notions of beauty and virtue, and turned from the trivial, the frivolous, the ephemeral. The name these aspirants gave to their visionary society—a working organization, finally, with a flesh-and-blood membership and headquarters in New York—was the American Academy of Arts and Letters.

The cornerstone of what was to become the Academy's permanent home, a resplendent Venetian Renaissance edifice just off Riverside Drive on West 155th Street, was laid on November 19, 1921, by Marshal Ferdinand Foch of France. The commander-in-chief of the Allied forces in the First World War, Foch was summoned to wield a ritual trowel not only as the hero of the recent victory over the Kaiser, but—more gloriously still—as an emissary of French cultural prestige. The nimbus of power that followed him from Paris to this plot of freshly broken ground along the remote northern margins of Manhattan was kindled as much by his membership in the French Academy as by his battlefield triumphs.

The venerable French Academy, founded by Cardinal Richelieu to maintain the purity of the French language, and limited to forty "Immortals," had preceded its New World counterpart (or would-be counterpart) by some two and a half centuries. Though this august company of scholars and men of letters was to serve as inspiration and aristocratic model, American democratic principles demanded a wider roster based on a bicameral system: hence membership in the American Academy was open to as many as fifty, and these fifty were selected by ballot from the two hundred and fifty distinguished authors, painters, sculptors, architects, and composers of the National Institute of Arts and Letters, the lower (and older) body. And while the "chairs" of the French Academy were phantom chairs—metaphoric, platonic—American pragmatism (and one Mrs. Cochran Bowen, who donated the requisite five thousand dollars) supplied *real* chairs, with arms and backs of dark polished wood, each with a plaque for its occupant's name.

The homegrown Richelieu of this grand structure of mind and marble was Robert Underwood Johnson, a powerful magazine editor and tireless poet who, though not precisely the organization's founder, was present at the Academy's earliest meetings, and as Permanent Secretary was its dominating spirit for the first three decades. In 1920 he disappeared, temporarily, having been appointed United States Ambassador to Italy. A 1922 newspaper photograph of Johnson—occasioned by a dispute with the Internal Revenue Department over unpaid taxes on ambassadorial meals and lodgings—shows a determined elderly gentleman with a steady yet relentless eye and a rather fierce pince-nez, the ribbon of which flows down over a full white beard and high collar. Unfortunately, no mouth is visible; it would be instructive to see the lips that so often speechified at Academy events, or adorned the hour with original verse. In still another portrait—a wood engraving by Timothy Cole, artist and Academy member—the Johnsonian mouth is again concealed under a cloud of furry whiskers, but the stiff cravat, scimitar nose, straight spine, and erect head are eloquent enough. They declare a fine facsimile of a Roman bust, attentive to what is noble and what is not—the face and figure of a man of established importance, a man who knows his worth: editor of *The Century*, Ambassador to Italy, Director of the Hall of Fame, Secretary of the American Academy of Arts and Letters.

Above all it is the face and figure of the nineteenth century, when the ideal of the publicly Noble could still stir the Western world. Together with the Harmonious, the Noble spoke in lofty

statuary, in the balanced configurations of painting and music, in
the white pilasters of heirloom architecture—but nowhere more
melodiously than in the poetry that descended (though somewhat
frayed by overhandling) from Keats.

The cornerstone affixed by Marshal Foch—in high-laced boots
and full uniform—on that rainy November afternoon in 1921 was
a hollow repository. In it Brander Matthews, Chancellor of the
Academy and a professor of literature at Columbia University,
placed numerous historic articles and documents—congratulatory
messages from the President of the United States, from the Governor of New York, from the Academies of Belgium, Rome, Spain,
and Brazil; papers recording the Special Symposium on Diction;
"Utterances by Members of the Academy Concerning the War of
1914–1918," bound in purple; replicas and photographs of medals,
including one presented to Marshal Foch by the American Numis-
matic Society (located next door); minutes of meetings; commemorative addresses; and a holographic copy of a dedicatory poem by
Robert Underwood Johnson:

The Temple

If this be but a house, whose stone we place,
  Better the prayer unbreathed, the music mute
  Ere it be stifled in the rifted lute;
Better had been withheld those hands of grace,
Undreamed the dream that was this moment's base
  Through nights that did the empty days refute.
  Accurs'd the fig-tree if it bear no fruit;
Only the flower sanctifies the vase.

No, 'tis a temple—where the mind may kneel
  And worship Beauty changeless and divine;
  Where the sage Past may consecrate the stole
Of Truth's new priest, the Future; where the peal
  Of organ voices down the human line
  Shall sound the diapason of the soul.

And there it was: the echoing legacy of Keats. But Keats's season of mists and mellow fruitfulness had long since passed into fog
and desiccation; the Romantic exhalations of the last century—a
century more than twenty years gone—could not be kept going

by pumping up a useless bellows that had run out of breath. The cornerstone may have received the pious mimicry of "The Temple" as its chief treasure, but modernism (one of its names was Ezra Pound) was pounding at the Temple's gates, shattering the sage Past and slighting the old forms of Beauty.

The Temple was not unaware of these shocking new vibrations: it derided and dismissed them. In 1925, in an address before the Academy-Institute (as the two closely allied bodies came to be called), three years after the publication of *The Waste Land*, Robert Underwood Johnson pointed to T. S. Eliot as one of the "prominent apostles" of "this so-called modern American poetry," and scolded him for prosiness and lack of taste and humor, while praising "the dignity and beauty of Landor's invocation to an English brook." (Walter Savage Landor, it might be noted, was born in 1775 and died in 1864, when Johnson was eleven years old.) Quoting lines from Marianne Moore, Johnson asked, "What is the remedy for this disease?" "The Academy's chief influence," he concluded, "will come from what and whom it recognizes, what and whom it praises, and what and whom it puts forth."

In the extraordinary literary decade that followed the Great War, the Academy neither recognized nor praised nor put forth nor took in T. S. Eliot, Ezra Pound, Marianne Moore, William Carlos Williams, Hart Crane, Wallace Stevens, Conrad Aiken, H.D., Louise Bogan, John Crowe Ransom, or E. E. Cummings—revolutionaries, in their varying degrees, of voice, theme, and line. Not since Whitman had there been such a conflagration of fresh sound in American verse; it engulfed the poets of the Harlem Renaissance, Langston Hughes and Jean Toomer among them, and burned brilliantly, though in another language, among the American Yiddish Imagists of the *In Zikh* movement farther downtown. Beauty, it seemed, was turning out to be neither changeless nor divine: it could take the form of the Brooklyn Bridge, and manifest itself in idioms and accents that an unreceptive Temple, immaculately devoted to the difference between "can" and "may" (the Academy's task, Johnson said, was to preserve this distinction), might be oblivious to at best, or at worst recoil from.

Established in 1898 as an outgrowth of the American Social Science Association, the National Institute of Arts and Letters flourished alone until 1904, when it gave birth to the American Academy of Arts and Letters, its hierarchical superior. The Academy was incorporated by an Act of Congress on April 17, 1916; its first president, who served from 1908 to 1920, was William Dean Howells, one of the few early Academicians whose names are recognizable to later generations. *The Rise of Silas Lapham* may not be much read today—not, say, as *The Great Gatsby* is read, zealously and regularly—but Howells (who was long ago dropped from routine high school curricula) is nevertheless permanently lodged in American literary history. He was succeeded as president (from his death in 1920 to Sloane's death in 1928) by William Milligan Sloane, a professor of history at Columbia University, the author of a mammoth four-volume *Life of Napoleon Bonaparte* and of seven other equally ambitious works. A public presence—an eminence—in his time, Sloane must now be researched in the *Dictionary of American Biography.*

And so it is with numerous others. The cycle of generations dims if not eclipses even the most illustrious, and if an examination of the Academy-Institute's membership reveals nothing else, it surely affirms the melancholy wisdom of Ecclesiastes. Yet one need not go to the Preacher to learn how there is "no remembrance of former things"; sometimes biblical perspective comes without waiting so much as a day. In 1923—the very year the Academy moved into its just-completed Renaissance palace—Burton Rascoe, a journalist with the *New York Tribune*, targeted the Temple's newest anointed: "[W]hen Mr. Johnson handed me a list of the fledglings upon whom the organization had just conferred harps and wings and other eternal impediments, I was even more startled to observe that scarcely one of the twenty outstanding literary personages of America was included, but a whole roster of nobodies whose careers were so limited and obscure that I had to spend an hour or so in the morgue after I got back to the office to find out what they had done or written." Rascoe's literary nobodies of 1923 included John Spencer Bassett, James Bucklin Bishop, Owen David, Burton J. Hendrick, Rollo Ogden—names that, if they meant nothing to Rascoe, are merest dust to us. But Eugene

O'Neill was on that same list, and Don Marquis (the celebrated progenitor of Archie the Cockroach); and if Rascoe—himself reduced now to one of the nobodies—had looked back a few years, from 1918 on (i.e., from the end of the war), he would have encountered literary somebodies we still remember, and sometimes even read: James Gibbon Huneker, Edgar Lee Masters, Irving Babbitt, John Erskine, Joseph Hergesheimer, and Bernard Berenson.

Still, the forgotten Burton Rascoe is not mistaken about the forgettable among his own contemporaries, or about the deadly absence of "outstanding literary personages." During the Academy's third decade of life—the vital cultural period between 1918 and 1927—the single major American writer to attain membership was Edith Wharton. (A belated elevation that took place in 1926, after an effort toward securing the admission of women finally prevailed over an acrimonious opposition.) Whereas in the world beyond the Temple—to confine our inquiry at this moment to literature only—there was an innovative ferment so astounding (and exhilarating) that no other segment of the twentieth century can match it. Consider: 1918 saw the publication of Willa Cather's *My Ántonia*, Lytton Strachey's *Eminent Victorians*, the first installments of James Joyce's *Ulysses*, volumes by Rebecca West and H. L. Mencken; *The Education of Henry Adams* won the Pulitzer Prize; the Theater Guild was founded in New York; in Germany, the Dada movement began; in Russia, Aleksandr Blok was writing poetry in praise of the Bolshevik Revolution (without suspecting that its dissolution eight decades later would draw equal praise).

The following year brought *Winesburg, Ohio*, by Sherwood Anderson; *Jurgen*, by James Branch Cabell; *The Arrow of Gold*, by Joseph Conrad; *La Symphonie pastorale*, by André Gide; *Demian*, by Hermann Hesse; *The Moon and Sixpence*, by Somerset Maugham—and Carl Sandburg won the Pulitzer. Finally, the next eight years—1920 to 1927—introduced a torrent of works by F. Scott Fitzgerald, John Galsworthy, Katherine Mansfield, Max Beerbohm, H. G. Wells, Sigrid Undset, John Dos Passos, Aldous Huxley, D. H. Lawrence, George Bernard Shaw, Luigi Pirandello, Bertolt Brecht, T. S. Eliot, Sinclair Lewis, François Mauriac, Virginia Woolf, Stefan Zweig, Rainer Maria Rilke, Italo Svevo, Robert

Frost, Colette, S. Ansky, E. M. Forster, Edna Ferber, Thomas Mann, Maxwell Anderson, Michael Arlen, Theodore Dreiser, Maxim Gorky, Franz Kafka, Gertrude Stein, Edwin Arlington Robinson, Ernest Hemingway, W. E. B. Du Bois, T. E. Lawrence, Sean O'Casey, William Faulkner, Jean Cocteau, William Butler Yeats, Thornton Wilder, Henri Bergson. Mixed though these writers are in theme, genre, nationality, and degree of achievement, they represent, on the literary side, what we mean when we speak of the Twenties—an era staggering in its deliverance from outworn voices and overly familiar modes and moods. Not all were "experimental"; indeed, most were not; but all claimed an idiosyncratic distinction between their own expectations of language and art and the expectations of the author of "The Temple."

Some of the Americans among them did finally gain admission to the Academy-Institute, but not without opposition. To combat the new streams of expression, Harrison Smith Morris—a writer elected to the Institute in 1908—proposed a Resolution:

> The National Institute of Arts and Letters in its long established office of upholder of Taste and Beauty in Arts and Letters in America, welcomes the approach of a return to the standards made sacred by tradition and by the genius of the great periods of the past.

> The National Institute feels that the time has arrived to distinguish the good from the bad in the Arts, and to urge those who have loved the literature and painting that are accepted by the winnowing hand of time to turn away from the Falsehoods of this period and again to embrace only the genuine expressions of man's genius.

> And the National Institute calls upon all those who write or speak on this essential subject of our culture as a nation, to ask their hearers to join in abhorrence of the offences, and to insist on the integrity of our arts.

Though the archives of the Academy do not yield information on how the members voted (or at least I have been unable to uncover the results), the Resolution itself was in profound consonance with the views held by the Permanent Secretary, Robert

Underwood Johnson himself. And Johnson in effect ran things, despite the status of the men at the top—Howells, then Sloane, later Nicholas Murray Butler; Johnson was the Academy's primary engine. A first-rate organizer and administrator, he single-handedly acquired an endowment for the Academy—or, rather, he acquired the friendship and loyalty of Archer Milton Huntington, an extraordinarily wealthy donor with a generous temperament and a serious interest in Spanish culture. Huntington, a railway magnate's son, owned the empty plot of land on West 155th Street (across the street from a cemetery), and offered it free; he also pledged $100,000 in endowment funds if enough money could be raised by 1919 to build on the land.

Spurred on by this promise, Johnson went in zealous pursuit of the extra money, but came back with empty pockets. Huntington extended the deadline; still no other large-scale benefactor appeared. Huntington withdrew his terms and supplied the building funds himself; in addition, he showered the Academy with periodic gifts ($475,000 in 1923, $100,000 in 1927, $600,000 in 1929), so that within a very short span a membership that was only recently being dunned for dues found itself cushioned and cosseted by prosperity.

At the annual meeting of 1925, Johnson spoke of Huntington as "a permanent friend of the Academy who desires to remain permanently anonymous." This was certainly true; yet Huntington—who quickly became a member of the Academy, and whose second wife, a sculptor, was herself eventually elected—was not without intimations of immortality. In an autographed poem dedicated to the Academy and entitled "Genius," and in a style reminiscent of Johnson's own, he wrote in praise of "this oriflamme of glory":

> High mystery prophetic that men cry!
> The splendid diadem of hearts supreme,
> Who shape reality from hope's vast dream
> And gild with flame new pantheons in the sky!
> Thus are we led to nobly raise on high
> An edifice of deeds that may redeem
> The lowliness of being, 'neath the gleam
> Of mists all colorless where life must lie.

(There was a follow-up stanza as well.)

Huntington was Johnson's organizational masterstroke—a funding triumph with recognizably lofty verbal credentials, capable of gilding new pantheons with cash. But Johnson's executive instincts pulled off a second administrative coup—in the shape of Mrs. Grace Vanamee, who was enlisted as the Permanent Secretary's permanent deputy in the fall of 1915. A widow in her forties, Mrs. Vanamee was a kind of robust Johnsonian reverberation: if he was exuberantly efficient, so was she; if he was determined that no concern, however minuscule, should go unresolved, so was she. Mrs. Vanamee was, in brief, an unflagging enthusiast. She is reputed to have been a woman of large dimensions (though there is no one alive who can claim to have set eyes on her), and even larger energies. Like Johnson, she could successfully concentrate on several activities at once. On the side, so to speak, Johnson oversaw New York University's Hall of Fame; Mrs. Vanamee directed the Organization of Soldiers' Families of America. A public lecturer herself, she was also chair of the Republican Women's State Speakers' Bureau and founder of the Women's National Republican Club; during the war she served as secretary of the Italian War Relief Committee, for which she earned a medal from the Italian Red Cross.

Her career as celebrated Academy factotum (a combination of executive director and chief housekeeper) began in a "sordid little office" at 70 Fifth Avenue, equipped with an ancient second-hand typewriter bought for twenty dollars. Huntington soon provided a more suitable venue, a building he owned on West Eighty-first Street, which was rapidly refurbished with offices, an auditorium, and living quarters for Mrs. Vanamee. There was, in addition, a President's Room decorated with a mahogany desk and green leather chairs and fine carpeting, at a cost of fifteen hundred dollars. Only two years later, when the West 155th Street edifice was ready to be occupied, all this would be dismantled.

But in the meantime, Mrs. Vanamee was in charge of caring for the now lavishly outfitted interim building—though not alone. A certain Frank P. Crasto emerges here as her indispensable assistant and sidekick; it is possible that he may represent our history's love-interest. (The archives, it goes without saying, are silent on this point; but in Crasto's obituary, intimacy is given a delicate license; he is described as Mrs. Vanamee's "foster-brother.") Mrs. Vanamee's early widowhood was enlivened by an open and famously zippy character, and her correspondence with this or that member of the Academy occasionally bordered on the flirtatious. In the middle of so much dense Victorian formality, she was even capable of an indiscreet anecdote: if not for Mrs. Vanamee, posterity would still be in the dark about the Pinching of the Trowel. In her account of Marshal Foch and the West 155th Street building's cornerstone ceremony—"President Sloane almost white with excitement, Mr. Johnson radiant because his dreams had come true"—she describes how "the little Maréchal was tired and had to hurry away, and as he did so to our great amusement and consternation we saw that he had absent-mindedly thrust the lovely little silver trowel into his hip pocket, but we never saw it again."

This cheery neglect of reverence for the great French military leader did not extend to Frank P. Crasto, himself a military man. Mrs. Vanamee identified him as "a Captain in the Reserves [who] knows what it is to inspect buildings and equipment and to maintain discipline as well as order and cleanliness," and added, with the esteem due such things, that "he understands all about printing, and is an expert proofreader." He was also found to be useful in handling the heavy work. Captain Crasto became Major Crasto, and Major Crasto was promoted to Colonel Crasto—ascending titles that Mrs. Vanamee noted with veneration. His maintenance responsibilities were perhaps less lofty than his officer status would suggest—at the Academy Board meeting of May 11, 1921, for instance, he reported that one hundred and thirty-eight of the three hundred and ten light bulbs at West Eighty-first Street were out. Eventually he was raised to the post of Librarian; but his rise in Mrs. Vanamee's affections had evidently occurred long before. In times of sickness they spelled each other. In 1923, when she was seriously ill in a Brooklyn hospital (but she lived until 1946), all inquiries concerning her condition were directed to the Colonel, and it was she who in 1925 packed him off on a recuperative steamer trip to New Orleans after a heart episode: "there is nothing pressing at the Academy," she urged. One gets the inescapable impression of a pair of turtle doves under the Temple's eaves.

Mrs. Vanamee, the Colonel, and, of course, the Permanent Secretary all moved on together to West 155th Street. Huntington carried out his plan to sell the West Eighty-first Street building (he intended to use the profits as endowment funds) despite pressure from Witter Bynner of the Poetry Society of America, who hoped to rent it as a meeting place for "all the Poetry Societies of America." The idea was discussed by the Academy Board early in 1922 and quickly rejected. Brander Matthews dismissed such a convention of poets as "a large body of very small people," and Robert Underwood Johnson declined to place "the Academy's stamp of approval on the lack of standards of the Poetry Society." (Its membership at the time included Stephen Vincent Benét, Carl Sandburg, and Edwin Arlington Robinson, all of whom Johnson scorned.)

It was in this same year that Sinclair Lewis, elected to Institute membership, angrily rejected it, unwilling to place *his* stamp of approval on the Academy or any part of it. Seven years later, accepting the Nobel Prize for Literature before the Swedish Academy in Stockholm, he excoriated its American counterpart: "It does not represent literary America of today. It represents only Henry Wadsworth Longfellow." (And in 1979 Witter Bynner had *his* revenge, albeit posthumously, with the establishment of the Academy's Witter Bynner Prize for Poetry.) The Academy was offended by Lewis but unruffled. The Board went on to review a roster of quotations that might be appropriate to stand as a frieze across the brow of the new building. Aperçus by Cicero, Lucian, Pericles, Plato, Aristotle, and Emerson were proposed, none of which satisfied—whereupon Johnson remarked that a member might be moved (he may have been thinking of himself) to write something original. The wording for the frieze was not determined until 1924, a year after the opening of the building. Brander Matthews made the selection: HOLD HIGH THE FLAMING TORCH FROM AGE TO AGE. When the architects asked for a second quotation, Matthews supplied them with ALL ARTS ARE ONE ALL BRANCHES ON ONE TREE. (The sources for both lines are unknown.)

The estimated cost of the finished Temple as presented to the Academy by the architects—McKim, Mead, and White, all three of whom were members—was $380,223.04, though the final bill probably exceeded half a million. The doors were heavy bronze. An early sketch of the façade before completion shows a pair of neoclassical sculptures in embrasures, and while these draped female figures, goddesses or Muses, at length vanished from the plans and were never executed, their spirit stuck fast. Stanford White was the designer of New York University's neoclassical campus on University Heights, and Charles F. McKim presided over Columbia's Beaux Arts buildings on Morningside Heights; both were visionaries of an ideal acropolis conceived as an echo (or rebirth) of older cities grown legendary through literature and art.

It was the same echo that had sounded in Robert Underwood Johnson's ear since his days at Earlham College, a small Quaker institution in Indiana that emphasized Latin and "the human element of Virgil, Horace, Tacitus, Cicero." Even the college-boy jokes were in Latin: a classroom was dubbed *Nugipolyloquidium*, "a place of talkers of nonsense." Out of all this came the lingering faith that the classical is the eternal, and that the past, because it *is* the past, holds a sacred and permanent power—a view that differs from the historical sense, with its awareness (in contradistinction to Truth and Beauty) of evolution, displacement, violence and oppression, migration of populations, competing intellectual movements, the decline and fall of even contemporary societies and cultures. The achievement of such a serene outlook will depend on one's distance from strikes, riots, destitution, foreign eruptions, the effects of prejudice, immigrants pressing in at Ellis Island, and all the rest.

Inland Earlham in 1867, when Johnson was a freshman there, is deservedly called "tranquil"—"Tranquil Days at Earlham" is a chapter in Johnson's autobiographical *Remembered Yesterdays*, self-published in 1923 (just when Marshal Foch was pocketing the silver trowel); and tranquility was the goal and soul of Johnson's artistic understanding. "We were charmed by the mountain scenery of the Gulf of Corinth, every peak and vale of which is haunted by mythological associations," he writes in a chapter entitled "Delight and Humor of Foreign Travel." "The Bay of Salamis gave us a thrill and at Eleusis we seemed to come in close touch with classic days, for here was the scene of the still unexplained Eleusinian mysteries." Living Greeks—at their rustic best, since "the urban Greek is undersized and unimpressive"—are admired solely as an ornamental allusion: "Some of them resembled fine Italian types, one or two reminding me of the elder Salvini," an Italian tragedian. More gratifying than these Greeks in the flesh are the crucial landmarks: "I stayed up until one o'clock at night to catch sight of the beacon on the 'Leucadian steep' which marks the spot from which Sappho is reputed to have thrown herself." "One may well imagine that three fourths of the time we spent in Athens was passed on the Acropolis."

This was the sensibility that dreamed and labored over and built the American Academy of Arts and Letters. Johnson came to this task—this passion—after forty years at *The Century*, the magazine that succeeded *Scribner's Monthly*. Its editor-in-chief was Richard Watson Gilder, a poet hugely overpraised by his contemporaries ("An echo of Dantean mysticism . . . He wanders in the highest realms of spiritual poetry") and wholly dismissed by their descendants. As editor-cum-poet, he was uniquely qualified to be mentor and model for Johnson, whom Gilder appointed associate editor in 1881. Gilder's own mentor and model was Edmund Clarence Stedman, himself a mediocre poet of the idealist school; both Stedman and Gilder were Academy members. Although Alfred Kazin (a present-day Academician) describes Gilder as "a very amiable man whom some malicious fortune set up as a perfect symbol of all that the new writers [of the Twenties] were to detest," he was, for Johnson and his generation, the perfect symbol of all that belles-lettres and an elevated civilization required.

Nor were Johnson and his generation misled. *The Century* was the most powerful literary periodical of its time, a genuine influence in the formation of American letters. In 1885, for example, the February issue alone carried—remarkably—excerpts from Mark Twain's *Huckleberry Finn*, Howells's *The Rise of Silas Lapham*, and James's *The Bostonians*. Gilder was a believer in purity of theme, which drew him away from certain subjects; Johnson was Gilder's even more cautious copy. In 1904, when, despite the editorial risk, Gilder wanted to publish Edith Wharton—he was shrewd enough to see that she was "on the eve of a great popular success"—Johnson demurred: Wharton had written stories about divorce. At Gilder's death in 1909 Johnson took over as editor-in-chief. The decline of *The Century* is usually attributed, at least in part, to his inability to respond to changing public taste and expectation. The trustees, at any rate, found him inflexible; he resigned in 1913.

He was then sixty years old, in full and effective vigor, with a strong activist bent and an affinity for citizenly service. He was an advocate, a man of causes. At *The Century* he had promoted the conservation of forests and was instrumental in getting Congressional sanction for the creation of Yosemite National Park. It was he who persuaded a coolly reticent General Ulysses S. Grant to set down an emotional memoir of the battle of Shiloh. As secretary of a committee of authors and publishers, Johnson lobbied for international copyright and fought against the pirating of foreign books. His ardor spilled over into nine volumes of verse, all self-published, on subjects both sublime and civic, often interwoven: "The Vision of Gettysburg," "The Price of Honor: The Colombian Indemnity," "The New Slavery (On the Expatriation by Germany of Civil Populations of Belgium)," "Armenia," "Henrik Ibsen, The Tribute of an Idealist," "To the Spirit of Luther: On Learning of the Reported Appeal of Germany to Matrons and Maidens to Give Themselves 'Officially' to the Propagation of the Race, Under Immunity from the Law." There are poems on the Dreyfus Affair: "The Keeper of the Sword (Apropos of the Dreyfus Trial at Rennes)" and "To Dreyfus Vindicated." The talent may have been middling, but the good will, and the prophetic vigilance, were mammoth.

If, as Emerson insists, the shipbuilder is the ship, then Robert Underwood Johnson was, long before its founding, the American Academy of Arts and Letters. There can be no useful history of the Academy that fails to contemplate Johnson's mind. Whatever ignited his enthusiasm, whatever struck him as repugnant—these formed the mind of the Academy. It was not that Johnson was dictatorial—on the contrary, he was elaborately courtly, and punctilious as to protocol. (As Permanent Secretary, he sent himself a deferential letter announcing his election to the Academy, and, with equal deference, wrote back to accept the honor.) He did no violence to the opinion of others; rather, his opinion was generally the opinion of the membership, and vice versa. It may have been the Muses themselves who nurtured such unanimity; or else it was the similarity of background of these cultivated gentlemen, similarly educated, similarly situated in society, each with his triplet of rhythmically interchangeable names, all of them patriots, yet all looking toward an older Europe for continuity of purpose— with one urgent European exception.

The exception was Germany in the Great War. The Academy, most notably in the person of Robert Underwood Johnson, threw itself indefatigably into the war effort against Germany, contributing $100,000 to Italy and over one hundred ambulances presented in the name of the poets of America. Though the hostilities had come to an end with the November armistice of 1918, the Academy's hostility remained white-hot into the following year, with the publication of its *World War Utterances*. Here patriotism overreached itself into unrestrained fury. In an essay called "The Incredible Cruelty of the Teutons," William Dean Howells—the most benignly moderate of novelists—asked: "Can anyone say what the worst wickedness of the Germans has been? If you choose one there are always other crimes which contest your choice. We used at first to fix the guilt of them upon the Kaiser, but event by event we have come to realize that no man or order of men can pervert a whole people without their complicity."

Luminary after luminary joined the cry, under titles such as "Can Peace Make Us Forget? A Plea for the Ostracism of All Things German"; "The Shipwreck of Kultur"; "The Crime of the *Lusitania*"; "Germany's Shame." "The nation which had invited our admiration for its *Gemütlichkeit* instantly aroused our abhorrence for its *Schrecklichkeit*," wrote Brander Matthews. And Nicholas Murray Butler, condemning Germany's "principle of world domination," compared German conquest and subjection of peoples to Alexander the Great, the legions of Rome, Charlemagne, Bonaparte, and, finally, "the Hebrews of old." (As the author of Columbia University's notorious and long-lasting Jewish quota, Butler—quite apart from his Academy activities, where such views were never expressed—apparently also feared conquest by later Hebrews.) Woodrow Wilson, who had campaigned for the Presidency with the slogan "He kept us out of war"—to the disgust of his more belligerent colleagues at the Academy—now spoke of Germany as "throwing to the winds all scruples of humanity" while engaged in "a warfare against mankind." In his "Note on German Music and German Ideas," Horatio Parker, one of the period's nearly forgotten composers, could not resist making a plea for German music, especially Bach, Richard Strauss, and Mendelssohn ("It is as useless to deny the beauty and greatness of classical masterpieces by Germans as it is to deny the same qualities in their mountains"); nevertheless he concluded that "prejudice of the public and of officials in this country against *modern* German music is perhaps justifiable."

In these exhortations to hatred and ostracism, the Academy's impulse was no different from the anti-German clamor that was everywhere in the American street. From our distance, the bitter words may seem overreactive and hyperchauvinist. Still, reading these papers now three-quarters of a century old, one feels a curious displacement of rage—a vertiginous sense of the premature, as of an hourglass set mistakenly on its head. The sinking of the *Lusitania*, merciless act of war though it was, was not yet Auschwitz. If Howells, say, had written as he did, not in 1918 but in 1945, after the exposure of the crematoria, how would we judge his judgment? It is sometimes an oddity of history that the right thing is said at the wrong time.

And it may be that, in the third decade of its life, many right things were spoken at the Academy at the wrong time. When the war was over, Johnson turned his energies once again to the celebration of a type of high culture. And again there looked to be a displacement of timing. In 1919, race riots broke out in Chicago and a dock workers' strike hit New York; the eight-hour workday was instituted nationally; President Woodrow Wilson won the

Nobel Peace Prize and presided over the first meeting of the League of Nations in Paris; the Red Army took Omsk, Kharkov, and the Crimea; Mussolini founded the Italian fascist movement; Paderewski became Premier of Poland. Henri Bergson, Karl Barth, Ernst Cassirer, Havelock Ellis, Karl Jaspers, John Maynard Keynes, Rudolf Steiner—indelible figures—were all active in their various spheres. Short-wave radio made its earliest appearance, there was progress in sound for movies, and Einstein's theory of relativity was borne out by astrophysical experiments. Walter Gropius developed the Bauhaus in Germany and revolutionized painting, architecture, sculpture, and the industrial arts. Kandinsky, Klee, and Modigliani were at work, and Picasso designed the set of Diaghilev's *The Three Cornered Hat.* Jazz headed for Europe; the Los Angeles Symphony gave its initial concert; the Juilliard School of Music opened in New York, and the New Symphony Orchestra, conducted by Edgard Varèse, inaugurated a hearing for modern music. A nonstop flight across the Atlantic was finally accomplished. Babe Ruth hit a 587-foot home run. The Nobel Prize for Literature went to Knut Hamsun.

In short, 1919 was the beginning of a deluge of new forms, new sounds, new ventures, new arrangements in the world. And in such an hour the Academy undertook to mark the centennial of James Russell Lowell, who had died twenty-eight years before. In itself, the choice was pleasant and not inappropriate. A leading American eminence of the nineteenth century, a man of affairs as well as a man of letters, a steady opponent of slavery, Lowell was poet, critic, literary historian. He was vigorous in promoting the study of modern languages, which he taught at Harvard. He was, besides, *The Atlantic Monthly's* first editor and (with Charles Eliot Norton) a founder of *The North American Review.* He served as American ambassador to the Court of Spain, and afterward as emissary to Britain. His complete works—both verse and prose— occupy ten volumes. According to Lowell's biographer, Horace E. Scudder—member of the Institute and author of a laudatory *Encyclopaedia Britannica* article on Lowell that is virtually contemporaneous with the Academy's celebratory event—Lowell "impressed himself deeply on his generation in America, especially upon the thoughtful and scholarly class who looked upon him as their representative." Johnson unquestionably looked on Lowell as his representative; Lowell's career—poet, editor, ambassador—was an ideal template for Johnson's own.

The centennial program, subtitled "In Celebration of the Unity and Power of the Literature of the English-speaking People," was intended to emphasize the ongoing link with the Mother Country. To further this connection, invitations went out to, among others, Prime Minister Herbert Asquith, Robert Bridges (the Poet Laureate), Rudyard Kipling, James Barrie, Conan Doyle, Gilbert Chesterton, Gilbert Murray, Arthur Quiller-Couch, Edmund Gosse, Alfred Noyes, and John Galsworthy. Ambitious though this roster was (it ran after nearly every living luminary of that scepter'd isle), only the last two accepted and actually arrived—Galsworthy with the proviso that he would attend the gala luncheon *"so long as this does not entail a speech."* Stephen Leacock came with a troop of notables from Canada, and Australia was represented by one lone guest.

Still, a demonstration of the unity and power of literary Anglo-Saxonism was not, as it turned out, the whole purpose of the centennial. Nor was it precisely as an act of historic commemoration that Johnson sought to honor Lowell. On February 13, 1919, a New York newspaper, *The Evening Post,* explained: "James Russell Lowell, who was born a hundred years ago next week . . . would not have liked vers libre or modern verse in general, says Robert Underwood Johnson. . . . Mr. Johnson knew Lowell personally." The *Post* went on to quote the Permanent Secretary's reminiscences—"I remember hearing Lowell once say, when asked if he had read the latest novel, 'No, I have not yet finished Shakespeare' "—and followed with a considerable excerpt from the rest of Johnson's remarks:

> Mr. Lowell represented in himself, as it is sometimes necessary to remind the current generation, the highest plane of learning, scholarship, and literary art, the principle of which he expounded in season and out of season in his critical writings. . . . His critical works furnish a body of doctrine in literary matters which is certainly preëminent in American criticism at least. In

these days, when the lawlessness of the literary Bolsheviki has invaded every form of composition, it is of tonic advantage to review Lowell's exposition of the principles of art underlying poetry and criticism. . . . No man studied to better purpose the range of expression afforded by the English classics or would have been more outraged by the random and fantastic productions which are classified with the poetry of the present time under the name of vers libre. While no doubt he recognized the force of Whitman, he refused to recognize him as a poet, and once retorted, when it was suggested that much of Whitman's poetry was between prose and poetry, that there was nothing between prose and poetry.

Johnson concluded with a pledge that the Academy would take on the "agreeable duty to endeavor to accentuate the treasures of American literature which have fallen into neglect," and hoped that the occasion would "incite our college faculties and their students to a study of the heritage which we have in the beautiful poetry and the acute and high-minded criticism of James Russell Lowell."

To suppose that the times were ripe for a return to the prosody of Lowell was a little like a call to reinstate Ptolemy in the age of Einstein. The Lowell centennial was not so much a memorial retrospective—i.e., an unimpeachable review of a significant literary history—as it was that other thing: an instance of antiquarianism. Or—to do justice to Johnson's credo—it was a battle-cry against the onrushing alien modernist hordes, the literary Bolsheviki.

The difficulty was that the Bolsheviki were rampant in all the arts. Young American composers—Virgil Thomson, Marc Blitzstein, Elliott Carter, Marion Bauer, Roger Sessions, Herbert Elwell, Aaron Copland, George Gershwin—were streaming toward Nadia Boulanger's studio outside Paris for instruction in harmony (much as young American writers were streaming toward Gertrude Stein's Paris sitting room for lessons in logic), and coming back home with extraordinary new sounds. Boulanger introduced Copland to the conductor Walter Damrosch (later President of the Academy at a time when its laces were far less strait), who joked about Copland's *Symphony for Organ and Orchestra:* "If a gifted young man can write a symphony like that at twenty-three, within five years he will be ready to commit murder." What Copland called the "jazz spirit," with its irregular rhythms and sometimes exotic instruments, was received by the more conventional critics as a kind of symphonic deicide—the old gods of rational cadence struck down by xylophones, tam-tams, Chinese woodblocks. Copland was charged with releasing a "modernist fury" of "barnyard and stable noises." "New York withholds its admiration," Virgil Thomson wrote of the critical atmosphere, "till assured that you are modeling yourself on central Europe."

But experiment was unstoppable: George Gershwin was blending concert music and jazz in works commissioned by Damrosch, and Serge Koussevitsky, conducting the Boston Symphony, was presiding over Copland's barnyard noises. Edgard Varèse, who came to the United States from Paris in 1915, reversing the flow, declared his belief in "organized sound," or "sound-masses," and employed cymbals, bells, chimes, castanets, slapsticks, rattles, chains, anvils, and almost every other possible percussion device, "with their contribution," as he put it, "of a blossoming of unsuspected timbres." His scores were often marked with "hurlant," indicating howling, roaring, wild and strident clamor: any sound, all sounds, were music.

In the prosperity and optimism of the Twenties, proponents of the "new" music were turning their backs (and not without contempt) on traditionalists like Frederick Shepherd Converse, Edward Burlingame Hill, George Whitefield Chadwick, Reginald De Koven, Arthur Foote, Victor Herbert, and John Powell, all members of the Academy, and all continuing to compose in nineteenth-century styles. The maverick among them was John Alden Carpenter, nearly the only Academician to venture into blues, ragtime, and jazz. But in the world beyond the Academy, the matchless Louis Armstrong and other eminent black musicians were revolutionizing the American—and European—ear, and by 1927 Duke Ellington's band in Harlem's Cotton Club was devising original voices for trumpet and trombone. The Twenties saw an interpenetration of foreign originality as well: Sergei Rachmaninoff arrived after the Russian Revolution, and in the winter of 1925 Igor Stravinsky appeared with both the New York Philharmonic and the Boston Symphony. Three years earlier, Darius Milhaud was lecturing at Harvard, Princeton, and Columbia. Ernest Bloch, noted for chamber music and an enchantment with Hebrew melodies, became an American citizen in 1924. Arnold Schoenberg, inventor of twelve-tone technique and a refugee from Nazi Germany, emigrated to the United States in 1933, but his influence had long preceded him.

Meanwhile, Henry Cowell, a native Californian, was not only trying out novel sounds on the piano—sometimes treating it like a violin—but was inventing a new instrument, the rhythmicon, "capable of producing very complex combinations of beat patterns." The quarterly Cowell founded, suitably named *New Music*, was hospitable to the work of the most arcane innovators, including Charles Ives—whose composition teacher at Yale in 1894 had been the mild but uncomprehending Horatio Parker. It is one of the ironies of the Academy's later history, and also one of its numerous triumphs over its older self, that grants and fellowships are now awarded to young composers in Charles Ives's name, and out of the royalties of his estate—though Ives's polytonality, quarter tones, and disjointed melody lines would surely have appalled the Academicians of the Twenties. In February of 1923, Richard Aldrich, a member of the Institute since 1908, and music critic for *The New York Times*, wrote in a bitter column called "Some Judgments on New Music":

> It is nothing less than a crime for a composer to write in any of the idioms that have been handed down, or to hold any of the older ideas of beauty. . . . Any who do not throw overboard all the baggage inherited from the past, all transmitted ideas of melody and harmony, are reactionaries, pulling back and hindering the march of music. . . . Whatever is presented to [the receptive new audiences] as acrid ugliness or rambling incoherence is eagerly accepted as emanations of greatness and originality. It never occurs to them that it might be simple, commonplace ugliness.

These are lines that might have emerged from Robert Underwood Johnson's own inkpot. But it fell to John Powell, a Virginian elected to the Institute in 1924, to catch the Johnsonian idiom entire—the modernists, Powell said, were "nothing more or less than cheap replicas of the recent European Bolshevists." Powell was a composer of moods, beguiled by the picturesque and the nostalgic, especially as associated with Southern antebellum plantation life. The introductory wail of his *Rapsodie nègre* is intended to capture a watermelon peddler's cry—a telltale image that, apart from its melodic use, may possibly bear some relation to his distaste for racial mixing and new immigrants. His musical preference was for what he termed "the Anglo-Saxon Folk Music School," and he shunned *Cavalleria Rusticana* and *Tristan and Isolde* not because he disliked opera, but because he disapproved of marital infidelity.

The new music, with its "acrid ugliness" and "rambling incoherence," may have been the extreme manifestation of what the Academy idealists were up against. Among the other arts, though, the idealists did have one strong ally, which steadfastly resisted— longer than music and longer than painting—the notions of freedom of form and idiosyncratic or experimental vision that modernism was opening up to the individual artist. Sculpture alone continued to profess public nobility and collective virtue in service to a national purpose. "Sculpture" meant statuary dedicated to historical uplift and moral seriousness. Even architecture, through its functional aspect, was more inclined to engage in individual expression—but virtually every statue was intended as a monument. The Armory Show of 1913, the catalyst that revolutionized American painting, barely touched the National Sculpture Society, which had settled on Augustus Saint-Gaudens and his successors, in their advance from marble to bronze, as "The Golden Age of American Sculpture." (Saint-Gaudens died in 1907.) Colossal multifigured structures, exhibition palaces (often fashioned from temporary materials and afterward dismantled), fountains, celebratory arches, symbolic themes indistinguishable from spiritual credos—all these were in full consonance with Robert Underwood Johnson's dream of an American Temple. Nearly fifty years before the Armory Show, the sculptor Erastus Dow Palmer had declared: "No work in sculpture, however wrought out physically, results in excellence, unless it rests upon, and is sustained by, the dignity of a moral or intellectual intention."

This dogma remained intact until the rise of the modernists, who repudiated not only its principles but its techniques. The Paris Beaux Arts tradition depended on studio assistants; a sculptor was a "thinker," a philosopher who conceived the work and modeled it in clay, after which lower-level technicians were delegated to carry out its translation into finished form. Modernism, by contrast, brought on a rush of hand carving—the kinetic and aesthetic interaction of sculptor with tools and material. But it was not until the Twenties were almost out that individual style began to emerge as a recognizable, though clearly not yet dominant, movement. It was a movement that purposefully turned away from Old World models, and looked to the "primitive," to African and pre-Columbian as well as Sumerian and Egyptian sources. While the Academy itself clung to the civically earnest, advanced taste was (once again) headed for unfamiliar territory. Thomas Hastings, a Beaux Arts adherent elected to the Academy in 1908, had designed a Victory Arch—adorned with abundant inspirational statuary—for the soldiers returning after the First World War to march through. In 1919 it was executed in temporary materials, and the soldiers did march through it. But public sentiment failed to support a permanent rendering in stone, and the Arch was taken down. Monuments to a civic consensus were slipping from popularity; work steeped in lofty aims met indifferent, or perhaps jaded, eyes.

Yet the new sculptors were not recognized by the Academy, and the strikingly fresh shapes and experiments of the Twenties streamed past the Temple only to attract its vilifying scorn. Saul Baizerman, whose innovative studies of contemporary life, *The City and the People*, were hammered out between 1920 and 1925, was never invited into the Institute, while even more notable sculptors of the period had to wait for a later generation's approbation. Bruce Moore was not admitted until 1949; William Zorach became a member only in 1953, and Robert Laurent only in 1970, the year of his death. Within the Academy of the third decade, it was Daniel Chester French (admitted in 1908) who was pre-

ëminent: the prized sculptor of the Lincoln Memorial in Washington, D.C., the creator of a female *Republic* (with staff, globe, and
dove) and of Columbia University's *Alma Mater*, himself a grand
symbol of the grand symbolic statuary that preceded the modernist flood and was finally—if belatedly in the Academy—
overwhelmed by it.

In a tribute delivered on French's death in 1931, Royal Cortissoz,
an Academician who was art critic for *The New York Herald Tribune*
from 1891 on, observed with just precision that French "was thoroughly in harmony with [the Academy's] spirit" in a life "dedicated from beginning to end to the production of noble work. . . .
A beautiful seriousness of purpose animated him." As an example
he offered French's figure of *Memory*, "a seated nude reminiscent
of antique ideas." Cortissoz was reflecting exactly what William
Milligan Sloane had prescribed in his address at the opening of the
Temple in 1923:

> We are a company seeking the ideal . . . we do not forget that
> our business is conservation first and foremost, conservation of
> the best and but incidentally, if at all, promotion of the untried.
> We are to guard tradition, not to seek out and reward innova-
> tion . . . we are sternly bound as an organization to examine
> carefully any intellectual movement striving to break with
> tradition. . . . Our effort in word and work must be to discover
> and cherish the true American spirit and keep it pure, in order
> to prevent inferior literature and art from getting the upper
> hand.

What, then, was Cortissoz about when he labeled modern art
"a gospel of stupid license and self-assertion," if not preventing the
inferior from getting the upper hand? Still another Academician,
the painter and critic Kenyon Cox, wrote: "There is only one word
for this denial of all law, this insurrection of individual license
without discipline and without restraint; and that word is anarchy." The Armory Show, Cox announced, was a "pathological
museum" where "individualism has reached the pitch of sheer insanity or triumphant charlatanism." Gauguin was "a decorator
tainted with insanity." Rodin displayed "symptoms of mental de-

cay." If Cortissoz thought Matisse produced "gauche puerilities," Cox went further, and condemned "grotesque and indecent postures" drawn "in the manner of a savage or depraved child."

Eleven years after the Armory shock, the Academy, still unforgiving in 1924, published three papers attacking "Modernist Art," one each by Cortissoz and Cox, and the third by Edwin Howland Blashfield. All three blasts had appeared in periodicals in 1913 and 1914, in direct response to the Armory Show, but the Academy—while asserting that modernism's influence was "on the wane"—saw fit to reprint them in the interests of dislodging "eccentricities" from "the tolerance of critics." Here again was Kenyon Cox: "The real meaning of the Cubist movement is nothing else than the total destruction of the art of painting"; Cézanne "seems to me absolutely without talent"; "this kind of art [may] corrupt public taste and stimulate an appetite for excitement that is as dangerous as the appetite for any other poisonous drug"; "do not allow yourselves to be blinded by the sophistries of the foolish dupes or the self-interested exploiters of all this charlatanry." And Cortissoz on the Post-Impressionists: "work not only incompetent, but grotesque. It has led them from complacency to what I can only describe as insolence"; their "oracular assertion that the statues and pictures are beautiful and great is merely so much impudence." Blashfield, finally, after deploring "a license to omit painstaking care, coherent thinking, an incitement to violence as compelling attention," simply ended with a cry of self-defense: *"there is no dead art."*

Thus the Temple on the coming of the New. And thus the Academy's collective impulse toward vituperation—delivered repeatedly, resentfully, remorselessly, relentlessly; and aimed at the New in music, painting, sculpture, literature. And not only here. Whatever was new in the evolving aspirations of women toward inclusion and equality was repudiated. New immigrants (no longer of familial Ango-Saxon stock, many of whom were to enrich American literature, art, and music) were repudiated. Any alteration of nineteenth-century standards of piety or learning was repudiated. In a 1922 address, Owen Wister, author of *The Virgin-*

ian, ostensibly lauding "the permanent hoard of human knowledge," offered a list of "certain menaces to our chance for great literature":

> We are developing ragtime religion. Homer and Virgil were founded on a serious faith. . . . The classics are in eclipse. To that star all intellect has hitched its wagon. Literature has become a feminine subject in our seats of learning. What female Shakespeare has ever lived? Recent arrivals pollute the original spring. . . . It would be well for us if many recent arrivals would become departures.

Across the water Virginia Woolf, too, was speculating on the absence of a female Shakespeare, though from another viewpoint. And in the very bowels of the Academy, in a letter to President Sloane on October 22, 1921, loyal Mrs. Vanamee herself—in the name of the logic of precedent—was protesting the exclusion of women:

> You will be astonished to learn that I found a volume of Institute Minutes which was once loaned to Mr. Johnson and in looking through it this morning we found a record of [Julia Ward] Howe's election to the Institute. It seems she was regularly [i.e., routinely] nominated and regularly elected for at that time [1907] there was no ruling against women's being elected to the Institute. Mrs. Howe's name has always been included among the names of "Deceased Members of the Institute." Of course this makes the ruling of yesterday entirely out of order.

Mrs. Vanamee recommended that "any record of what occurred" (meaning the entire set of minutes of the meeting ruling against admission of women) be expunged in a little act of hanky-panky. Accordingly, the culpable minutes were somehow spirited away, never again to emerge—but the issue continued to fester, and it would be another five years before enough ballots could be counted in favor of admission. Julia Ward Howe's membership—for the three feeble years before her death at age ninety-one—was argued against as "an error of procedure." Besides, as the author of "The Battle Hymn of the Republic" she was less a woman than a national monument, one of those ideal female symbol-figures specialized in by Daniel Chester French.

In the ballots of 1923—asking directly, "Do you favor the admission of women to the National Institute of Arts and Letters?"— sometimes a simple "no" was not enough to satisfy the spleen of an elderly gentleman born before or during the Civil War. "NO I DO NOT," roared the painter Whitney Warren. "A categorical NO," announced the composer Arthur Bird, and followed up with a tirade:

> To express my decided antipathy against this proposed innovation you will notice that I have added *categorical*. I have lately in the Chicago Musical Leader ventilated my opinion on this subject in a short exposé. The occasion of a woman attempting to conduct the Philharmonic orchestra here at a symphony concert gave me a long awaited opportunity to mouth a short but vigorous sally . . . against the attempts of a certain clan of womanhood to try to do things the feminine gender is by nature utterly incapable of doing and hooting at those things for which it is by nature predestined. What on earth *have or ever will have women* to do with science, art and letters (in the highest sense of the words) or are they satisfied to play a very mediocre second fiddle? It is needless to hide the naked fact, conceal the plain truth, that the moment the fair sex drops its skirts, throws aside guiltiness, modesty, refinement, all that gentility that we know and love so much, *don the leather breeches, beat the drum,* then lackaday to all the poetry of this life, away with the sentiments so expressive in Heine's poem so prettily and cleverly translated by our Longfellow, "The sea hath its pearls," etc. Then we shall say "For women must work and fight, men weep and spin." Id est—the world turned upside down.

Tirades on the one hand, gloatings on the other. "I rejoice exceedingly," the writer James Ford Rhodes wrote in 1918 to Robert Underwood Johnson (who, surprisingly, favored women's admission), "that you were beaten on the women question. What would you do with the 'wimmin' at the dinners at the University Club? . . . A hysteria is going over the country, showing itself in women's suffrage and Prohibition." (The Temple may have been able to do without women at dinner, but it rarely permitted itself to do without booze, and regularly circumvented the Eighteenth Amendment—*viz.*, "My dear Cass, Please send the bottle of Gin for the Institute dinner, carefully wrapped up so as to conceal its identity." "My dear Thorndike, Will you please send the bottle of Gin, carefully wrapped up so that it will not look suspicious.")

In the midst of all these fulminations and refusals and repudiations (always excepting the gin), there was, nevertheless, one moment early in the Academy's third decade that hinted at a glimmer of doubt, perhaps even of self-criticism. It was, in fact, a kind of bloodless insurrection or palace coup, and took place behind Robert Underwood Johnson's formidable back. The rebel in the case was Hamlin Garland, author of *A Son of the Middle Border*, a school classic of the last generation. Wisconsin-born, Garland grew up in the drudging privations of farm life, at home in the unpolished—and impoverished—regions of Iowa, California, and the Dakotas. Unlike Johnson (out of whom the last traces of Indiana had long since been squeezed), Garland could never have been mistaken for a formal Easterner. His perspectives were wider and more sympathetic than many of his colleagues'; he was a liberal who wrote seriously on social reform. His name was irrefutably linked with narrative realism, but he was a realist in the more everyday sense as well: he looked around and saw an Academy of fatigued and retrograde gentlemen stuck fast in a narrow mold. "We must avoid the appearance of a club of old fogies," he warned, and kept an eye out for a chance to invigorate the membership.

The chance came in 1920, when President Wilson (an Academy member since 1908) appointed Johnson to be Ambassador to Italy, and Garland stepped in as the Academy's Acting Secretary. In Johnson's absence, Garland's first target was Johnson himself: "We cannot become a 'one man organization,' no matter how fine that man may be." To Brander Matthews he wrote, "Now is the time to make the Academy known. If we let this chance pass we shall be a Johnson Institution for the rest of our lives. . . . We can't be run by a volunteer member seventy years of age. . . . We are called . . . that Johnson thing." He noted "the age and growing infirmity of many of our members who are losing interest in the organization" and "the fact that our membership is scattered as well as aged and preoccupied. . . . We should draw closer," he advised, "and take the future of the Academy much more seriously than we have heretofore done. . . . We must not lose touch with youth. We should not be known as 'a senile institution.' We must assume to lead in the progress of the Nation."

Yet Garland's ideas for Academy programs turned out to be less than revolutionary: "The Academy by a Lecture Foundation should offer to the Nation a series of addresses on American Arts and Letters in which the most vigorous propaganda for the good as against the bad should be carried forward. We should stand against all literary pandering, all corrupting influences"—an exhortation that might easily have been uttered by any of the old fogies had it not concluded with a call to "make it plain that we are for progress, that it is our plan to hasten and direct the advance. That we intend to recognize the man of genius whether in the Academy or not."

He proposed the election of honorary foreign members, so that the Academy's "penumbra can extend throughout the world." As for the native membership, he warned against "the choice of a scholar who is known only to a few other scholars." "There is always the danger of electing too many men who are merely college professors. The Academy," he insisted, "cannot afford to elect a classicist in preference to the man of original genius." And there was only one kind of genius he really wanted: "The Academy membership must be kept predominantly literary or the Academy will lose power. The moment the Academy is overbalanced on the art side it loses standing, a result which may be unjust but it is true." He pushed for fame: "A man may be chosen who is recognized by the great public as a figure. Edwin Markham for example does not have to be explained. He is in Who's Who. Some of the Academy elections have to be explained even to members." He pushed for zeal: "men who will come to the meetings. . . . Every time the Academy takes in a man who has a sort of contempt for what it is trying to do it weakens the organization." He pushed above all for the Academy as "an inspiration to young men," and called for the establishment of annual awards to "young workers in the five arts."

And as a final push, though Johnson was still safely in Italy, Garland considered how to suppress him on his return: "Johnson is ex-officio on all committees," he conceded, but "should not be Chairman." In the course of time Garland proposed an even more radical solution—the Academy should get rid of Johnson altogether: "The returning secretary is an old man, preoccupied (as the rest of us are) with personal work of his own. He cannot give his entire mind to the Academy and as he is a member, it is not desirable that he should. It is not a good thing to have any one member known as the manager of the organization. The managing Secretary should be an outside man on a salary."

At the end of the day Garland was happy to have Johnson back. The truth was that Johnson *could* give his entire mind to the Academy, and had always been eager to do exactly that. The administrative minutiae that Johnson reveled in ultimately made Garland grumble—he was clearly sick of contending with old-fogey letters like the two that arrived a month apart in the fall of 1921, from Abbott Lawrence Lowell, the President of Harvard:

> I do not know whether I shall be able to be present at the meeting on November 2nd; but I want to suggest that it would be well for the Academy, which stands for Letters, to use the best English in its communications to members, and say "I shall," or "shall not, be present",—not "I will, or will not."

> I do not know what the duties of the Education Committee of the American Academy of Arts and Letters are. I am very glad to serve on the Committee; but it seems to me that it would be a great mistake for the Academy to attempt to do anything or express an opinion about education.

Like Lowell, the membership, reluctant to be more activist than they had been under Johnson, resisted Garland's pressure for broader concern and greater participation. "The lack of interest and cohesion is pitiful," he wrote to President Sloane. And to Matthews he complained, "I am just downright discouraged. . . . The truth is we are a lot of 'elderly old parties' who don't care very much whether school keeps or not—we'd rather not if it involves any janitor work on our part. . . . I cannot be a party to a passive

policy." The Academy, it seemed, liked it well enough that Johnson ran a one-man establishment, and Garland himself was feeling
more and more the imposition on his own literary productivity. "I
am carrying so much of the detail work of the Academy at this
time," he moaned one year into his service as Acting Secretary,
"that I have no leisure for my own writing." Two years later he
was in a state of full surrender, and could hardly wait for the finish
of Johnson's ambassadorial stint. "As I see it now there will be no
one but Johnson to carry on the work and I withdraw all opposition to him." And: "I've been a nuisance to little effect and shall
turn the Office of Secretary over to Johnson the moment he
reaches the building. It is a thankless task for any man."

Thankless for any but Robert Underwood Johnson. Though his
beard may have grown whiter, he resumed his position at the
helm as energetically as before: it was as if Italy had never inter-
vened. Despite Garland's efforts to introduce notions of "progress," everything Johnson had left behind was still in place, every
prejudice intact, the familiar projects ongoing: the preoccupation
with standards of English diction; public addresses entitled "The
Literature of Early American Statesmanship," "Kinship and Detachment from Europe in American Literature," "The Emotional
Discovery of America," "The Relations of American Literature
and American Scholarship in Retrospect and Prospect" (all these
in 1924, to mark the Academy's twentieth anniversary); the annual
Evangeline Wilbour Blashfield Lecture, in honor of the wife of
Edwin Howland Blashfield, sculptor of *The Evolution of Civilization*.
At her death she was eulogized not merely for "nobility of character" but more particularly for faith "in the furtherance of sane and
useful movements in literature and the Arts."

Perhaps the most Johnsonian display of taste burst out in 1924,
the year Robert Frost won the Pulitzer Prize for poetry and the
Academy voted not to award its Gold Medal to anyone at all. According to the minutes of October 10, Johnson protested this decision, "favoring as the recipient Miss Edith M. Thomas, whose
seventieth birthday has just occurred. Mr. Johnson spoke in high
appreciation of the substance and style of Miss Thomas's work,
which he regarded as the summit of contemporary American po-

etry." Not that this was Johnson's first salvo on behalf of the summit. He had begun to urge Miss Thomas's cause six years earlier; apparently he regarded her as his most incendiary weapon in the war on free verse. "Aside from her professional merits and the nobility of her character," he pressed, "the spiritual tone of her work . . . would be all the more timely because of the widespread misconceptions in the public mind concerning the art of poetry, due to the vogue of formless, whimsical and eccentric productions, which by reason of their typographical form are generally classified as poetry by publishers, librarians, critics and readers. That the Academy should honor a poetic artist of so fine a strain as Miss Thomas would be to throw the force of its influence against the lawlessness of the time that has invaded all the Arts." And even by 1926—it was now four years since the landmark appearance of *The Waste Land*—Johnson was still not giving up on Edith Thomas: "I believe that in some respects she has seen more deeply and reported more melodiously the evanescent phases of the borderland of the soul than any other American poet except Ralph Waldo Emerson."

In 1925 the vote for the newly established William Dean Howells Medal, given "in recognition of the most distinguished work of fiction published during the preceding five years," went to Mary E. Wilkins Freeman for her depiction of "Old New England, New England before the coming of the French Canadian and the Italian peasant. . . . The body of her work remains of the Anglo-Saxon order." (Other American fiction published in that annus mirabilis of 1925 included *The Professor's House*, by Willa Cather, who was elected to the Institute in 1929; *In Our Time*, short stories by Ernest Hemingway, never admitted to membership; *The Great Gatsby*, by F. Scott Fitzgerald, also never admitted; *An American Tragedy*, by Theodore Dreiser, another non-member; *Manhattan Transfer*, by John Dos Passos, admitted in 1937; and *The Making of Americans*, by Gertrude Stein, who of all American writers was least likely to be nominated.) At the same time the vote in the Institute for the Gold Medal for Belles Lettres landed on William Crary Brownell, an Academy member who had the distinction of serving as Edith Wharton's editor at Scribner's. Wharton herself was still unadmitted. In 1926, the Gold Medal for Sculpture was presented to Herbert Adams, the Academician who had designed the Academy's bronze doors, with their inscription: GREAT MEN ARE THEY WHO SEE THAT THOUGHTS RULE THE WORLD. In 1927, William Milligan Sloane won the Gold Medal for Biography and History; Johnson had successfully nominated the Academy's President for the Academy's own award.

The Academy was also engaged in other forms of self-recognition. There was the question of a bookplate, insignia, regalia—all the grave emblems of institutional Importance. The bookplate—an airy Pegasus rearing among clouds, framed by a wreath resting on a book, below which appears the Academy's motto: OPPORTUNITY, INSPIRATION, ACHIEVEMENT—was devised by the architect Henry Bacon and engraved by Timothy Cole. The airiness was Cole's contribution—"a delicate light style," he said, "that I have been at great pains to secure"—but Bacon rejected it, preferring the "heavy strong manner" of Piranesi, the eighteenth-century Italian neoclassicist. Bacon died in the middle of the dispute, so Pegasus continued to fly lightly, as Cole rendered him.

No lightness attached to the issue of regalia, however—odd-looking caps and shroudlike gowns were supplied to the Academicians (a photograph attests to their discomfort) and then discarded. From 1923 on, there were various experiments with insignia; at one point the current small rosette was in disfavor for grand occasions, and a great floppy badge was introduced—a giant purple satin ribbon trimmed with gold scallops and tiny bows. (A box of these relics, accompanied by cards of unused ribbon, matching thread, and even needles and pins, is still being thriftily stored in the Academy's archives.) And there were Roman-style busts of the Academicians themselves: F. Wellington Ruckstull, an Academy sculptor, was commissioned to immortalize both Nicholas Murray Butler and Wilbur Cross, a governor of Connecticut whose name, familiar as a highway leading to New England, may prove that asphalt is more lasting than bronze.

But it would be misleading to infer that the Academy was fixed only on itself in these years. One ambitious plan for the general enlightenment was to establish an art museum in every state lacking one. "The commanding motive," Johnson explained in 1925, was to bring "knowledge of the best painting and sculpture to populations that are not able to visit the great centers." Doggedly optimistic, Johnson traveled from city to city searching for donors and making speeches—"I am well, but a bit tired of my own voice," he reported to Mrs. Vanamee. The idea fell through, possibly because, as Johnson noted, "there is an impasse between the artistic and the commercial temperament." A second attempt to widen the Academy's purview—its affiliation with the American Academy in Rome—was more efficacious, and endured.

And the course of public lectures the Academy launched in Boston, Cleveland, Chicago, Philadelphia, and other venues frequently aspired to a global embrace: "The Literature of Japan"; "The Spirit of Italy"; talks on Scandinavia, France, Russia; and, following the war, an entire series on "The Failure of German Kultur" (though these were rather more punitive than embracing). Relations were kept up with the Belgian and French Academies. Letters of invitation—and homage—went often to British men of letters. In 1919, Maurice Maeterlinck, the 1911 Nobel Laureate, visited the Academy as an honored literary guest from Belgium. The novelist Vicente Blasco Ibáñez came from Spain.

Spain, Italy, Belgium, France, Canada, and Britain all sent laudatory messages to the Academy's William Dean Howells memorial meeting in March of 1921; Rudyard Kipling's contribution, representing England, brought a vigorous insight into the American literary past—with more conviction, possibly, than some of the narrowly Anglophile Academicians themselves (always conscious of what they saw as American marginality with regard to European models) could wholeheartedly summon. Despite the international tributes solicited from overseas, and despite the number of speakers and subjects ("Howells the Novelist," "Howells the Dramatist," "Howells the Humorist," etc.), some indeterminate trace of the intramural nevertheless clung to the Howells commemoration—a touch of the gentleman's club; Howells, after all, had been the Academy's first president. The event rises out of the record less as a national literary celebration than as an Academy period piece. The speakers, Academy members all, were once again identifiable by their common idiom—the idiom of backward-looking gentility, hence of diminishment. Press attention was meager.

Three years later, H. L. Mencken, in an article headlined "No Head for Howells' Hat" in the Detroit *News* of March 23, 1924, took up a different approach to Howells. "Suppose," he wrote, "Henrik Ibsen and Anatole France were still alive and on their way to the United States on a lecture tour, or to study prohibition and sex hygiene, or to pay their respects to Dr. Coolidge . . . who would go down the bay in a revenue cutter to meet them . . . who to represent American literature?" Represent it, he explained, "in a tasteful and resounding manner." "So long as Howells kept his legs," Mencken went on, "he was chosen almost automatically for all such jobs, for he was dean of the national letters and acknowledged to be such by everyone. Moreover, he had experience at the work and a natural gift for it. He looked well in funeral garments. He had a noble and ancient head. He made a neat and caressing speech. He understood etiquette."

But the price of Mencken's esteem for Howells, however soaked in the Mencken satire, was disesteem for the Academy:

> Who is to represent [American literature] today? I search the country without finding a single candidate, to say nothing of a whole posse. Turn, for example, to the mystic nobles of the American Academy of Arts and Letters. I pick out five at random: William C. Brownell, Robert Underwood Johnson, Hamlin Garland, Bliss Perry, and Henry Van Dyke. What is wrong with them? The plain but dreadful fact that no literary foreigner has ever heard of them—that their appearance on the deck of his incoming barge would puzzle and alarm him and probably cause him to call for the police.
>
> These men do not lack the homely virtues. They all spell correctly, write neatly and print nothing that is not constructive. In the whole five of them there is not enough sin to raise a congressman's temperature one-hundredth of a degree. But they are devoid of what is essential to the official life; they have, so to speak, no stage presence. There is nothing rotund and gaudy about them. No public and unanimous reverence bathes them. What they write or say never causes any talk. To be wel-

comed by them jointly or severally would appear to Thomas Hardy or Gabriele d'Annunzio as equal to being welcomed by representatives of the St. Joe, Mo., Rotary Club.

On the heels of the Howells commemoration came the Academy's 1922 memorial to John Burroughs, the naturalist, a member since 1905. This was marked by a lengthy address entitled "The Racial Soul of John Burroughs," by Henry Fairfield Osborn (who was *not* an Academy member)—a talk of a certain brightness and charm until it discloses its dubious thesis: the existence of "racial aptitudes." "The *racial* creative spirit of man always reacts to its own historic racial environment, into the remote past." "Have we not reason to believe that there is a *racial soul* as well as a racial mind, a racial system of morals, a racial anatomy?" In short, it was his "northern heredity" that drew Burroughs to become "the poet of our robins, of our apple trees, of the beauties of our forests and farms," and "the ardent and sometimes violent prophet of conservation." There is no evidence that any of Osborn's listeners demurred from a theory linking conservation of forests to northern European genes. And a decade later similar ideas of race, applied less innocently than to an interest in robins, would inflame Europe and destroy whole populations.

In the spring of that same year—1922—the Academy turned once again to Europe, anticipating Mencken's nasty vision of distinguished "literary foreigners" being welcomed at the docks by a Temple nonentity. The nonentity in this instance was not an Academician but rather a Mr. Haskell, unknown to history and apparently a Columbia University factotum sent to the pier by Nicholas Murray Butler to meet the S.S. *Paris*. Aboard were Maurice Donnay and André Chevrillon, Director and Chancellor respectively of the Académie Française. The pair had been imported to attend the three-hundredth anniversary of the birth of Molière—"In Celebration of the Power and Beauty of the Literature of France and Its Influence upon That of the English-speaking Peoples"—and were fêted at luncheons and dinners in New York, Princeton, Boston, Philadelphia, and Washington. The official Academy dinner included oxtail soup, appropriately dubbed "Parisienne"; the appetizer was a quatrain by Richard Watson Gilder:

Molière

He was the first great modern. In his art
The very times their very manners show;
But for he truly drew the human heart
In his true page all times themselves shall know.

The public meeting honoring Molière—or his latterday representatives—was held at the Ritz-Carlton Hotel on April 25, 1922. A
day earlier the visitors had been taken uptown to see the site of
the new Temple, and then were conducted back to the temporary
Academy building at 15 West Eighty-first Street for tea and a
speech by Butler: "I well recall that in his subtle and quite unri-
valed study of French traits, our associate, Mr. Brownell, pointed
out that while among the French the love of knowledge is not
more insatiable than with us, it is infinitely more judicious. . . .
precision, definiteness, proportion, are certain marks of what is
truly French." "The aim of the American Academy," he continued,
"must for long years to come be to rescue a people's art and a people's letters from what is vulgar, from what is provincial, from
what is pretense, and to raise a standard to which the lovers of the
beauty of loveliness and the lovers of the beauty of dignity may,
with confidence and satisfaction, repair."

Precision, definiteness, proportion were truly French; vulgarity,
provinciality, pretense were truly American. The literary foreigners may have been flattered by what seemed to be homage born
of New World insecurity, but since Butler's list of American flaws
covered not only homegrown philistinism but also international
modernism ("pretense"), the French were surely implicated in the
latter. It was France, after all, that had produced Matisse and
Milhaud and Jules Laforgue (who had influenced Eliot)—not to
mention the French infatuation with jazz, and Paris's harboring of
suspect American types like Gertrude Stein. And if the laughing
ghost of Molière had come to the feast, would it have chosen to
side with the deadly predictable purveyors of "the beauty of loveliness" or with the syncopated ironists of modernism?

In 1925 Robert Underwood Johnson was still incorrigibly at war with the new poets. The recoil from modernism he enshrined as a cause; and what was Johnson's cause was bound to become the Academy's cause, very nearly its *raison d'être*. (The first cracks in anti-modernism would not occur until late in the decade, and then—torrentially—in the 1930's and 1940's.) On November 23, 1925, in a letter to *Who's Who in America*, presenting himself as an incarnation of the Temple's eternality, Johnson requested that he be identified as "an antagonist of free verse and author of a criticism of it in an address before the Academy entitled 'The Glory of Words.'" "The modernists," he complained in that talk, "wish to exalt into poetic association words that heretofore have not been considered poetic. . . . Naturally such an attempt is conspicuously deficient in the glory of words." The "metrical product of the revolutionists," he went on, was "unimaginative," "monotonously conventional," and "objectionably sophisticated—individualism run to seed." And: "They are determined to make silk purses out of sows' ears." "Because the Muses no longer rule there must be no allusion to Parnassus; the Muses are not 'factual' and must go by the board." "The chief promise of poetry is to express the pervasive and permanent spiritual forces of all time."

Although Johnson's zeal on behalf of Miss Thomas had failed to win her an Academy honor, his fight against Robert Frost did not abate. To Booth Tarkington he wrote:

> I am very strongly opposed to Frost's nomination on principle (I have never met him and have no personal feeling). . . . I think both he and Edwin Arlington Robinson who has been nominated are in the main mediocre in their work . . . they are not worthy of consideration for the Academy. . . . We have other men in the Institute who ought to be put forward for the quality of their poetry—Percy MacKaye, Clinton Scollard, Richard Burton, Brian Hooker, Don Marquis, Charles deKay and John Finley. Each one of these men has done beautiful work.

To our ears these are largely unrecognizable minor deities. Johnson's own Parnassus has not gathered them to its bosom. And if Polyhymnia, having anointed (sparingly) Edward MacDowell and Victor Herbert, remains cool to Frederick Shepherd Converse

and George Whitefield Chadwick, while smiling palely on Horatio Parker chiefly for his connection with Charles Ives, what of the
painters' Muse? Edith Thomas as poet and John Powell as composer may be confined to the category of antiquarian curios, but
(for instance) Joseph Pennell and Childe Hassam are not. (Anyone
examining the superbly evocative Pennell drawings that accompany Henry James's *Collected Travel Writings*, reissued in 1993 by
the Library of America, will be stirred by what we call permanence in art: that which cannot date.)

Repeatedly infuriated by the encroachments of new modes of
literary expression and helpless before its tide—Robinson and
Frost were both admitted to the Academy, in 1927 and 1930
respectively—Johnson was determined that the Temple should
make an indelible statement at least in the graphic arts. One effort
toward that end, the attempt to put a museum in every state, fizzled. A second idea both survived and prospered: this was to establish a collection by Academicians and other American painters.
Johnson worked closely with the earliest Committee on Art, then
known as the Committee on Art Censorship—a name that may
suggest the prescriptive tastes of its three members: the painter
and critic Kenyon Cox, the sculptor Herbert Adams, and the architect Cass Gilbert. Paintings were solicited from private collectors
and through bequests. Since one of Johnson's motives was to promote and augment the influence of the Academy, it is no wonder
that portraits dominated, or that the collection was based, by and
large, on the products of its own members. Johnson was relentless
in going after contributions, especially from the freshly widowed
wives of deceased Academicians. The collection expanded to
cover etchings, lithographs, engravings, small sculptures, photographs, memorabilia, and manuscripts.

To display the Academy's riches, the year 1927 saw four public
events: separate exhibits honoring Academicians Childe Hassam,
Timothy Cole, and Joseph Pennell, and an "Exhibition of Manuscripts Representing the First Century of American Independence"—which included the notebooks of John Burroughs and
letters by Academy members Henry Adams, Charles Francis
Adams, Thomas Bailey Aldrich, Julia Ward Howe, William Dean

Howells, Thomas Wentworth Higginson (the very Higginson who had chided Emily Dickinson for "spasmodic" and "uncontrolled" verse), Henry James, Henry Charles Lea, Edmund Clarence Stedman, and Richard Henry Stoddard. Manuscripts by Emerson, Hawthorne, and Whitman were also on exhibit. As a mendicant on behalf of the Academy, Johnson was astoundingly tireless, and his solicitations ended only with his death in 1937. With Johnson gone, the Academy's policy for both artists and writers (and for musicians and composers as well) moved from mainly self-reflecting acquisition to outward-looking prodigality: awards to the young at the start of their careers.

A few days after the Timothy Cole event, Huntington presented the Academy with a gift of $100,000 as an endowment for future exhibits. The permanent collection, and the new plan for ongoing showings by painters, were designed to set a standard for American cultural aspiration. So were the concerts and recitals sponsored by the Academy during the decade of the Twenties: what was to be emphasized, George Whitefield Chadwick urged, was "the development of *American Music* (not by foreign musicians, no matter how accomplished)." But the pressure for indigenous American achievement—a sign of the early Academy's sense of its own inferiority before the age and weight of Europe's cultural cargo—was nowhere more pronounced than in the preoccupation with American speech. President Sloane warned of "a stream of linguistic tendency, prone to dangerous flood and devastating inundation," alluding no doubt to the postwar immigration. Yet native-born journalists were almost as perilous a threat as foreigners spilling into the country: "How are we to justify the diction of the press," William Roscoe Thayer inquired, "through which pours an incessant stream of slang, vulgarism, grammatical blunders, and rhetorical crudity?" Responding, the press—in the shape of the Boston *Herald* of December 15, 1926—pretended to take up the case of an instance of ambiguity in the use of "is" and "are," which was being placed before the Temple for adjudication: "After having brought half the dilettantes and intellectuals of the nation in futile disagreement, one of the worst sentences ever written will soon arrive at the Academy of Arts and Letters in search of further trouble."

Further trouble? Such playfulness—or mockery—could hardly sit well with the Permanent Secretary. The function of the Academy, Johnson grandly noted, was to reject "invasions from the ribbon counter" and to "stand against the slovenly, and for the dignified and effective use of words." This meant also the *sound* of words. In a radio talk invoking the Academy's various causes, Mrs. Vanamee testified to the excitements of clear enunciation:

> There is a medal for good diction on the Stage which was awarded to Walter Hampden in 1924 and last spring to Miss Edith Wynne Matthison whose perfect diction was never more perfectly in evidence than in her superbly simple and touching acceptance of the medal from the hands of Robert Underwood Johnson, the Secretary of the Academy, and after he and its Chancellor, Dr. Nicholas Murray Butler had paid high tribute to Miss Matthison's work.

Mrs. Vanamee was plainly not in line for a medal honoring Style.

THE RIBBON COUNTER, along with the Academy's defunct ribbon badge, has vanished; it is a different Academy today. For one thing, though born of the Institute, the Academy has swallowed up its progenitor. What was once two bodies, joined like Siamese twins in any case, is now a single organization—diverse, welcoming, lavishly encouraging to beginners in the arts. Yet what Hamlin Garland remarked on long ago remains: a quantity of seasoned gray heads—few of whom, however, are polemically inclined to retrogressive views. Crusty elitism is out. The presence of women goes unquestioned. Ethnic parochialism is condemned. No one regards experiment as a revolutionary danger. And by now modernism, which seventy years ago seemed so disruptive to the history-minded, is itself an entrenched tradition with a lengthening history of its own—even fading off into the kind of old-fashionedness that derives from repetitiveness, imitation, overfamiliarity. Modernism has grown as tranquil as Robert Underwood Johnson's Parnassus; and what postmodernism is, or will become, we hardly know.

Do these white-bearded, high-collared gentlemen of the old Academy—who live out the nineteenth century's aesthetic and intellectual passions right up to the lip of the Great Depression—strike us as "quaint"? Condescending and unholy word! Unholy, because it forgets that death and distance beckon us, too: our turn lies just ahead. Possibly we are already quaintly clothed, as unaware that we are retrograde as Kenyon Cox and Royal Cortissoz before Matisse, or Robert Underwood Johnson in the face of T. S. Eliot and Marianne Moore. Despite our ingrained modernist heritage, we may, after all, discover ourselves to be more closely linked to the print-loyal denizens of the Twenties Temple than we are to the cybernetic future. If a brittle and browning 1924 Mencken clipping testifies to the cultural irrelevance of the official humanists of two generations ago, the loss of a fixed and bound text, if it occurs—bringing a similar disorientation to fixed expectations—may be as cataclysmic for us as Cubism was to the votaries of Beaux Arts.

And if time has reduced Robert Underwood Johnson and his solemnly spiritualized colleagues to toys for our irony, what does that signify? Probably that (given our modernist habits) we value irony more than dignity, and what does *that* signify? The "mystic nobles," as Mencken called them, of the Academy's third decade lacked irony; but they also lacked cynicism. When they sermonized on "nobility of character," they believed in its likelihood, and even in its actual presence. When Johnson honored "Beauty changeless and divine," he took it for granted that the continuity of a civilization is a sacred covenant. A review of *American Poetry: The Nineteenth Century*, a pair of Library of America volumes published in 1993 and edited by John Hollander, a contemporary Academician, adds this perspective: "Just as the spare acerbity of early modernism must have looked bracingly astringent to writers and readers grown weary of nineteenth-century rotundities, so today . . . these relics of another age are deeply refreshing."

We who are postmodern inheritors of the violent whole of the twentieth century no longer dare to parade—even if we privately hold them—convictions of virtue, harmony, nobility, wisdom, beauty; or of their sources. But (setting aside irony, satire, condescension, and the always arrogant power of the present to diminish the past), the ideals of the Temple, exactly as Johnson conceived them, *are* refreshing to an era tormented by unimaginable atrocity and justifiable cynicism. Nor are those ideals precisely "relics." Suppose Johnson had chosen Frank Lloyd Wright as architect for the new building; what might the Academy have looked like then? If it is good to have the Guggenheim Museum's inventiveness, it is also good to have the Academy's Venetian palace, just as Stanford White and Charles McKim dreamed it.

Or what if the Academy's art committee had allied itself with, say, Alfred Stieglitz's "291" gallery, the heart and muscle of the modernist cause? What if Robert Frost and Charles Ives had been admitted to membership in 1918? Or H. L. Mencken?

Such speculations instantly annihilate the history of the Temple's credo between the Great War and the Great Depression. Worse, they wipe out the name and (noble) character of the redoubtable Robert Underwood Johnson, and who would want that?

"IT TAKES A
GREAT DEAL
OF HISTORY
TO PRODUCE
A LITTLE
LITERATURE"

H. G. Wells once accused Henry James of knowing
practically nothing. In the Jamesian novel, Wells charged, "you
will find no people with defined political opinions, no people with
religious opinions, none with clear partisanships or with lusts or
whims, none definitely up to any specific impersonal thing." Wells
concluded: "It is leviathan retrieving pebbles."

James was desperately wounded. He was at the close of his
great span of illumination—it was less than a year before his
death—and he was being set aside as useless, "a church lit but
without a congregation." Replying to Wells, he defended himself
on the question of the utility of art. Literature, he asserted, is "for
use": "I regard it as relevant in a degree that leaves everything behind." There followed the famously characteristic Jamesian credo,
by now long familiar to us. "It is art," he wrote, "that *makes* life,
makes interest, makes importance . . . I know of no substitute
whatever for the force and beauty of its process." And though he
was speaking explicitly of the novel's purpose as "the extension of
life, which is the novel's great gift," there is evidence enough that

he would not have excluded the literary essay, of which he was equal master, from art's force and beauty. Thus, what Henry James knew.

To which Wells retorted: "I had rather be a journalist, that is the essence of it."

In the quarrel between Wells and James, James's view has been overtaken by times and habits far less elevated in their literary motives (and motifs) than his own, and by radical changes in the aims of education and in the impulses that drive the common culture. What James knew was the nobility of art—if, for him, the novel and the literary essay were not splendors just short of divine, then they were, anyhow, divining rods, with the capacity to quiver over the springs of discovered life. What Wells knew was something else—the future; us; what we are now. He welcomed the germinating hour of technology's fecundity, and flourished in it. James, we recall, switched from pen and ink to the typewriter, not because he was attracted to machines—he was not—but because he suffered from writer's cramp. He never learned to type himself; instead, he dictated to a typist—a technological regression, in a way, to the preliterate oral; or else an ascendance to the dominant priestly single voice. Wells, by contrast, was magnetized by the machine-world. Imagine him our contemporary: his study is mobbed by computer, printer, modem, e-mail, voice-mail, photocopier, fax, cable—the congeries and confluence of gadgets and conveniences that feed what the most up-to-date colleges advertise as "communications skills."

The truth of our little age is this: nowadays no one gives a damn about what Henry James knew. I dare to say our "little" age not to denigrate (or not only to denigrate), but because we squat now over the remnant embers of the last diminishing decade of the dying twentieth century, possibly the rottenest of all centuries, and good riddance to it (despite modernism at the start and moonwalking near the middle). The victories over mass murder and mass delusion, West and East, are hardly permanent. "Never again" is a pointless slogan: old atrocities are models (they give permission) for new ones. The worst reproduces itself; the best is singular. Tyrants, it seems, can be spewed out by the dozens, and their atrocities by the thousands, as by a copy machine; but Kafka, tyranny's symbolist, is like a fingerprint, or like handwriting, not duplicatable. This is what Henry James knew: that civilization is not bred out of machines, whether the machines are tanks or missiles, or whether they are laser copiers. Civilization, like art its handmaid (read: hand-made), is custom-built.

Let this not be mistaken for any sort of languorous pre-Raphaelite detachment from science or technology, or, heaven forfend, as a complaint against progress and its reliefs. Gratitude for anaesthesia and angioplasty and air travel, and for faxes and computers and frozen food and the flush toilet and all the rest! Gratitude, in truth, for Mr. Gradgrind and the Facts, and for those who devise the Facts—especially when those facts ease the purely utilitarian side of life. What distinguishes the data of medicine and science is precisely that they *can* be duplicated: an experiment that cannot be repeated will be discarded as an unreliable fluke, or, worse, as a likely forgery. In the realm of science, what is collective has authority. It is the same with journalism: if two reporters witness an incident, and the two accounts differ, one must be wrong, or must at least promote distrust. A unique view, uncorroborated, is without value. Wells, in discrediting James, was in pursuit of public and collective discriminations, as opposed to the purely idiosyncratic; he was after consensus-witnessing, both in science and society, and a more recognizable record, perhaps, even of lust and whim. Defined political and religious opinions, clear partisanships, persons definitely up to some specific impersonal thing.

Defined, definite, specific—how, what, when, where: the journalist's catalogue and catechism. Naming generates categories and headings, and categories and headings offer shortcuts—like looking something up in the encyclopedia, where knowledge, abbreviated, has already been codified and collected. James's way, longer and slower, is for knowledge to be detected, inferred, individually, laboriously, scrupulously, mazily—knowledge that might not be found in any encyclopedia.

"I had rather be a journalist, that is the essence of it"—hark, the cry of the common culture. Inference and detection (accretion heading toward revelation) be damned. What this has meant, for literature, is the eclipse of the essay in favor of the "article"—that shabby, team-driven, ugly, truncated, undeveloped, speedy, breezy, cheap, impatient thing. A while ago, coming once again on Robert Louis Stevenson's "Virginibus Puerisque"—an essay not short, wholly odd, no other like it, custom-made, soliciting the brightness of full attention in order to release its mocking charms—I tried to think of a single periodical today that might be willing to grant print to this sort of construction. Not even "judicious cutting," as editors like to say, would save Stevenson now. Of course there may be an instantly appropriate objection to so mildewed an observation. Stevenson is decidedly uncontemporary—the tone is all wrong, and surely we are entitled to our own sounds? Yes, the nineteenth century deserves to be read—but remember, while reading, that it is dead.

All right. But what of the "clear partisanship" of a book review encountered only this morning, in a leading journal dedicated to reviews? "Five books, however rich and absorbing, are a hefty number for the reader to digest," the reviewer declares, commenting on Leon Edel's multivolume biography of Henry James; "a little amateur sleuthing some years ago suggested to me that the number of people who bought Mr. Edel's quintet bore little relation to the number who succeeded in battling their way through them." (Amateur sleuthing may be professional gall. "Succeeded in battling," good God! Is there a paragraph in Edel's devoted work, acclaimed as magisterial by two generations, that does not seduce and illuminate?) Edel, however, is not under review; he is only a point of contrast. The book in actual question, a fresh biography of James—in one volume—is, among other merits, praised for being admirably "short." It is attention span that is victor, even for people who claim to be serious readers.

And writers may give themselves out as a not dissimilar sample. Now and then you will hear a writer (even one who does not define herself as a journalist) speak of her task as "communication," as if the meticulous making of a sentence, or the feverish uncovering of an idea, or the sting of a visionary jolt delivered by what used to be called the Muse, were no more artful than a ten-minute telephone conversation. Literature may "communicate" (a redundancy, even a tautology), but its enduring force, well past the routine of facile sending and receiving, is in the consummation, as James tells us, of life, interest, importance. Leviathan rises to kick away the pebble of journalism.

Yet the pebble, it seems, is mightier than leviathan. The ten-minute article is *here*, and it has, by and large, displaced the essay. The essay is gradual and patient. The article is quick, restless, and brief. The essay reflects on its predecessors, and spirals organically out of a context, like a green twig from a living branch. The article rushes on, amnesiac, despising the meditative, reveling in gossip and polemics, a courtier of the moment. Essays, like articles, can distort and lie, but because essays are under the eye of history, it is a little harder to swindle the reader. Articles swindle almost by nature, because superficiality is a swindle. Pessimists suppose that none of this is any longer reversible. That the literary essay survives in this or that academic periodical, or in a handful of tiny quarterlies, is scarcely to the point. It has left the common culture.

Some doubt whether there *is* a common culture now at all, whether it is right to imagine that "the West" retains any resonance of worthy meaning; or even that it should. To claim commonality is, paradoxically, to be written off as elitist. Politically, through exploration, exploitation, and contempt, the West has spread elitism and exclusion; but it has also spread an idea of democratic inclusiveness so powerful—all of humanity is made in the image of the One Creator—that it serves to knock the politics of contempt off its feet all over the world. The round earth, like an hourglass, is turned upside down these days, spilling variegated populations-in-motion into static homogeneous populations, south into north, east into west; the village mentality, with its comfortable reliance on the familiar, is eroded by the polychrome and polyglot. America, vessel of migrations, began it. Grumbling, Europe catches up. While the kaleidoscope rattles and spins, and tribe assaults tribe, no one can predict how all this will shake itself out; but the village mentality is certainly dead. The jet plane cooked its goose.

· · ·

"It Takes a Great Deal of History to Produce a Little Literature"

BETWEEN THE LAST paragraph and this one, I took a quick trip to Paris. This is not the sort of thing a hermitlike scribbler usually does; generally it is a little daunting for me to walk the three short blocks to Main Street. But the rareness of such a plummeting from one society into another, perhaps because one's attention becomes preternaturally heightened, somehow illumines the notion of commonality. I crossed an ocean in an airplane and found, on the opposite shore, almost exactly what I left behind: the same congeries of concerns. The same writers were being talked about, the same world news (starvation, feuding, bombing) was being deplored; only the language was different. So there really *is* a "West"—something we mostly forget as we live our mostly Main Street lives. Suppose, then, the language were not different but the same?

And if "commonality" requires more persuasive evidence than a transoceanic flight, there is, after all, the question (the answer, rather) of English—setting aside Shaw's quip about America and Britain being separated by a common language. The mother-tongue, as the sweet phrase has it, is a poet's first and most lasting home, his ineradicable patriotism.* In my teens I read Katherine Mansfield: what did a New York–born Jewish girl whose family had fled the boot of the Russian Czar have in common with a woman born in New Zealand forty years earlier? And what did this woman of the farthest reaches of the South Pacific have in common with an island off the continent of Europe? How rapidly the riddle is undone: Keats and Shelley and Coleridge and Wordsworth, to begin with. The great tree-trunk of English literature . . . no, that grand image ought to give way to something

---

*I know a European writer of genius, in love with his language, whose bad luck it was to have been born just in time to suffer two consecutive tyrannies. It is a wonder that this writer lived past childhood. At the age of five, under Hitler, he was torn from his home and shipped to a concentration camp. Having survived that, he was spiritually and intellectually crushed by the extremes of Communist rule, including a mindless and vicious censorship. Currently, after the fall of the dictator, and having emigrated to America, he is being vilified in the press of his native land for having exposed one of its national heroes as a programmatic antisemite. After so much brutalization by the country of his birth, it would be difficult to expect him to identify himself as a patriot. But that is what he is. He is a patriot of his mother-tongue, and daily feels the estrangement of exile. *Pro patria dulce mori!*

homelier. Call it the drawstring of English letters, which packs us all into the same sack, at the bottom of which—as we tumble around all mixed up down there, North Americans, Australians, Nigerians, South Africans, Jamaicans, numbers of Indians, and on and on—lies a hillock of gold.

The gold is the idea (old-fashioned, even archaic, perhaps extinct) of belles-lettres. Some will name it false gold, since English, as language and as literature, came to the Caribbean, and to New York, and to all those other places, as the spoor of empire. (Spooky thought: if not for the Czar of All the Russias, and if not for mad King George III, and if not for their anachronistic confluence, I would not now be, as I am, on my knees before the English poets. Also: no native cadences of Hawthorne, Melville, Emerson, Thoreau, Dickinson, Faulkner, Mark Twain, Cather!) The Shropshire Lad for a while bestrode the world, and was welcome nowhere. But Milton and Mill and Swift and George Eliot and E. M. Forster came along as stowaways—"Areopagitica," and *A Vindication of the Rights of Woman*, and "A Modest Proposal," and *Daniel Deronda*, and *A Passage to India*. These hardly stand for the arrogance of parochialism—and it is just this engagement with belles-lettres that allows parochialism to open its arms, so that the inevitable accompaniment of belles-lettres is a sense of indebtedness. "It takes a great deal of history to produce a little literature," James noted; everything that informs belles-lettres is in that remark, and also everything that militates against the dismissal of either the term or the concept.

If I began these reflections in curmudgeonly resentment of the virtual annihilation of what Henry James knew—of the demise of the literary essay—it is only to press for its rescue and reclamation. Poetry and the novel will continue to go their own way, and we can be reasonably confident that they will take care of themselves. But the literary essay needs and merits defense: defense and more—celebrants, revivification through performance. One way or another, the literary essay is connected to the self-conscious progression of a culture, whereas the essay's flashy successor—the article, or "piece"—is in every instance a pusher of Now, a shaker-off of whatever requires study or patience, or what used to be called, without prejudice, ambition. The essayist's ambition is no more and no less than that awareness of indebtedness I spoke of a moment ago—indebtedness to history, scholarship, literature, the acutest nuances of language.

Is this what is meant by "elitism"? Perhaps. I think of it as work, if work is construed (as it ought to be) as "the passion for exactitude and sublimity." The latter phrase I borrow from a young essayist in London—my daughter's age exactly—who, because of a driven Parnassian ardor and because he is still in his twenties, has, I trust, the future of belles-lettres secreted in his fountain pen. In the newest literary generation, the one most assailed by the journalist's credo of Now, it is a thing worth marveling at: this determination to subdue, with exactitude and sublimity, the passionless trivia of our time.

Grateful acknowledgment is made to the following for permission to reprint previously published material:

American Academy of Arts and Letters: Excerpts from unpublished letters and documents from the Hamlin Garland file. Hamlin Garland papers. The poem "Genius" by Archer Milton Huntington. Archives of the American Academy of Arts and Letters, New York, NY.

Black Sparrow Press: Excerpts from "The Foot" by Alfred Chester, copyright © 1970 by Alfred Chester, from *Head of a Sad Angel: Stories 1953–1966*; excerpts from "Letter from the Wandering Jew" by Alfred Chester, copyright © 1971 by Alfred Chester, from *Looking for Genet: Literary Essays & Reviews*. Reprinted by permission of Black Sparrow Press.

The Detroit News: "No Head for Howells' Hat" by H. L. Mencken (*The Detroit News,* November 23, 1924). Reprinted by permission of *The Detroit News.*

Harcourt Brace & Company and *Faber and Faber Limited:* Excerpts from *The Waste Land,* "Burbank with a Baedeker: Bleistein with a Cigar," "Gerontion," "Sweeney Among the Nightingales," and "Ash-Wednesday" from *Collected Poems 1909–1962* by T. S. Eliot, copyright © 1936 by Harcourt Brace & Company, copyright © 1963, 1964 by T. S. Eliot; excerpts from "Burnt Norton" and "The Dry Salvages" from *Four Quartets* by T. S. Eliot, copyright © 1943 by T. S. Eliot, copyright renewed 1971 by Esme Valerie Eliot. Rights outside the United States administered by Faber and Faber Limited, London, from *The Complete Poems and Plays of T. S. Eliot.* Excerpts of three letters from *The Letters of T. S. Eliot, 1898–1922,* Volume One, edited by Valerie Eliot, copyright © 1988 by SET Copyrights Limited. Rights outside the United States administered by Faber and Faber Limited, London. Reprinted by permission of Harcourt Brace & Company and Faber and Faber Limited.

Harvard University Press: Excerpts from letters from *Henry James: Selected Letters,* edited by Leon Edel, copyright © 1974, 1975, 1980, 1984, 1987 by Leon Edel and Alexander R. James. Reprinted by permission of Harvard University Press.

Permissions Acknowledgments

A Note About the Author

CYNTHIA OZICK lives in Westchester County, New York, with her husband. She has won numerous prizes and awards for her short stories, novels, and essays, and her work has been translated into most major languages. Three of the essays collected here are included in *Best American Essays 1993, 1994,* and *1995.* She has recently ventured into playwriting.

A Note on the Type

This book was set in Monotype Dante, a typeface designed by Giovanni Mardersteig (1892–1977). Conceived as a private type for the Officina Bodoni in Verona, Italy, Dante was originally cut only for hand composition by Charles Malin, the famous Parisian punch cutter, between 1946 and 1952. Its first use was in an edition of Boccaccio's *Trattatello in laude di Dante* that appeared in 1954. The Monotype Corporation's version of Dante followed in 1957. Although modeled on the Aldine type used for Pietro Cardinal Bembo's treatise *De Aetna* in 1495, Dante is a thoroughly modern interpretation of the venerable face.

Composed by Creative Graphics, Allentown, Pennsylvania
Printed and bound by R. R. Donnelley & Sons,
Harrisonburg, Virginia
Designed by Anthea Lingeman